PRELIMINARY EXCAVATION REPORTS:

Sardis, Bir Umm Fawakhir, Tell el-ᶜUmeiri, The Combined Caesarea Expeditions, and Tell Dothan

THE ANNUAL OF
THE AMERICAN SCHOOLS OF ORIENTAL RESEARCH

Volume 52

Edited By
William G. Dever

PRELIMINARY EXCAVATION REPORTS:

Sardis, Bir Umm Fawakhir, Tell el-ᶜUmeiri, The Combined Caesarea Expeditions, and Tell Dothan

Edited by

William G. Dever

American Schools of Oriental Research

PRELIMINARY EXCAVATION REPORTS
SARDIS, BIR UMM FAWAKHIR, TELL EL-'UMEIRI,
THE COMBINED CAESAREA EXPEDITIONS,
AND TELL DOTHAN

Edited by
William G. Dever

© 1995
American Schools of Oriental Research

Library of Congress Cataloging in Publication Data
Preliminary excavation reports : Sardis, Bir Umm Fawakhir, Tell el
—'Umeiri, the Combined Caesarea Expeditions, and Tell Dothan /
edited by William G. Dever.
     p. cm. — (The Annual of the American Schools of Oriental
Research ; v. 52)
    ISBN 0-7885-0099-6 (cloth)
    1. Excavations (Archaeology)— Middle East. 2. Middle East—
Antiquities. I. Dever, William G. II. Series.
DS56.P74   1995
939.4—dc20   95–6929
                                    CIP

Printed in the United States of America
on acid-free paper

Contents

The Sardis Campaigns of 1990 and 1991

CRAWFORD H. GREENEWALT, JR.
Department of Classics
University of California
Berkeley, CA 94720

CHRISTOPHER RATTÉ
Department of Classics
Florida State University
Tallahassee, FL 32306

MARCUS L. RAUTMAN
Department of Art History and Archaeology
University of Missouri
Columbia, MO 65211

Antiquities explored and uncovered in 1990 and 1991 were primarily Late Roman and Archaic and consisted of architecture and artifacts in two regions of the city site excavated in previous seasons, and three (Archaic) tombs of the city cemetery, Bin Tepe, and a locale to the northeast. Excavation uncovered more urban features of the Late Roman city (two colonnaded thoroughfares and residential units of the fourth to seventh centuries C.E.), more of the Archaic fortifications that protected part of the lower city in the sixth century B.C.E. and of a building with several clearly-defined seventh century B.C.E. features. A mistaken notion about the design of the Classical or Hellenistic Metroon is corrected. The design and construction of the Pyramid Tomb at Sardis were clarified; and a sixth century B.C.E. date was determined from masonry and ceramic evidence for the tumulus at Bin Tepe that has been called the Tomb of Gyges.

INTRODUCTION

The results of excavation and related archaeological exploration at Sardis in the field seasons of 1990 and 1991[1] are the subject of this report; the season's programs also included conservation, graphic recording, study, and site enhancement projects.[2] Information in this report is derived largely from more detailed manuscript reports written in the field by expedition staff members; copies of those reports are filed in the Sardis Expedition Office at Harvard University.

Excavation concentrated on two regions of the city site: Sectors MMS, MMS/S, and MMS/N, located at the foot of the Acropolis (fig. 1, nos. 63–65) and Sector ByzFort ("Byzantine Fortress"), a flat-topped spur on the north flank of the Acropolis (fig. 1, no. 23). The Pyramid Tomb was reexcavated (fig. 1, no. 14). Cleaning and study provided new information about the tumulus called Karnı-yarık Tepe, located at Bin Tepe, 10 km north of Sardis, and about a tumulus farther away, at Sarı-çalı, northeast of Gölmarmara.

SECTORS MMS, MMS/S, MMS/N

Sectors are located at the foot of the Acropolis, directly south of the Roman Bath–Gymnasium complex; one or more of them has been under excavation each year since 1977 (Greenewalt, Ratté, and Rautman 1994 and references). The principal features uncovered in all three are Late Roman, i.e., fourth to early seventh centuries C.E., and Archaic, i.e., seventh to mid-fifth centuries B.C.E. Sectors MMS and MMS/S are marked in the modern landscape by low artificial hills (fig. 2), which are substantially created by the ruins of a huge Archaic building, "Colossal Lydian Structure" (figs. 14, 15). The division between the two hills is probably created by the Late Roman colonnaded street (fig. 3), which cut through the Archaic building. Sector MMS/N is directly north of MMS, across the modern highway.

C.H.G.

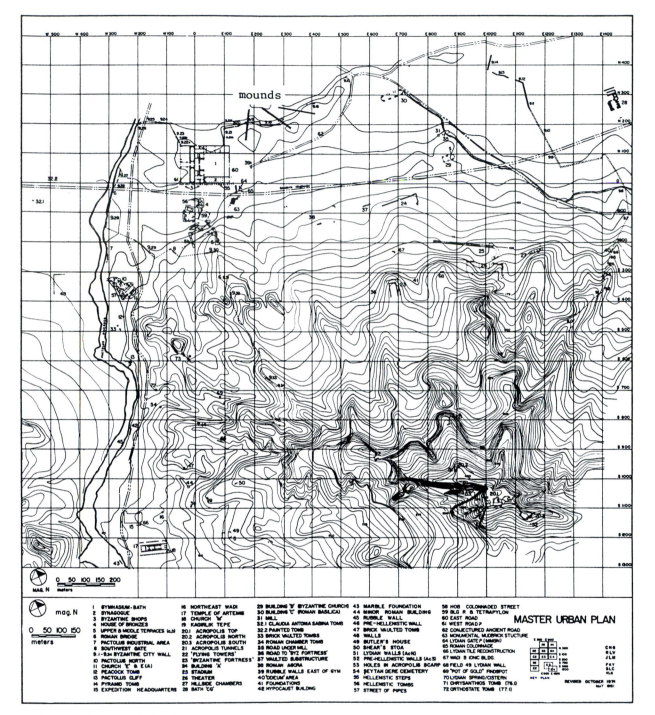

Fig. 1. Sardis, general site plan.

Sectors MMS, MMS/S, and MMS/N, Roman Levels

Extensive Roman and Late Roman remains lie across the three MMS sectors. Located near the city's large western bath complex, this urban quarter included broad streets flanked by colonnaded porticoes, behind which stood small shops, tabernae, and elegant townhouses in the fourth to seventh centuries (fig. 3). Excavation in 1990 and 1991 continued to explore this Late Roman residential neighborhood and document its earlier history.

Fig. 2. Sectors MMS/S, MMS, MMS/N, view looking northeast. The artificial mounds of sectors MMS/S and MMS are in the foreground, on the nearer side of the modern highway. A chain of artificial mounds that extend east from the Roman Bath-Gymnasium complex appears in the middle distance, center and right.

The following discussion proceeds from north to south.

Sector MMS/N. Lying just north of the present highway, Sector MMS/N stands midway between the large public buildings of the Bath–Gymnasium and Synagogue to the northwest and the residential area of MMS to the south. In Roman times the sector included a marble-paved plaza standing at the east end of the broad Marble Road, with a monumental colonnade extending along its south side (see Crawford 1990: 3–5). Previous work identified the major features of this portico, including a row of large columns erected in two sections and two superimposed mosaic floors (Greenewalt, Ratté, and Rautman 1994: 6). After recording and study in 1990 and 1991, parts of these surfaces were lifted in order to explore earlier features of Roman and Archaic date.

In its latest, sixth-century C.E. phase, the MMS/N portico comprised two distinct parts unified behind the long primary colonnade (fig. 4). The colonnade's deep foundations attest its use throughout late antiquity, although variations in the size and interval of surviving bases suggest its piecemeal construction and repair. The colonnade's western part faces a substantial, 8-m-long wall that extends from a broad doorway with threshold east to a large projecting pier. East of the pier is a stylobate on which at least five columns or piers stood on large Ionic bases and one inverted pier-capital. To the south of the second colonnade lies the raised floor of the inner portico, which was covered by a thick layer of fallen brick and tile (Greenewalt et al. 1983: fig. 14). Excavation of this debris exposed a small part of the inner portico and traces of its mosaic floor.

At least two large mosaic panels occupied the inner portico. Behind the first four columnar intervals are small panels with interlocking circles and scales, a border of interlacing cables, and a field of Solomon knots, interlocking circles, and interlace patterns. Farther east begins a second large panel with a three-strand guilloche frame surrounding large roundels filled with interlacing cables and enclosing Solomon knots. The range of motifs corresponds with the previously suggested sixth-century date for the mosaic. Coins and pottery recovered from above its surface date from the sixth and early seventh centuries C.E., when the portico's superstructure finally collapsed.[3]

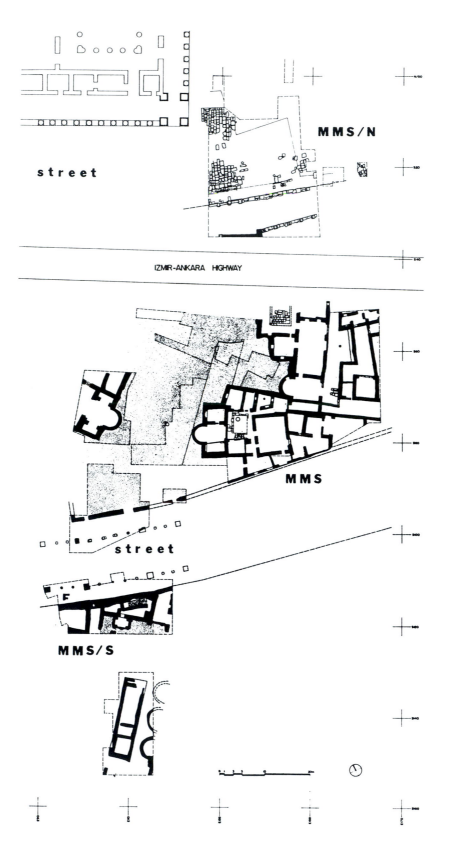

Fig. 3. Sectors MMS/N, MMS, and MMS/S. Late Roman features, simplified plan.

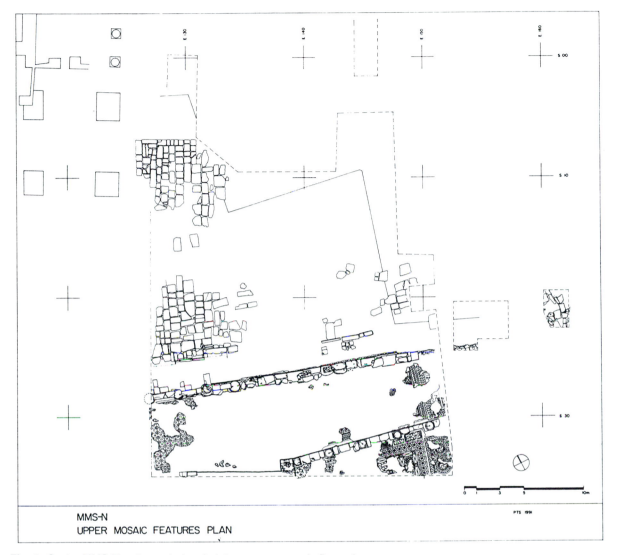

**MMS-N
UPPER MOSAIC FEATURES PLAN**

Fig. 4. Sector MMS/N, colonnaded ambulatory, upper mosaic floor, plan.

The floor of the main portico was covered with polychrome mosaics at a slightly lower level. Previously exposed parts employ guilloche and interlacing cable patterns together with a fragmentary inscription (Greenewalt et al. 1983: 13, fig. 16). Further excavation of this ambulatory yielded little more of the mosaic, which was seriously eroded in antiquity. Coins and pottery from its bedding reinforce a sixth century date for its installation.

Excavation below this surface and its packing revealed extensive remains of a lower mosaic floor in the main portico (fig. 5). This bichrome mosaic consists of two well-preserved panels that meet just north of the back wall's projecting pier. The two panels are closely related in design and share an ivy leaf border on the north side that continues to the main stylobate. The more westerly of the two large panels lies about 1 m in front of the portico's back wall between doorway and pier, separated from the wall by a narrow roughly cobbled surface. The panel consists of a compound guilloche border surrounding a field filled with loosely knotted squares enclosing Solomon knots, ivy leaves, and quatrefoils (Greenewalt, Ratté, and Rautman 1994 : 6, fig. 4; a related pattern, used elsewhere at the Marble Road is presented in Crawford 1990: fig. 24). While remaining regular in its details, the mosaic's south and east sides splay out toward the nearby pier.

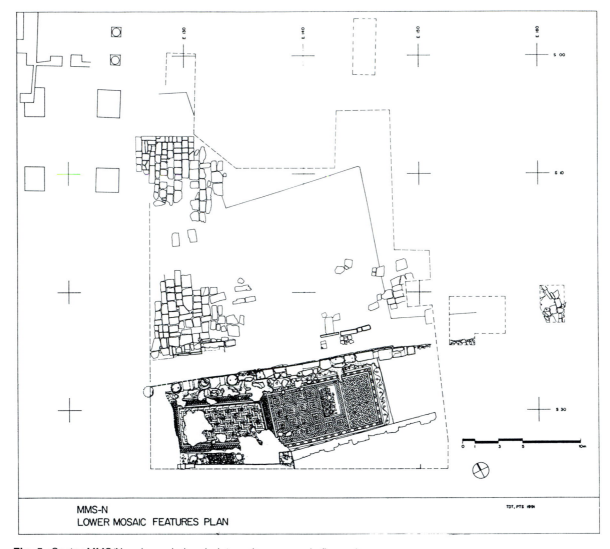

Fig. 5. Sector MMS/N, colonnaded ambulatory, lower mosaic floor, plan.

The second panel lies between the two colonnades beyond the wall pier. The outer ivy leaf border stops abruptly along the line of a possible ledge or raised step at its east edge. The main panel consists of a bead-and-reel border surrounding a field in two parts. To the east is a panel of cables forming interlacing circles. The larger, more westerly field is subdivided by interlacing cable bands into a regular grid of small compartments with diagonal Solomon knots. The northeast corner of this decorative grid is interrupted by a 2.7 × 1.7 m box containing a well-preserved inscription of seven lines (fig. 6). The Greek text records the decoration with mosaics of the *embolos* during the term of the prefect Flavius Archelaos, who is named as "most illustrious" companion (*comes*) of the first rank (IN90.21).[4] The text reads as follows:

Ἐκεντήθη ὁ ἔνβολος
καὶ πάντα τὸν κόσμον
εἴληφεν ἐπὶ φλαβίου
Ἀρχελάου, τοῦ λαμ(προτάτου) κόμ(ητος)
πρώτου βαθμοῦ, διέπον-
τος τὴν ἔπαρχον
ἐξουσεῖαν.

The colonnaded street was paved with mosaic and received all the decoration when Flavius Archelaos, companion of the first rank of his Serene Highness, held the Office of Prefect.

Fig. 6. Sector MMS/N, colonnaded ambulatory, lower mosaic floor, inscription (IN90.21).

Most of this lower mosaic was lifted after recording and study. The mortar bedding yielded a number of coins issued in the fourth and the beginning of the fifth centuries C.E.

Excavation beneath the main portico's lower mosaics exposed a group of foundations that survived the area's early fifth-century development. In the western portico area several unattributed foundations were built immediately above Archaic levels (below, pp. 13–18). Among the earliest Roman features is a 7-m-long row of closely fitted marble blocks that continues the approximate line of the Marble Road's south colonnade. Lying just south of the later stylobate, this solid foundation abuts a large square pier built of reused Archaic blocks, carefully mortared around a rubble core. A correspondingly deep parallel foundation about 5 m south may have supported the back wall of an earlier portico. A deep mortared drain and three large terracotta pipes ran from west to east between the foundations. Isolated patches of mortar bedding suggest an opus sectile floor may have paved this area.

At a later date this area was turned to other less public purposes. Four new foundations enclosed a 5 × 6 m trapezoidal space that may have served a shop or tab-erna. To the west a small (1.2 × 0.4 m) latrine was added to the adjacent space, facing away from the street and emptying into the earlier drain. Similar foundations found east of the square mortared pier suggest the steady encroachment onto this public space by domestic or industrial structures. Despite the lack of intact floors, layers of packed fill suggest a fourth-century date for these features. The latrine deposit included Roman pottery and coins dating to the late fourth century C.E. All of these structures were removed and paved over during the new colonnade's construction shortly after 400 C.E.

Sector MMS. The central MMS area lies across the present highway immediately south of Sector MMS/N. Roman features belong to an irregularly-shaped residential block that extended south of the plaza at MMS/N and was bounded to west and south by broad, colonnaded streets (fig. 7). Excavation in 1990 and 1991 revealed several new rooms of this residential quarter and selectively explored their underlying features.

Room IV is a narrow, irregularly shaped space near the highway that offered an opportunity both to explore earlier phases of the Late Roman complex

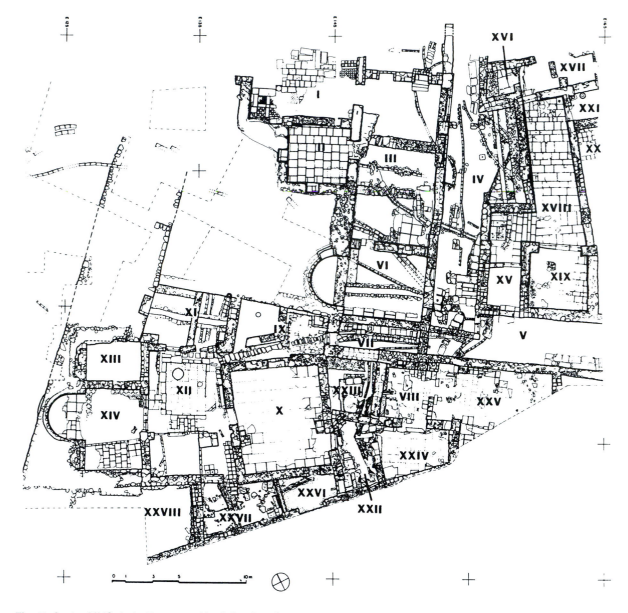

Fig. 7. Sector MMS, Late Roman residential units, plan.

and to ascertain the condition of Archaic levels east of Colossal Lydian Structure. In its original form Room IV comprised a long corridor leading south from a presumed entrance near MMS/N to meet the perpendicular Room V (Greenewalt 1990: 3–6). A broad, unroofed alcove lay along its east side, while to the west multiple doorways opened onto the adjacent Rooms III and VI. In the latest occupied state, a flight of four steps with a landing rose 0.65 m at the room's south end. Excavation beneath the final floors of Room IV clearly documented the intensity of local activities from the sixth century C.E. down

to Hellenistic times, and pointed to deeper unexplored Archaic strata.

Gently sloping layers of mudbrick debris from Colossal Lydian Structure underlie several isolated foundations of possible Hellenistic date. By the third or early fourth century C.E. a deep foundation stood along the west side of this space, underlying Room IV's west wall, and was perhaps accompanied by a shallow portico with piers facing east. A deep covered drain ran in front of both wall and piers from south to northeast. Also to an early phase belongs a small ironworking hearth in front of the piers; standing nearby was an amphora base filled

Fig. 8. Sector MMS, north wall of Late Roman street and adjacent residential spaces, looking northeast.

with lime, which may have been used in the smelting process.

Around the early fifth century C.E., this open area was absorbed by the quarter's residential development. The rebuilt west wall continued to organize the area, with new walls shaping spaces to either side: small rectilinear rooms stood to the west, while along its east face stretched Room IV, already acting as a kind of corridor. During that phase a narrow vestibule with a water feature stood at the room's north end, while along the east side opened a slightly less spacious alcove with a doorway to the east. Room IV retained this basic shape throughout the fifth and early sixth centuries C.E., when a network of pipes and drains served the domestic needs of successive generations. As noted elsewhere in the sector, each campaign of renovation took its toll on earlier features, which were often isolated by construction pits and foundation trenches. Room IV's floor level did not rise appreciably before its final phase of occupation in the sixth century.

Excavation in the south part of the MMS sector exposed several additional rooms of the residential complex and identified its southern boundary (fig. 8). The thick north wall of the MMS street cuts diagonally through the area along the approximate line of a long-used village track.[5] Of the section exposed in 1991, the western part of the wall cuts through Colossal Lydian Structure and retains collapsed mudbrick debris to the north. An arched opening announces the east face of the Archaic wall, similar to the opening along its west face (Greenewalt, Cahill, and Rautman 1987: 17, fig. 4; below, p. 18). Built of mortared rubble with brick bands and pierced by occasional doorways, the

street wall continues along its northeasterly course to define the quarter's southern edge.

Rooms XXVI–XVII and Space XXVIII lie between the large domestic spaces of the more southerly residential unit and the nearby street wall. Piers and partitions variously subdivided this band of small irregularly shaped spaces. Room XXVII apparently served as the primary entrance to the house: two doorways once opened from the street to the south, while through its north doorway one reached the central Court XII. At one time Room XXVII was subdivided by a central partition. Its narrow western part may have functioned briefly as a small shop, independently accessible from the street and joined further west to an open area or garden (Space XXVIII) that gradually accumulated domestic debris. By the late fifth century this partition had been removed and the more westerly street doorway blocked. In the latter phase a short row of steps rose to the now higher level of Space XXVIII. The floor of Room XXVII was roughly paved, including a reused block bearing two lines of Greek text commemorating the *mystai* of Zeus (IN91.10= S91.5/9919). In its final phase a short section of a column shaft rolled against the east wall apparently served as a makeshift bench at the entrance to the domus. Room XXVI is a 4.1 × 2.5 m trapezoidal space squeezed between the street wall and the large Room X to the north. Above its well-preserved plaster floor traces of painted plaster survive on the walls. A shallow 2.0 × 0.4 m alcove in the south wall faces the doorway to Room X and might have contained a *kline* or cabinet.

Fig. 9. Sector MMS, Late Roman Rooms VIII, XXIV, XXV, looking west.

Rooms VIII, XXIV and XXV make up a suite of large spaces paved with marble and enclosed by plastered walls (fig. 9). With an excavated area of almost 40 m², Room XXV is one of the sector's largest interior spaces. The partially cleared room probably continues south to the street wall. At its northwest corner stood a water basin, preserved today only in foundations but with an original capacity of some 425 liters. From that space one entered Room VIII through a broad opening flanked by narrow piers. Room VIII's north wall apparently contained cupboards that faced the broad doorway to Room XXIV to the south. Room VIII was similarly furnished with a marble paved floor, plastered walls, and at its southwest corner a marble-lined water basin of perhaps 440 liters.

Immediately to the west of Room XXIV stands Room XXII, a small, trapezoidal space of approximately 12 m² (fig. 10). Two openings in the street wall suggest that in the early fifth century C.E. this space may have served as a vestibule giving access to Rooms VIII, XXIV, and XXV to the east, and the small Room XXIII to the north. At a later date these streetside entrances were closed off and a small latrine was installed at the room's southwest corner. Figure 11 reconstructs the facility with a single seat of wood or stone. The latrine was supplied by the overflow from the water tank in Room XXIV, which drained through a horizontal wall pipe in the south wall into a short open trough formed by an inverted roof cover tile, before continuing to the latrine itself. A marble floorboard preserves cuttings for a gentle flow of water and a receptical for the requi-

site sponge. From there water emptied through the tiled latrine box into a deep, well-built drain beneath the floor. A stone platform nearby may at one time have supported a companion water basin. By the later sixth century the latrine niche had been filled with unmortared rubble and a small hearth stood in the room's northwest corner (Greenewalt, Ratté, and Rautman 1994: 10).

Room XXIII is a small, enclosed space north of Room XXII. Excavation below its final floor revealed a dense sequence of occupation layers similar to those in Room IV (pp. 8–9). Several small pits and construction trenches accompanied the installation of new walls and successive lines of terracotta pipe through the space to supply the basin in Room XXIV. Briefly communicating with Room X to the east, Room XXIII apparently served for most of its life as a storage chamber (Greenewalt, Ratté, and Rautman 1994: 10).

MMS/S. The broad, colonnaded street bordering the MMS houses also separates that sector from MMS/S, which includes the street's south portico and the hill rising behind it. Previous work on the hill's north and east slopes identified Archaic, Hellenistic, and Roman remains that mostly predate the street's construction in the early fifth century C.E. Excavation in 1990 and 1991 continued to explore the area's early history and its transformation during late antiquity (fig. 12).

A group of small, rectilinear buildings crowned the north edge of the MMS/S ridge in the fourth century C.E. Known only by their foundations, the northernmost spaces were cut by construction of the tall south street

Fig. 10. Sector MMS, Late Roman Rooms XXII, with latrine in southwest corner, later hearth in northwest corner.

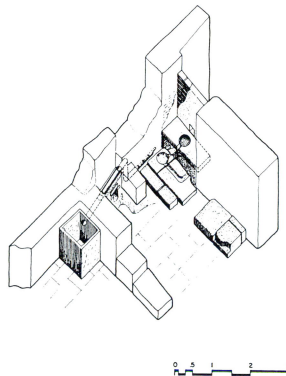

0 .5 1 2 3m

Fig. 11. Sector MMS, Late Roman latrine in Room XXII, reconstruction.

wall. Several parts of the complex were reoccupied during the fifth to seventh centuries. Those spaces stood high above the street surface and looked across it to the north. From the roadway one entered through the arched streetside doorway and turned left to climb a 1.5-m-wide flight of steps behind the street wall. Carefully built of bricks and reused marble blocks, these fourteen steps rose 4.4 m to a packed earthen landing. Turning west, one continued to a small, vaulted space. This 3.0 × 2.3 m room was trapezoidal and had small corner piers supporting a low cross vault. Few traces survive of the room's original function. Beneath the plaster floor against the east wall was an infant burial. Pottery and a half-follis of Anastasius (512–518 C.E., 1990.283) indicate that the space remained open into the sixth century.

A larger room at the sector's northeast corner was partially cleared in an earlier season (Greenewalt et al. 1983: 8). Renewed excavation in 1991 exposed this spacious (4.0 × 7.5 m) oblong space to its final occupation phase (fig. 13). Below the room's final floor level lie earlier walls and surfaces, some of which may predate the construction of the nearby street wall. The room was substantially rebuilt, apparently in the fifth century, with

brick and rubble walls rising to a height of over 2.5 m. Two doorways opened to the east, one located next to the street wall, the other near the room's center; the second doorway, with a threshold, was closed during the room's final phases. A broad 2.3 × 1.1 m alcove in the south wall was covered by a shallow barrel vault and might have contained a *kline* or cupboard. The room was neatly paved with terracotta tiles and its plastered walls carried painted bands and floral patterns. While lacking other furniture, such arrangements suggest the room served as a cubiculum. Coins of Phocas indicate that the space remained open into the early seventh century (607/608 C.E., C79.23; 602–610 C.E., 1991.67, 1991.95).

Another group of Roman spaces stood 10 to 30 m to the south along the lower east slope of the MMS/S ridge. Two parallel foundations set about 4 m apart follow the hill's north–south contours and support a terrace that steps down to the east, enclosing within their mass the Archaic wall (below, p. 19). Between the two foundations traces of perpendicular walls survive, together with fragmentary tile and opus sectile floors; several lines of

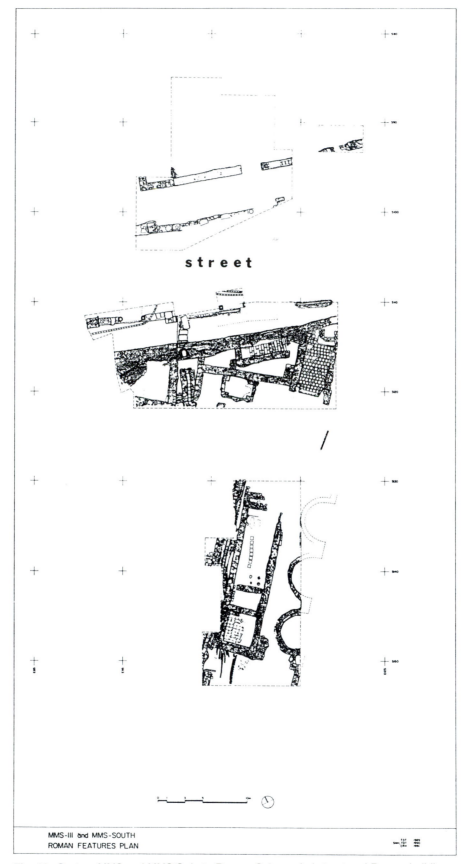

Fig. 12. Sectors MMS and MMS/S, Late Roman Colonnaded street and Roman buildings to the south, plan.

Fig. 13. Sector MMS/S, Late Roman room, looking south.

terracotta pipe continue to the south. About 2 to 5 m east stand two broad and very deep semicircular foundations that open off a third parallel terrace wall; a similar foundation in the scarp to the north suggests the presence of a third curving wall. The grand scale of those large apsidal features contrasts with the ridgetop's small domestic buildings and seems more appropriate for a public structure, perhaps a nymphaeum or honorific monument that opened onto a parallel street located to the east.

M.L.R.

Sector MMS/S, Hellenistic Material

Mixed fills in sector MMS/S contained a significant quantity of Hellenistic pottery, which included fragments of relief bowls (four inventoried), of molds for relief bowls (eight inventoried) and for a lamp, of terracotta figurines (twelve inventoried), of West Slope and related painted wares (two inventoried), of echinus bowls (five inventoried), and of fish plates (one inventoried). Contemporaneous architectural features were negligible.

Sector MMS, MMS/S, MMS/N, Archaic Features

The principal Archaic feature exposed in excavation was the huge building called "Colossal Lydian Structure." Its length was traced for another 36 m (15 m to the south, 21 m to the north), making a total traced length of 130 m, not counting topographical evidence for continuation to the south (Greenewalt, Ratté, and Rautman 1994: 14–26; here

fig. 2, lower right). The narrow proportions in addition to the great thickness and massive construction of the Structure (Greenewalt, Sterud, and Belknap 1982: 18–24; Greenewalt et al. 1983: 1–8) are additional evidence that the Structure was a fortification wall, as discoverers Ramage and Ramage claimed in 1976. Similarities to another huge Archaic building, of which side surfaces have been uncovered a few meters to the north, indicate that the wall continued north beyond a gate that separated two of its segments (figs. 14, 15). The following discussion proceeds from north to south.

Sector MMS/N, Features. Excavation in 1990 and 1991 exposed the north end of the Structure, which is located north of the modern highway under the south colonnaded ambulatory of the Roman avenue (figs. 3, 14). Excavation exposed remains of the northwest corner, which included about 5 m of the west side and 15 m of the north side (from that corner), and a west extension aligned with the north side and exposed for 5 m from the corner (figs. 14–17). Only lower courses survive. The foundations consist of three or more courses of roughly-trimmed fieldstone; the corner stone[6] is large and has an inset vertical arris at the corner (fig. 17). On the north side, the foundations support one or two courses of ashlar masonry in white limestone and sandstone, with chisel-drafted borders and pick-dressed centers (figs. 16, 17).

A single course survives on the north side proper, two courses on the west extension. Sandstone occurs only at the west end of the west extension. Bevels occur

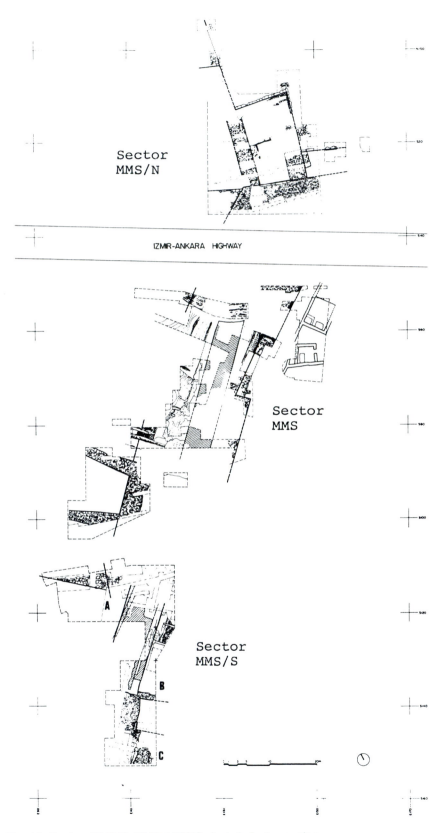

Fig. 14. Sectors MMS/N, MMS, MMS/S, Archaic features, plan.

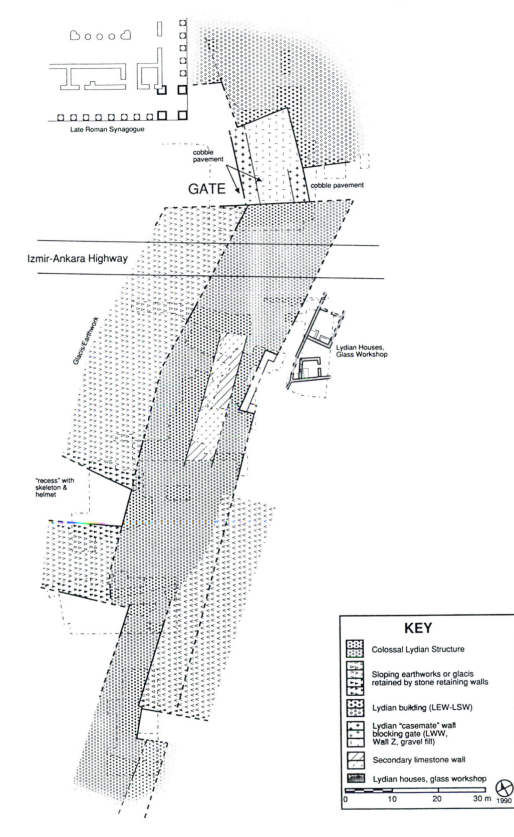

Fig. 15. Sectors MMS/N, MMS, MMS/S, Archaic features, interpretive restored plan.

Fig. 17. Sector MMS/N, view looking south. Colossal Lydian Structure: northwest corner abutted by the west extension (right).

Fig. 16. Sector MMS/N, view looking east. Colossal Lydian Structure: north side (lower courses of the face and field stone packing behind) with west extension (foreground). At middle left, "shell walls" (Lydian West Wall, Wall Z) of the casemate wall gate blockage abut the north side of the Structure. Roman features are screened.

on the left sides of three blocks (for their significance, see Ratté 1989: 50–53). Roughly-picked circles, with diameters of 0.045–0.06 m, occur on three blocks of the north side proper.

The north side slopes down from east to west, and the lowest ashlar course was staggered in three steps along the north side proper and the western extension (and is missing for the highest, most easterly step). These faces of the Structure are backed with a packing of fieldstones. Near the northwest corner, the packing was disturbed in Roman times

and is also intruded by the Roman trapezoidal foundation (built of limestone blocks that were evidently reused from the Structure, above, p. 7; fig. 16). Outside the western extension, a surface of mortared stones that abuts the lowest exposed course of the extension (fig. 17) and on which rested Roman pottery fragments, also attests Roman intrusion in the Structure.

A short but massive "casemate wall," formed by two stone "shell walls," each ca. 3.5 m thick (Lydian West Wall, Wall Z), and an intermediate fill of gravel, blocked the space between Colossal Lydian Structure and the large Archaic building with W-shaped, zig-zag facade, i.e., Lydian East Wall–Lydian Sandstone Wall, to the north (fig. 15).

When those features were last reported their interpretation as components of a casemate wall was posed as a question (Greenewalt et al. 1983: 14); without further evidence or discussion, it has come to be assumed (e.g., Greenewalt 1989: 265).

Remains of the south end of the casemate wall were excavated in 1991. The two "shell walls" abut the north side of Colossal Lydian Structure (the west face of the more westerly wall, i.e., Lydian West Wall, however, had been destroyed, probably during building in Roman times; fig. 16); and some of the gravel fill also ran up against the north side of the Structure.

A widespread deposit of debris that consists primarily of reddish crushed and fragmentary brick rests immediately north of Colossal Lydian Structure, running up against its north side and underlying parts of the casemate wall that were exposed in 1991 (i.e., both "shell walls" and gravel fill). What appears to be the same debris had previously been noticed west of the casemate wall (Greenewalt, Sterud, and Belknap 1982: 20) and south of the large Archaic building with zig-zag facade (Lydian East Wall–Lydian Sandstone Wall), at its eastern end where it is closest to Colossal Lydian Structure, and had been tentatively identified as "Brick Fall," i.e., debris that consists predominantly of brick and is evidently remains of Colossal Lydian Structure superstructure that had been destroyed and dumped in the mid-sixth century B.C.E., presumably when Sardis fell to the armies of Cyrus the Great of Persia (Cahill in Greenewalt, Cahill, and Rautman 1987: 22–24; Greenewalt 1992b: 8). The deposit encountered in 1991 was only partly excavated, and its identity as Brick Fall was not established.

Sector MMS/N, Interpretation of Features. Similarities in orientation and construction (i.e., with distinctively-dressed ashlar masonry in limestone and sandstone) between the north side of Colossal Lydian Structure and the large building with zig-zag facade to the north (Lydian East Wall–Lydian Sandstone Wall; figs. 14–17; cf. Greenewalt, Cahill, and Rautman 1987: 31–33, figs. 14–16) indicate a close relationship between the two buildings that is consistent with the interpretation of them as forming two sides of a gate, and of the large building with zig-zag facade as a continuation of the Colossal Lydian Structure fortification wall. The wall at MMS/N had been "shaved down" by later building, probably that of the Roman avenue; and the absence of topographic evidence for the wall for the next 100 m to the north (i.e., in contrast to the evidence of the mounds created by Colossal Lydian Structure in the modern landscape south of the modern highway; fig. 2, foreground) may also be explained as a consequence of post-Archaic building, probably that of the Roman Bath–Gymnasium complex. The chain of mounds that extends eastward from the northeast corner of the Bath–Gymnasium complex (figs. 1, 2) is created at least in part by the ruins of a huge Lydian building (faced with ashlar masonry in white limestone; Greenewalt, Cahill, and Rautman 1987: 80–84); the chain may represent continuation of the same fortification wall to which Colossal Lydian Structure and the building with zig-zag facade belong, and may have provided a precedent for the Late Roman line of defense that was built against the north side of those mounds (Hanfmann and Waldbaum 1975: 37, where the mound chain is called "terrace of earth and fill"). Whether that interpretation conflicts with the nature of Archaic occupation at sectors HoB and PN (fig. 1, nos. 4, 10), which would have been located outside the fortifications, and with the apparent implication in Herodotus's account (5.101) that the central part of Sardis flanked the Pactolus stream remains to be discussed. Today the stream flows some 400 m west of Colossal Lydian Structure.[7] The defenses to which the Structure belongs may have enclosed only part of the lower city of Sardis (like the inner citadel at Carchemish); is it reasonable to suppose that it excluded the "market" and houses at sector HoB, the gold-refining installations at sector PN, and the residential zone and agora known to Herodotus?[8]

If the debris that underlies the casemate wall is Brick Fall, the casemate wall must be later than the great destruction of Colossal Lydian Structure and presumably postdates the Persian conquest of ca. 546 B.C.E. (the casemate wall had previously been understood to be a pre-destruction feature). It would have been built to block the gate; but it is blockage in the sense of a major, long-term renovation that eliminated the gate and extended the fortification across the gate passage. Is it a reflection of administrative change from Lydian to Persian rule? The accommodation of traffic from one side of the defenses to the other in the locale remains to be determined.

The function of the west extension of the north side of the Structure is unclear. Figure 15 suggests that it was a retaining wall for the earthwork/glaçis on the west side of the Structure proper, and is the counterpart of the retaining wall 60 m to the south (i.e., which forms the north side of the recess in

Fig. 18. Sector MMS/S A, view looking south. Colossal Lydian Structure: mudbrick west face (diagonal arrow), surface of Brick Fall (on which excavator sits), and post-destruction west face in three superimposed planes (the uppermost, largely concealed behind Roman Brick construction, is indicated by two arrows). In the foreground, Roman wall-like feature and stones.

which helmet and skeleton were recovered in 1987 and 1988; Greenewalt 1990: 10–14; Greenewalt, Ratté, and Rautman 1994: 20–21).

The obtuse angle of the northwest corner of the Structure proper is unusual for gate design, and may indicate that the east–west route through the gate passage (attested by gravel surfaces as well as by the passage space; Greenewalt et al. 1983: 14–15) is older than the fortification wall. The orientation of the wall in this locale might have been determined by topographical factors.

Sector MMS. The east face of Colossal Lydian Structure was traced for another 3.3 m, about 10 m south of the shallow recess near the Archaic residential complex (fig. 14; i.e., at ca. S. 84–88 on the 'B'

grid, fig. 14, and below Late Roman Space XXVIII, figs. 3, 7).

In this locale, the east face had been exposed for a length of ca. 2 m in previous excavation (Greenewalt, Rautman and Meriç 1986: 6). Of the adjacent segment exposed in 1991, only the top preserved two courses and the undistributed top of Brick Fall (above, p. 17, MMS/N) to the east were excavated.

One of several instances of interrelation between the Structure and Late Roman features occurs in this locale. The east face of the Structure continues to the north through an arched opening in the north wall of the Late Roman colonnaded street. Similarly, the west face of the Structure passed through an opening in the same wall, further to the west.[9] Another instance is the coincidence of location between a change of design and construction in the east face of the Structure (sloped and mudbrick on relatively low stone socle; vertical and stone) and a major wall of the late Roman residential complex (the massive north wall of Rooms IX and XI (Greenewalt et al. 1985: 73; see also Rautman in Greenewalt, Cahill, and Rautman 1987: 18). Those interrelations cannot all be fortuitous; for reasons that remain to be determined, Late Roman construction to some extent accommodated in its design the Archaic remains below.

Sector MMS/S. Significant features of Colossal Lydian Structure excavated in Sector MMS/S included a rectilinear recess on the east side, thick deposits of Brick Fall (above, p. 17, MMS/N) on both sides and considerable amounts of carbonized wood directly under Brick Fall on one side, and remains of the post-destruction rebuilt Structure. Those features appear in a 35 m-long stretch where excavation focused on three locales, from north to south, A,B,C (originally separate trenches; fig. 14).

In MMS/S A, both sides of the preserved top of the Structure were uncovered. The width at the preserved top is ca. 8 m (narrower by a meter than the preserved top of the Structure 55 m to the north, at the north end of the MMS hill; Greenewalt et al. 1983: 2). In MMS/S A, both sides as far as exposed are mudbrick. The west face is vertical, unlike other mudbrick faces of the Structure, which have a distinct batter. A 3 m-long segment of west face was excavated to a depth of 3 m below preserved top; the face is covered with mud plaster, as was determined in a small cut through the face (at the southeast corner of the trench), where the plaster, 0.015 m thick, and brick outlines behind the plaster were revealed in section (fig. 19).

The east face of the Structure in MMS/S is problematic.

Fig. 19. Sector MMS/S A, view looking south. Colossal Lydian Structure: mudbrick west face (at left and behind excavator), with mud plaster exposed, where it has been sectioned in the scarp, as a narrow, light-colored line (arrow). Brick Fall appears in the scarp ("strata" being brushed by excavator) and under excavator (where it remains unexcavated).

In MMS/S A and B, a more-or-less continuous line of mudbrick facing was traced for ca. 15 m (north of the recess; fig. 14), but apart from a short 2.3 m-long stretch where the face was exposed to a height of 18 courses and 1.7 m below preserved top (between ca. S. 130–133 on the 'B' grid), only one or two courses of facing were recognized. In front of those courses at lower levels occurred clear evidence of construction *in situ*: patches of laid brick; two "walls" made of loosely-aligned bricks, one brick wide and two or three bricks high, oriented roughly perpendicular to the east side of the Structure; and, at the deepest level penetrated in excavation, ca. 2 m east from the "face," a deposit of river stone packing.

In MMS/S C, a mass of coursed mudbrick construction was located in the west half of the trench (i.e., up to ca. E. 100 on the 'B' grid) but no face was recognized. In earthy fill to the east, occasional mudbrick fragments were detected; and at the deepest level a surface of river stone packing similar to that of MMS/S A was exposed.

For those features there are several possible explanations. In MMS/S A, the face might be at the line of mudbricks, and construction below too loose or sandy (because of being in pisé as well as poor-quality mudbrick?) for recognition; and the feature in front might be a bulwark or glacis. The two "walls" have close parallels in the earthwork on the east side of the Structure (Greenewalt et al. 1990: 142–43). Alternatively, the east side of the Structure might have contained a high step or shelf (like one for which there is evidence in the west side, Greenewalt et al. 1990: 114), in which the lines of bricks belong to the upper "back" face and the built features in front are core materials behind the lower "front" face. The river stone packing in MMS/S A and C might be backing for a stone face that is an extension of the east face located 38 m to the north in sector MMS (above p. 18); and is connected to the face of the recess in MMS/S B (below, this page). Above the river stone

packing in MMS/S C, construction materials of the Structure would appear to have been disturbed (perhaps during creation of the Late Roman triple apse building [cf. figs. 14, 3]).

Sector MMS/S, Recess. The northwest corner of the recess was partly excavated in 1989 (Greenewalt, Ratté, and Rautman 1994: 23–24). In 1990 and 1991 more of the inner end was excavated. Preserved tops of the sides were exposed to determine width and construction features; the north side was exposed to its full preserved height for a short stretch of 1.5 m (fig. 21); and ca. 10 m² of the floor (1.0–3.5 m east–west by 5 m north–south, against the north face) were excavated. The faces at the inner end were not fully exposed, partly to obtain sections through Brick Fall that filled the recess (below, p. 20) and partly to protect the stone faces from deterioration, because at the preserved top the stone faces showed cracks and signs of softening, apparently the result of exposure to heat. (Traces of burning were noticed on the top surfaces of stones of the north face [Greenewalt, Ratté, and Rautman 1994: 24]. Signs of deterioration were not noticed, however, in lower parts of the north face that were exposed.) The outer end of the recess is blocked by an apse of the Late Roman triple-apse building at the east end of the trench (figs. 3, 14).

The recess is 6.65 m wide, has vertical sides, and is faced with stone—roughly dressed blocks of schist and quartzite, as observed in 1989. The preserved top of the back face was 7 m above the recess floor. The uppermost four to five courses (together ca. 1 m high) had become dislocated,

Fig. 20. Sector MMS/S A, view looking north. Roman wall-like feature of field stones surrounded by Brick Fall (partly excavated).

apparently due to pressure from Roman construction above (cf. figs. 3, 14), and were tilted forward by as much as 0.50 m; they were removed for the sake of safety. The side faces of the recess appear to abut the back face. The relationship of the recess to the fabric of the Structure remains to be determined.[10] The floor of the recess evidently consisted of sandy soil.

Sector MMS/S, Brick Fall. The Brick Fall was exposed and excavated west of the west face of the Structure in MMS/S A, and in the recess of the east face (MMS/S B). From the Brick Fall itself, chronologically diagnostic material was not recovered (for diagnostic material recovered elsewhere in Brick Fall, Greenewalt and Heywood 1992: 3).

In MMS/S A, the top of the Brick Fall deposit[11] sloped down more or less evenly from the east face (fig. 18). Part of it, against the Structure face at the south end of the trench, was excavated to a depth of 2 m below the preserved top against the face; the section through it in the south trench scarp shows internal "strata" sloped down to the east (fig. 19). At the south end of the trench, Brick Fall appeared to be undisturbed. Further north, however, is a short wall-like feature of field stones (ca. 3.20 m long by 1.05 m wide by 1.75 m high) that was surrounded by Brick Fall (figs. 18, 20). A fragment of coarse ripple-ware pottery recovered inside it and coarse mortar that adhered to many of its stones suggest that the wall-like feature was created in Roman times. For post-Archaic disturbance of the earthy fill that rested directly over the south half to two-thirds of the wall-like feature, however, the only other evidence that was recognized was a lamp of Hellenistic type.[12]

In the recess, Brick Fall was removed to floor level in a space ca. 1.0–3.5 m east–west by 5 m north–south against the north face. That space was excavated ca. 1 m from the back face to make a section across the width of the recess (fig. 21, left), and ca. 1.65 m from the south face, to make a section perpendicular to the back face. The section across the width (which was made in 1990) showed brick debris sloped down from either side toward center; the incline from the south indicated the existence and proximity of the south face (which was located in 1991). The section perpendicular to the back face showed the debris sloped down from the back; as in other recesses of the Structure (Greenewalt, Cahill, and Rautman 1987: 23, fig. 7; Greenewalt and Heywood 1992: 4, fig. 4).

Resting on the floor of the recess underneath Brick Fall was a considerable amount of carbonized wood. When located at the end of the 1990 season, it was left *in situ* to be excavated the following year by P. I. Kuniholm and his staff of the Aegean Dendrochronology Project. Although the wood remains were covered with a layer of earth and a roof, by 1991 they had become too soft from (ground?) moisture for removal in entirety or for removal of reconstructable pieces. All wood examined by Kuniholm and his staff was oak. To Kuniholm, its thorough carbonization suggested that a time interval of at least a few days had elapsed between the burning of the wood and its burial under Brick Fall.

From the floor of the recess, underneath the wood remains, were recovered a few pottery fragments; for the most part they were ordinary plain wares (banded skyphoi), but they included one small fragment with

Fig. 21. Sector MMS/S B, view looking north. Colossal Lydian Structure: north wall of recess and back wall partly visible at top (arrow). Brick Fall (left) has been sectioned parallel to the back wall of the recess.

Fig. 22. Attic black-figure pottery fragments from sector MMS/S (see note 14).

orientalizing animal figure decoration, which provides further evidence that pottery with such decoration continued to circulate at Sardis as late as the middle of the sixth century B.C.E.[13]

Sector MMS/S, Post-destruction Rebuilding. In MMS/S A and B, stone construction of small-to-middle-sized field stones and small-sized blocks of sandstone and marble (some reused), set dry or in mud mortar, evidently belongs to a rebuilding of the Structure after the destruction of the mid-sixth century B.C.E. The date of the construction, which included two or more phases, was not determined; because of loose association with pottery of Archaic and Classical types it is presumed to fall within the later sixth-to-fourth centuries B.C.E. In fig. 14, the construction is shaded with diagonal lines, like the "Secondary Limestone Wall" in sec-

tor MMS (cf. fig. 15), which, however, contains many larger stones (Greenewalt et al. 1983: 6–8).

There are two east faces; the outer, which has a short return that abuts the inner, is evidently the later of the two. Of the west face there are three surerimposed planes (fig. 18): an upper face 2.5 m high, with preserved top less than 0.50 m below modern ground surface (indicated by two arrows in fig. 18); a middle face ca. 1 m to the west and 0.7 m high; and a lower face slightly recessed behind the middle face and ca. 1 m high. Earthly debris resting in layers that slope down to the west from those faces may represent an earthwork support or glacis contemporaneous with them.

Sector MMS/S, Attic and Eastern Greek Pottery. Of intrinsic interest are fragments of Attic and Eastern Greek painted pottery recovered from MMS/S, none of them in secure contexts; some of the Attic black-figure fragments appear in fig. 22.[14]

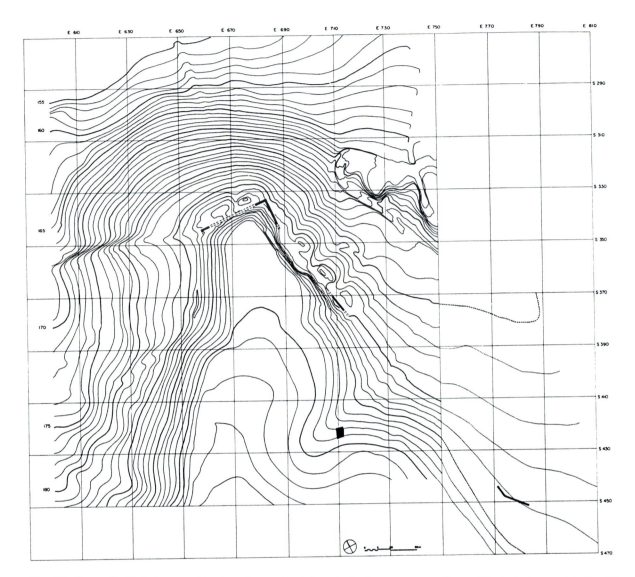

Fig. 23. Sector ByzFort, topographic plan. Heavy black lines indicate exposed sections of Archaic terrace (cf. fig. 27) and of sandstone foundations in concavity on east side of hill (cf. fig. 24).

METROON *PARASTADES*

The architectural role of ten marble blocks that had been reused in the Late Roman Synagogue and that had originally belonged to *parastades* of a Metroon (the word *parastada* appears in one of the Greek texts of Hellenistic correspondence that are inscribed on several blocks; Gauthier 1989) was discussed in Greenewalt 1990: 20–21. Because of the treatment of their sides, the blocks were presumed to belong to piers that projected at right angles from one or more wall surfaces. Since anta blocks in Andron B, i.e., the Andron of Mausolus, at Labraunda (Hellström and Thieme 1981) have

the same treatment, however, it is more reasonable to suppose that the Sardis blocks belonged to antae, the common meaning of *parastades*, in a Metroon of conventional Greek megaron design.

C.H.G.

SECTOR BYZFORT

After a hiatus of one season in 1990, excavation at Sector ByzFort—the flat-topped spur or foothill crowned by a large Archaic terrace on the lower north slope of the acropolis—was resumed for one and one-half months in 1992 (the spur is located at ca. E. 630–730 / S. 310–340 on the 'B' grid). The

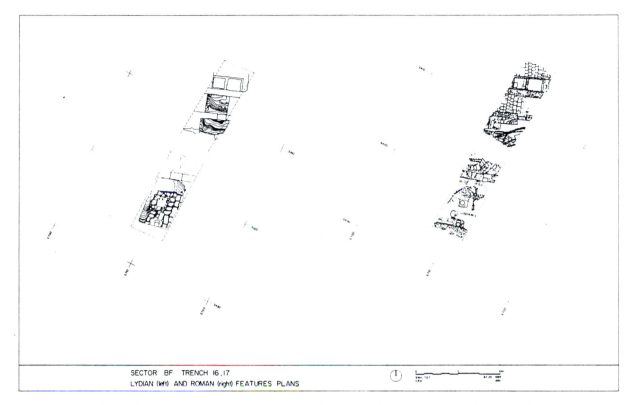

SECTOR BF TRENCH 16,17
LYDIAN (left) AND ROMAN (right) FEATURES PLANS

Fig. 24. Sector ByzFort, plans of trenches dug in 1988–1989 and 1991 in concavity on east side of hill.

goals of this season's work were to finish two projects started in 1988 and 1989: the exploration of the spur's east side, and the excavation of a sequence of Archaic deposits on the summit of the spur. The completion of those projects brings the program of investigation of Sector ByzFort, begun in 1983, to an end; no further digging is planned (for results of previous work, Greenewalt, Ratté, and Rautman 1994: 26–31and references).

East Side

In 1988 and 1989, a 4 × 10 m trench was dug into the east side of the hill, roughly halfway between the northeast corner of the Archaic terrace and the southernmost exposed section of the terrace's east face, for the purpose of investigating a concave dip or depression that interrupts the hillside at this point (the trench was located on the south side of this concavity at E. 718–722 / S. 416–426 on the 'B' grid; fig. 23). The trench revealed the south edge of what appeared to be a street running uphill from east to west (elevation approximately 188 m above sea level), and, facing

the street, part of a building 6 m wide, nestled against the base of a tall retaining wall (preserved height, 5.5 m above the level of the street; fig. 24). Pottery and coins found beneath the floors of the building facing the street suggested a date in the fifth century C.E. Further excavation showed that this late Roman building rested partly on undisturbed soil, partly on top of an earlier structure—a massive foundation built of sandstone blocks—whose date and function remained unclear.

In 1991, a second 4 × 10 m trench was opened up 2 m north of the trench dug in 1988 and 1989 (location of the new trench: E. 708–712 / S. 404–414; fig. 23). This trench revealed the north edge of the Roman street (thus shown to be roughly 5 m wide) and on the north side of the street, part of another Roman building (figs. 24, 25). The Roman building comprised two distinct areas: to the south, a room with a tile floor approximately 1 m below street level and a door opening through its south wall onto the street; to the north, on the other side of a party wall, an unconnected room whose tile floor lay 1.6 m below the floor level of the south room. A notable feature of the north room is a pair

Fig. 25. Sector ByzFort, view of trench dug in 1991 in concavity on east side of hill, looking south.

Fig. 26. Pilgrim flask (P91.10/9859) with hoard of bronze coins (1991.467–537) from Sector ByzFort.

of large basins or tanks, built up against the room's south wall (capacities of basins ca. 1250 liters each; cf. the basins excavated at Sector MMS in 1985 [Greenewalt, Rautman, and Cahill 1987: 57–60]; p. 10 here). The floors of these basins are paved with schist slabs; their sides are lined with terracotta tiles. The basins are connected by a pipe running through the party wall that divides them. A second pipe in the north wall of the west basin may have been used for drainage.

A pilgrim flask containing a small hoard of 71 bronze coins, most of the late fifth century C.E., was found beneath the floor of the south room (fig. 26).[15] Further excavation both in this area and beneath the street uncovered a complex network of pipes and drains; especially notable is a large covered drain 0.7 m wide and 0.75–1.0 m high, running beneath the street. These waterworks were set in mixed fill, beneath which lay undisturbed soil sloping down from north to south at elevations 2–5 m below street level. Apart from a single Ar-

chaic potsherd, no traces of earlier occupation were revealed.

The structures on both sides of the street thus appear to rest on a series of terraces climbing up the south side of the concavity that interrupts the ByzFort hill's east slope. The sandstone foundation uncovered in 1988 and 1989 beneath the building on the uphill side of the street remains enigmatic, and it is possible that these terraces predate, at least in part, the late Roman structures they support. But it so, the later construction has almost entirely obliterated the earlier structures and strata, and it is also possible that the east edge of the ByzFort hill originally—and in the Archaic period—formed a straight line, and that the present concavity is entirely the result of post-Archaic erosion and late Roman building. After excavation and recording were finished, the trenches dug in 1988, 1989, and 1991 on the east side of the hill were filled in.

Spur Summit

In 1989, excavation on top of the hill revealed a narrow stone (marble and sandstone) foundation or stylobate—Archaic in date and belonging perhaps to the porch of a small building or pavilion—resting in part on the fill of a large square pit (3.5 m along a side and 2.2 m deep; these features are located at ca. E. 671–676 / S. 348–352 on the 'B' grid; figs. 23, 27); included in the fill of this pit or cellar was a rich deposit of Lydian pottery, debatable to the mid-seventh century B.C.E. The goals of excavation in 1991 were to date the Archaic stylobate more precisely and to dig more of the seventh century B.C.E. pottery deposit in the fill of the cellar.

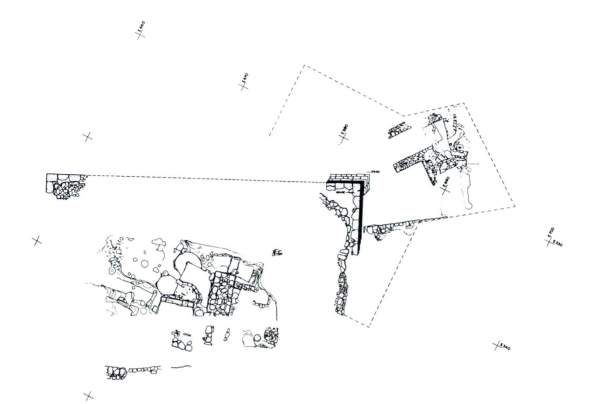

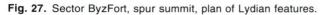

Sector BF   Lydian Features

Fig. 27. Sector ByzFort, spur summit, plan of Lydian features.

Fig. 28. Sector ByzFort, spur summit, view of fallen mudbrick wall, looking south.

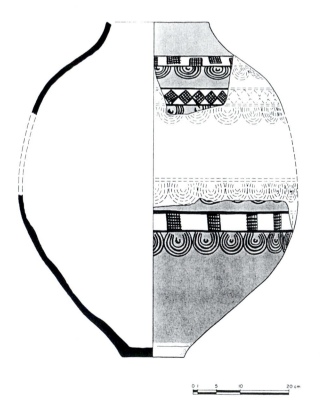

Fig. 29. Composite restoration drawing of jar from Sector ByzFort, based on P91.37/9927 and P91.40/9930.

Excavation of the area immediately behind (south of) and beneath the stylobate did not yield any precisely datable artifacts, but a few ceramic skyphos fragments seem more characteristic of the sixth than of the seventh century. Anathyrosis on the joint of one of the blocks of the stylobate, revealed when two of the stylobate blocks were removed so that more of the fill of the cellar could be excavated, also indicates a sixth rather than a seventh century date (Ratté 1989: 86).

The deposit of seventh century B.C.E. pottery in the fill of the cellar was contained in a layer of debris 0.3–0.7 m above the cellar floor. Excavation in 1991 showed that this layer rested on top of a fallen mudbrick wall that had tumbled face down into the cellar from the south (fig. 28). Nineteen courses of bricks (0.36 m long, 0.24 m wide, and 0.08 m thick) were preserved, five bricks wide at the widest point. The wall was only one brick thick; the bricks were separated by thin layers of mud mortar, and the face of the wall bore a thin layer of mud plaster. The fallen mudbrick wall proved in turn to rest on a second layer of debris, which itself lay directly on the floor of the cellar.

The two debris layers differed in the types of pottery recovered from them. The lower layer contained mostly large, undecorated storage vessels; the upper layer contained painted jars (a composite drawing of one such bichrome jar, restored from fragments of at least two different vessels, is illustrated in fig. 29),[16] and painted gray and monochrome dishes (Greenewalt, Ratté, and Rautman 1994: 32, fig. 26). Presumably the lower debris layer represents the contents of the cellar before the collapse of the mudbrick wall, and the upper layer includes debris tossed or fallen in from above. The pottery from both layers was, however,

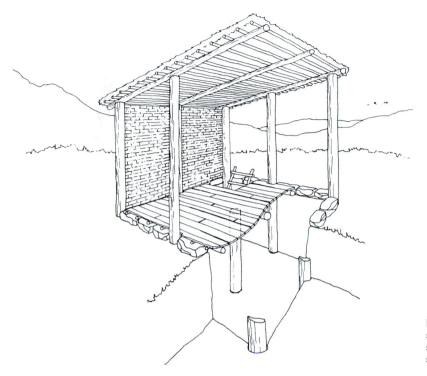

Fig. 30. Sector ByzFort, spur summit, conjectural restoration of superstructure of cellar, looking southwest.

for the most part fragmentary. The paucity of restorable vessels suggests that both the cellar and the living or working spaces above and around it had been cleaned out, or abandoned for some time before the mudbrick wall and the debris on top of it fell into the cellar.

Large postholes dug in the corners of the cellar, in the middle of each wall, and in the center of the floor, suggest that the building to which the cellar belonged rose at least one story above ground level. The mudbrick wall fallen into the cellar may have formed the south wall of the structure. The absence of any trace of the foundations of this wall suggests that the area around the cellar was leveled off at some later date. The superstructure of the cellar may not have been walled in on its east, north, and west sides—thus requiring posts in the absence of walls to carry the roof. Figure 30 offers a conjectural restoration of this structure.[17]

The results of excavation on the ByzFort summit in 1991 help to refine the chronology of Archaic occupation and construction proposed in Greenewalt, Ratté, and Rautman 1994: 29–31. Thus the cellar belongs to an initial building phase of the mid-seventh century B.C.E. A second building phase of the late seventh or early sixth century is represented by the large stone foundation built partly into the east half of the cellar, and by the leveling of the

undisturbed soil around these features. The Archaic terrace wall that encloses the ByzFort hill on its north and east sides belongs to a third building phase of the mid-sixth century; the stylobate on the top of the hill apparently belongs to the same phase.

The nature of the Archaic occupation of this sector remains enigmatic. In most places, later construction has erased all but the foundations of the Archaic structures, and in the areas exposed, plans of the buildings to which these foundations belong have proved impossible to recognize. Excavation of the area south of the trenches on the summit of the spur might yield more definitive results, but that area is impractically large. (It is an excellent candidate, however, for nonintrusive, subsurface surveying.) For these reasons, excavation of Sector ByzFort, now that the specific projects begun in earlier seasons have all been completed, has been called to a halt.

GRAVES AT SARDIS, BIN TEPE, AND ENVIRONS

Pyramid Tomb

The so-called Pyramid Tomb is a small limestone structure on the northwest slope of the acropolis of

Fig. 31. Pyramid Tomb, general view.

Sardis (fig. 31). The Pyramid Tomb was initially discovered in 1914 by the first American Expedition to Sardis (Butler 1922: 155–66, 167–70), rediscovered and reexcavated in 1960–1961 and 1969 by the current Harvard/Cornell project (Hanfmann 1983: 42 and references). A new study of the tomb was undertaken in 1990 in order to reexamine the monument in the light of recent discoveries, and to compile a new set of architectural drawings. After excavation, the tomb was partially reburied to protect it from weathering and vandalism.

As preserved, the tomb is a stepped platform, resembling the lower part of a stepped pyramid, 7.5 m² at foundation level. Above the foundations, the structure steps in evenly on all sides, rising over six steps to a maximum height of 1.9 m. The only remains of the superstructure of the tomb are a stone pavement, found by the first Sardis Expedition in the center of the tomb at the level of the top of the fifth step, and two wall blocks. Setting lines incised in the surface of the pavement indicate the positions of the walls of the tomb chamber to which the pavement and the two surviving wall blocks belonged. The dimensions of the chamber as measured from the setting lines are 1.46 × 2.26 m, from which figures it is possible to infer a foot measure of approximately 0.324 m. Thus the chamber measured 4.5 feet by 7 feet, and each of the steps of the tomb was roughly 1 foot high and 1 foot deep.

The tomb may be restored, as originally suggested by H. C. Butler, after the model of the tomb of Cyrus at Pasargadae (Butler 1922: 166, ill. 185,

168–70);[18] a new such restoration is illustrated in fig. 32. If, as seems likely, the Pyramid Tomb is a product of the same "Graeco-Persian" cultural movement that produced the tomb of Cyrus, it would presumably postdate the fall of Sardis in ca. 546 B.C.E.; if it is actually a copy of Cyrus's tomb, it would likely postdate the death of that king in ca. 530 B.C.E. In any event, the Pyramid Tomb may be more generally and independently dated within the sixth century on the basis of its masonry; especially diagnostic is the absence of any evidence for the use of the claw chisel, which indicates a *terminus ante quem* of ca. 500 B.C.E. (Nylander 1970: 53–56; Stronach 1978: 99–100); for a fuller report on the reexcavation of the Pyramid Tomb, see Ratté, 1992.

Karnıyarık Tepe

The burial mound known as Karnıyarık Tepe (diameter: 220 m, height: 50 m) is one of the largest mounds at Bin Tepe, the great tumulus cemetery in the Hermus plain opposite Sardis (fig. 33). In the mid-1960s, the Sardis Expedition devoted three field seasons to the exploration by tunneling of the interior of this mound (Hanfmann 1983: 57–58 and references); 65 m in from the edge of the mound, the excavators encountered a curving limestone wall, which seems to describe the circumference of a circle concentric with the outside of the tumulus (fig. 34). This wall is thus apparently the retaining wall or "crepis" of an earlier and smaller tumulus, buried beneath the present mound. Although the

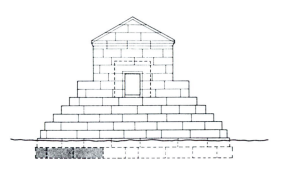

NORTH ELEVATION

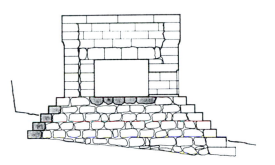

EAST ELEVATION

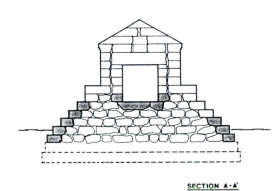

SECTION A-A'

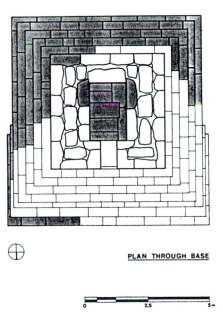

SECTION B-B'

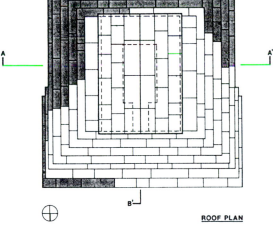

ROOF PLAN

PLAN THROUGH BASE

Fig. 32. Pyramid Tomb, conjectural restoration.

tunnels were continued to the center of the mound, the burial chamber or chambers were never found.

On the basis of a reference in a fragment of verse attributed to Hipponax (Degani 1983: 30–32, fr. 7) and of a symbol inscribed in numerous places on the face of the interior crepis wall (fig. 34), ten-

tatively identified as a royal monogram, G. M. A. Hanfmann suggested that Karnıyarık Tepe was the tomb of Gyges, who died in the mid-seventh century B.C.E. (Hanfmann 1965: 34). Hanfmann's identification was, however, speculative (the association with the poem by Hipponax depends on an

Fig. 33. Karnıyarık Tepe, general view.

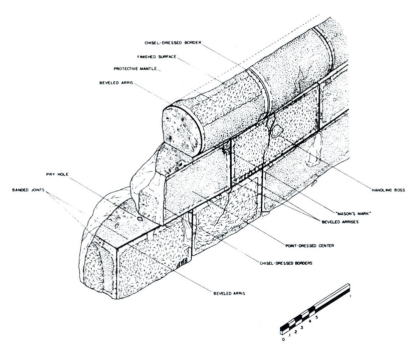

Fig. 34. Karnıyarık Tepe, isometric view of crepis wall.

uncertain emendation, and the reading of the symbol inscribed on the face of the crepis wall has been contested by no less an authority than R. Gusmani [1975: 69–70 and references]). Other evidence, especially the masonry of the crepis wall, indicates a sixth rather than a seventh century date.

In 1991, a new study of the crepis wall was undertaken in order to reexamine and record the technical details that indicate a later date; these include handling bosses, prymarks, a joining technique similar in some respects to anathyrosis, and very fine bevels or chamfers cut in both the horizontal and

vertical edges of the blocks (fig. 34). The earliest securely datable monuments in Lydia that exhibit comparable details are the tomb of Alyattes (Ratté 1989: 7–15, 157–89; Greenewalt et al. 1983: 26–27; Hanfmann 1983: 56–57 and references) and the limestone and sandstone walls at Sector MMS/N (Ratté 1989: 22–23, 237–44; Greenewalt, Rautman, and Cahill 1987: 72–84; Greenewalt et al. 1983: 13–15), both of which probably belong to the first half of the sixth century; Greek architectural comparanda such as the temple of Artemis at Ephesos (Hogarth 1908: 256–58, pl. 11; cf. Bammer 1988:

20–21) suggest a similar date. In addition to those architectural details, a new small find also indicates a date in the sixth century: a fragmentary stemmed dish found in the stone packing piled up behind the wall (figs. 35, 36).[19] Many similar dishes were found in the mid-sixth century Persian destruction layer at Sector MMS (Greenewalt, Cahill, and Rautman 1987: 28 fig. 12).

Thus the archaeological evidence suggests that Karnıyarık Tepe in both its original and its enlarged forms should be dated roughly 50 to 100 years later than the death of Gyges. It is not impossible that Karnıyarık Tepe was a cenotaph or memorial for Gyges, but it is more likely that it belongs to one of his descendants, not Alyattes, whose tomb is already accounted for, or Croesus, who if he was buried at Sardis was presumably denied the honor of a monument on this scale, but perhaps a prince—such as Atys, the elder son of Croesus—or princess of the royal house.[20]

Tumulus Tomb Near Sarıçalı

In July of 1990, several members of the Sardis Expedition visited a tumulus tomb (first noticed in 1989 on an expedition to a nearby marble quarry) in the region of the village of Sarıçalı, between Gölmarmara and Akhisar north of Sardis (fig. 37). The tumulus is approximately 50 m wide and 10 m high, and an open tunnel dug into the side of the mound gave access to a well preserved tomb chamber within.

The tomb chamber is approached by an unroofed dromos and a shallow antechamber, and is built of finely dressed and fitted marble blocks (figs. 38, 39). The chamber is oblong, with the entrance centered in one of the long sides; its dimensions (1.45 × 2.60 m) are similar to those of the chamber of the Pyramid Tomb (1.46 × 2.26 m), and the same unit of measurement (a foot of 0.324 m) may have been used in both structures; thus this tomb chamber measures 4.5 feet from front to back and 8 feet in width. The chamber was partially filled with earth, so it was impossible to measure its full height; it is at least 1.85 m. The walls and ceiling are smoothly chisel-dressed, except for "protective lips."—narrow fillet-like raised bands—along the tops of the walls and on both sides of the joints between the ceiling blocks; these details are also present in the chamber of the tomb of Alyattes, which in its workmanship this chamber closely resembles. A fragment of a funerary couch found inside the chamber bears a shallow, bed-like

Fig. 35. Stemmed dish (P91.9/9857) from Karnıyarık Tepe.

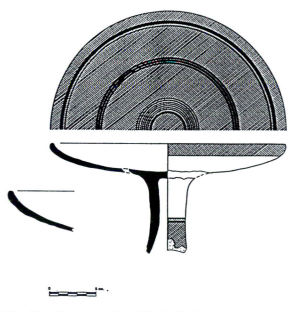

Fig. 36. Stemmed dish (P91.9/9857) from Karnıyarık Tepe, drawing showing profile and decoration.

depression on its upper surface, with a flat semicircular "pillow" at the head.

A missing wall block in one corner of the chamber led to an open space above the ceiling. This open space was, it seems, originally filled with rubble; above the rubble lay a thin deposit of fine lime mortar, surmounted by a thin layer of charcoal, and then a reed matting, of which the impression survives in a layer of fine clay pressed on top (fig. 40). Some of these details, like those of the stoneworking, also find parallels in the chamber of the tomb of Alyattes, which itself bears a layer of charcoal—apparently a waterproofing agent of some kind—on

Fig. 37. Tumulus tomb near Sarı-çalı, general view.

Fig. 38. Tumulus tomb near Sarıçalı, view of interior of tomb showing dromos, antechamber, and entrance to chamber.

Fig. 39. Tumulus tomb near Sarıçalı, view of interior of chamber.

top of the ceiling. The similarities between the tomb near Sarıçalı and the tomb of Alyattes—one of only a few other known Archaic Lydian tomb chambers made of marble (Ratté 1989: 31, 123, n. 9)—indicate a date in the sixth century B.C.E.; the absence here as in the tomb of Alyattes and the Pyramid Tomb of any evidence for the use of the claw chisel suggests a *terminus ante quem* of the end of that century.

C.R.

Fig. 40. Tumulus tomb near Sarıçalı, close-up view of impression of reed matting in clay above roof of chamber.

NOTES

[1] Excavation and other projects were conducted by the Archaeological Exploration of Sardis, or Sardis Expedition, which is jointly sponsored by the Harvard University Art Museums, Cornell University, the American Schools of Oriental Research, and the Corning Museum of Glass. The Expedition is supported financially by many corporate and individual donors. The conservation program is supported by a grant from the Samuel H. Kress Foundation. Study projects connected with publication of the results of fieldwork before 1977 are supported by the National Endowment for the Humanities, a federal agency that supports study in such fields as art history, philosophy, literature, and languages. Field work was authorized in 1990 and 1991 by the General Directorate of Monuments and Museums, a division of the Ministry of Culture of the Republic of Turkey. Each field season took place during three summer months. It is a pleasure to acknowledge fundamental permissions granted by the General Directorate of Monuments and Museums and the encouragement and support of its officers; especially Director General Mehmet Akif Işık, Excavations Department Mehmet Yılmaz, and Excavations Branch Directors Çelik Topcu and Osman Özbek. The Archaeological and Ethnographical Museum in Manisa also generously supported, assisted, and encouraged Expedition projects; the Expedition is particularly grateful to Director Hasan Dedeoğlu, Deputy Directors Fatma Bilgin and Mustafa Tümer, and curators İlhami Bilgin, Rafet Dinç, and Mehmet Önder. The Government Representatives were Remzi Yağcı (Museum of Anatolian Civilizations, Ankara) in 1990 and Mustafa Samur (Kayseri Museum), Turhan Kayabey (Balıkesir Museum), Ömer Çakır (Orodu Museum), and Emel Erten Yağcı (General Directorate of Monuments and Museums, Ankara) in 1991; their supportive advice and assistance greatly facilitated Expedition programs. Staff members for 1990 and 1991 were the following (for both seasons where no year is given): C. H. Greenewalt, Jr. (University of California at Berkeley; field director); Teoman Yalçınkaya (Yapıtek A. Ş., a division of Çimentaş, Izmir; administrative officer and agent); A. Ramage (Cornell; associate director and specialist for sector HoB stratigraphy and pottery, 1990); C. Ratté (Florida State University; assistant director, senior archaeologist, specialist for Lydian masonry); K. J. Frazer (Egypt Exploration Society; camp manager); J. A. Scott (Harvard; editor of publications for Phase I); K. J. Severson (Daedalus, Inc., Boston; senior conservator and conservation consultant); J. A. Sherman, E. B. Salzman, P. Griffin (all New York University, Institute of Fine Arts Conservation Center; conservators, respectively 1990, 1990 and 1991, 1991); H. G. Kökten (Aegean University; conservator, 1991); T. D. Thompson (Woollen, Molzan and Partners, Indianapolis; senior architect); S. M. Hickey, M. D. Antrim, P. Stinson, C. Harvey (all Ball State University; architects, the first two in 1990, the second two in 1991); C. S. Alexander (Harvard; draftsman); C. M. de Boucaud (Cornell; photographer); D. Zeidenberg (Harvard; registrar, 1990); L. Benson (University of Missouri-Columbia; registrar, 1991); N. D. Cahill (University of California at Berkeley, senior excavator, 1990); M. L. Rautman (University of Missouri-Columbia; senior excavator); G. Umholtz (University of California at Berkeley; senior excavator and epigraphist); R. T. Neer (Harvard; excavator and numismatist); M. Bechhoefer (Cornell; excavator, 1990); G. Gürtekin (Aegean University; excavator, 1991); E. R. McIntosh (Harvard, excavator 1991); F. K. Yegül (University of California at Santa Barbara; specialist for graphic recording of Artemis Temple); D. G. Favro (University of California at Los Angeles; specialist for Roman architecture, 1991); N. H. Ramage (Ithaca College; specialist for Attic pottery); S. I. Rotroff (Hunter College; specialist for Hellenistic relief wares, 1990); A. Oliver, Jr. (National Endowment for the Arts; specialist for Hellenistic pottery, 1990); M. J. Rein (Harvard; specialist for marble Cybele naiskos); A. B. Casendino (Childs Bertman Tseckares and Casendino, Inc., Boston; consultant for site enhancement,

1991); H. R. Goette (German Archaeological Institute, Athens; specialist for Artemis Temple capitals, 1990). The considerable clerical work required by regulations of the Ministry of Labor and the Social Security Commission was done efficiently and cheerfully by Celalletin Şentürk (Manisa Museum). To all these for patience, hard work, high professional standards, and team spirit, hearty and heartfelt thanks.

[2] Conservation, in addition to routine treatment and mending of artifacts, included the following projects. Principal fragments of the Archaic iron and bronze helmet that were recovered in 1987 and 1988 were mounted for exhibition (Greenewalt and Heywood 1992: figs. 6–9). Broken parts of the southeast corner of the Pyramid Tomb were consolidated and restored in 1990. Painted plaster in a Late Roman room (cubiculum? sector MMS/S was consolidated and edged for protection in 1991. Ninety square meters of mosaic paving (in the south ambulatory of the Late Roman avenue, sector MMS/N) were lifted and stored for future backing. Three facsimile mosaic inscriptions in the Late Roman Synagogue were repainted in 1990. Fourteen modern drainage sinks in the Synagogue were cleaned and refurbished in 1991.

Other projects included graphic recording of the Artemis temple (by F. K. Yegül) and of Lydian masonry in Karnıyarık Tepe at Bin Tepe (by C. Ratté); studies of Iron Age stratification and pottery from sector HoB (by A. Ramage in 1990); of Attic pottery (by N. H. Ramage, 1990); of Hellenistic pottery (by S. I. Rotroff and A. Oliver, Jr., 1990); of the Archaic marble Cybele naiskos (by M. J. Rein, 1991); of Artemis temple capitals (by H. R. Goette, 1990); preliminary planning for reconstruction and site enhancement at sectors MMS, MMS/S, MMS/N (by A. B. Casendino in 1991); study of the Archaic iron and bronze helmet fragments, in preparation for a reconstruction by the Royal Armouries, H. M. Tower of London (by C. Smith and R. Smith, 1991).

[3] A pile of bricks stacked next to one column base and the absence of at least one stylobate block may reflect the area's selective despoliation prior to the collapse of its superstructure. Like the main ambulatory, the inner portico apparently had an upper story which included spouted and opaion roof tiles (Greenewalt, Ratté, and Rautman 1994: 39 n. 6 for the date).

[4] Area of text 2.55 × 1.55 m; height of letters 0.10–0.15 m. This reading follows the preliminary analysis of the inscription by G. Umholtz and P. Herrmann. Two *emboloi* are mentioned in another Late Roman building inscription from western Sardis (IN68.18); see Greenewalt, Cahill, and Rautman 1987: 47 n. 8 with references. Flavius Archelaos, also a "companion of his serene highness" as well as a *hegemon* (commander), is named in a dated inscription of 349 C.E., from Radeime in Syria; see *L'Année Épigraphique* 1933: 41 no. 171. P. Herrmann, who acknowledges D. Hoffmann for this reference, cautions that the name may not be very rare and that Flavius is a common name in late antiquity (personal communication).

[5] The presence of the street wall was anticipated by magnetometer prospection carried out in the area in 1985; see Greenewalt, Rautman, and Cahill 1987: 62, and for the street Greenewalt, Cahill, and Rautman 1987: 18–20.

[6] Whether the bottom course of the foundations was exposed anywhere in 1990 and 1991 is unclear.

[7] In excavation at sector HoB, 300 m west of the Archaic fortification, however, widespread deposits of water-laid gravel and sand in Archaic strata were interpreted by excavator G. F. Swift, Jr., as the result of flooding by the Pactolus (Hanfmann 1966: 8; 1967: 32). If his interpretation is correct—as A. Ramage, who has reviewed the stratification history believes—the course of the Pactolus in the seventh and sixth centuries B.C.E. must have come significantly further to the east of its present course.

[8] On the reconciliation of ancient literary testimonia with archaeological evidence, G. M. A. Hanfmann (1983: 75) pithily observed "... no verbal picture can ever match the concreteness and complexity of material realities. In this way, the spade is mightier than the word."

[9] This interrelation is not clearly described or illustrated in published Sardis reports. The relevant segment of the west face is also the back wall of the recess from which the helmet and skeleton were recovered in 1987 and 1988; fig. 15. The face appears as a simple line running diagonally through the opening in the north street wall in Greenewalt, Cahill, and Rautman 1987: 17 fig. 4 (at E. 108–109 / S. 93–96 on the 'B' grid). The opening in the street wall (2.25 m. wide) is reported by Rautman, 18 (in Greenewalt, Cahill, and Rautman 1987); a segment of the street wall west of the opening was dismantled in 1989, Rautman in Greenewalt, Ratté, and Rautman 1994: 11. A segment of Late Roman street wall east of the opening and the west face of Colossal Lydian structure (= back wall of the Structure recess) appear together in Greenewalt and Heywood 1992: 3, fig. 3, and in Greenewalt 1992b: 10, fig. 7.

[10] Some features, like the crude "face" oriented east–west within the Structure behind the recess (Greenewalt, Ratté, and Rautman 1994: 23–24) suggest several building phases.

[11] The top of the Brick Fall was cleared for a space of about 10 m², the trench scarp to the south (fig. 18) and Late Roman construction to the north and west (cf. figs. 3, 14) limited further excavation in those directions; and for safety reasons it seemed inadvisable to excavate significantly deeper than the lowest levels reached in 1991.

[12] Lamp L90.7/9786: with two narrow ridges and a collar around the filling hole; lug at proper right side towards front, long nozzle, no handle; poor glaze. Intact except for parts of collar, end of nozzle. Parallels are Scheibler 1976: 93 no. 573; Howland 1958: 95 no. 411 (classified under Type 29A).

A plan of the wall-like feature appears in Sardis Expedition drawing MMS 77.

[13] The fragment is a skyphos rim, with "marbling" in the interior and part of an animal in dark "glaze" on

cream slip on the exterior. The same combination of decorative conventions occurs on a boat-shape vessel, the remains of which were recovered from a residential complex that had been buried under Brick Fall in sector MMS (Cahill in Greenewalt et al. 1990: 152–53; Greenewalt 1989: 277 fig. 12). For other evidence of orientalizing styles at Sardis in the middle of the sixth century B.C.E., Greenewalt 1972.

[14] Figure 22 shows the following fragments. Top left, Siana (?) cup with bearded male figure (P90.43/9796); top right, small open vessel with lion ear and mane (P90.51/9809); center, closed vessel with combat scene (P90.22/9761); bottom left, closed vessel with feline body, according to G. Bakır ca. 570–560 B.C.E. (P90.23/9762); bottom right, closed vessel with scene showing the arming of Achilles by Thetis and her companions (P90.45/9801; for the subject, see Johansen 1967: 92–113). Other fragments from sector MMS/S include Attic black-figure cup with figural scene (P91.3/9835) and closed vessel with body of horse (P91.11/9860); Attic red-figure open vessel with egg-and-dart pattern and face, neck and shoulders of man to left on exterior (P90.7/9737; probably late fifth or fourth century B.C.E.); Ionian cup rim with leaf pattern (P91.2/9833); Ionian (?) black-figure open vessel with legs of walking animal to left (P90.52/9810); Fikellura amphora and amphoriskos with pattern decoration (P90.18/9753, R. M. Cook's Group Q, see Cook 1954: 8,

pl. 4; amphoriskos not inventoried); local (?) black-figure closed vessel with goose (?; P91.28/9911).

[15] Pilgrim flask: P91.10/9859; coins: 1991.467–537; the latest coins are nine issues of Zeno (476–491 C.E.).

[16] P91.37/9927 and P91.40/9930.

[17] Pieces of charcoal found on the floor of the cellar have been identified by P. Kuniholm and C. Griggs as beech, not a local tree (although it does occur, as Kuniholm informs us, in other parts of Asia Minor, especially in the mountains near the Black Sea). For dendrochronological analysis of these pieces, see Huber 1992: 41–45.

[18] Butler also proposed an alternative restoration of the tomb as a stepped pyramid; this intriguing but improbable idea was developed by S. Kasper in drawings illustrated in Hanfmann 1972: fig. 193, and Hanfmann 1983: fig. 68.

[19] P91.9/9857. Diam. 0.230 m, p. H. 0.085 m. The decoration consists of red glaze on the inside of the dish, on the outside of the rim, and on the lower part of the stem, with narrow bands painted on both the interior and the exterior in black over the red glaze, in a typical "black on red" style.

[20] According to Herodotus (1.34–46), Atys was killed in a hunting accident two years before Croesus began to prepare for war against Persia, thus in about 550 B.C.E. See Ratté in press for a fuller report on the dating and identification of Karnıyarıktepe.

BIBLIOGRAPHY

1988   L'Année Épigraphique. Rue des Publications Épigraphiques Relatives à l'Antiquité Romaine. Paris: Ernest Leroux.

Bammer, A.
1988   Neue Grabungen an der Zentralbasis des Artemision von Ephesos. *Jahreshefte der Österreichischen archäologischen Instituts in Wien, Beiblatt* 58: 3–32.

Butler, H. C.
1922   *Sardis I, The Excavations Part I, 1910–1914.* Leyden: Brill.

Cook, R. M.
1954   *Corpus Vasorum Antiquorum, Great Britain, 13. British Museum, 8.* London: British Museum.

Crawford, J. S.
1990   *The Byzantine Shops at Sardis.* Sardis Monograph 9. Cambridge, MA: Harvard.

Degani, E.
1983   *Hipponactis Testimonia et Framenta.* Leipzig: Teubner.

Gauthier, P.
1989   *Nouvelles Inscriptions de Sardes* II. Centre de Recherche d'Histoire et de Philologie de la IVe Section de l'Ecole pratique des Hautes Études, III. Hautes Études du monde Gréco-Romain, 15. Geneva: Droz.

Greenewalt, C. H., Jr.
1972   Two Lydian Graves at Sardis. *California Studies in Classical Antiquity* 5: 113–45.
1989   Excavations at Sardis, 1978–1988. *Türk Arkeoloji Dergisi* 28: 263–85.
1990   The Sardis Campaign of 1987, *Bulletin of the American Schools of Oriental Research, Supplement* 27: 1–28.
1992a   Sardis: Archaeological Research in 1990. *XIII. Kazı Sonuçları Toplantısı,* Ankara: T. C. Kültür Bakanlığı, Anıtlar ve Müzeler Genel Müdürlüğü.
1992b   When a Mighty Empire was Destroyed: The Common Man at the Fall of Sardis, ca. 546 B.C. *Proceedings of the American Philosophical Society* 136: 247–71.

Greenewalt, C. H., Jr.; Cahill, N. D.; Dedeoğlu, H.; and Herrmann, P.
1990   The Sardis Campaign of 1986. *Bulletin of the American Schools of Oriental Research* Supplement 26: 137–77.

Greenewalt, C. H., Jr.; Cahill, N. D.; and Rautman, M. L.
1987   The Sardis Campaign of 1984. *Bulletin of the American Schools of Oriental Research* Supplement 25: 13–54.

Greenewalt, C. H., Jr., and Heywood, A. M.
1992   A Helmet of the Sixth Century B.C. from Sardis. *Bulletin of the American Schools of Oriental Research* 285: 1–31.

Greenewalt, C. H., Jr.; Ramage, A.; Sullivan, D. G.; Nayır, K.; and Tulga, A.
1983   The Sardis Campaigns of 1979 and 1980. *Bulletin of the American Schools of Oriental Research* 249: 1–44.

Greenewalt, C. H., Jr.; Ratté, C.; and Rautman, M. L.
1994   The Sardis Campaigns of 1988 and 1989. *Annual of the American Schools of Oriental Research* 51: 1–43.

Greenewalt, C. H., Jr., Sullivan, D. G., Ratté, C., and Howe, T. N.
1985   The Sardis Campaigns of 1981 and 1982. *Bulletin of the American Schools of Oriental Research* Supplement 23: 53–92.

Greenewalt, C. H., Jr.; Rautman, M. L.; and Cahill, N. D.
1987   The Sardis Campaign of 1985. *Bulletin of the American Schools of Oriental Research* Supplement 25: 55–92.

Greenewalt, C. H., Jr.; Rautman, M. L.; and Meriç, R.
1986   The Sardis Campaign of 1983. *Bulletin of the American Schools of Oriental Research* Supplement 24: 1–30.

Greenewalt, C. H., Jr.; Sterud, E. L.; and Belknap, D. F.
1982   The Sardis Campaign of 1978. *Bulletin of the American Schools of Oriental Research* 245: 1–34.

Gusmani, R.
1975   *Neue epichorische Schriftzeugnisse aus Sardis (1958–1971).* Sardis Monograph 3. Cambridge, MA: Harvard.

Hanfmann, G. M. A.
1965   The Seventh Campaign at Sardis (1964). *Bulletin of the American Schools of Oriental Research* 177: 2–37.

1966   The Eighth Campaign of Sardis (1965). *Bulletin of the American Schools of Oriental Research* 182: 2–54.

1967   The Ninth Campaign at Sardis (1966). *Bulletin of the American Schools of Oriental Research* 186: 17–52.

1972   *Letters from Sardis.* Cambridge, MA: Harvard.

1983   *Sardis from Prehistoric to Roman Times: Results of the Archaeological Exploration of Sardis 1958–1975.* Cambridge, MA: Harvard.

Hanfmann, G. M. A., and Waldbaum, J. C.
1975   *A Survey of Sardis and the Major Monuments Outside the City Walls.* Sardis Report 1. Cambridge, MA: Harvard.

Hellström, P., and Thieme, T.
1981   The Androns at Labraunda. A Preliminary Account of their Architecture. *The Museum of Mediterranean and Near Eastern Antiquities,* Bulletin 16: 58–74.

Hogarth, D. G.
1908   *Excavations at Ephesus, the Archaic Artemisia.* London: British Museum.

Howland, R. H.
1958   *Greek Lamps and Survivals.* The Athenian Agora 4. Princeton: American School of Classical Studies at Athens.

Huber, J. J.
1992   A Dendrochronological Analysis of Two Iron Age Anatolian Sites: Structure R39 at Kaman-Kalehöyuk and MMS and ByzFort at Sardis. Honors Thesis, Cornell University.

Johansen, K. F.
1967   *The Iliad in Early Greek Art.* Copenhagen: Munksgaard.

Meiggs, R.
1982   *Trees and Timber in the Ancient Mediterranean World.* Oxford: Clarendon.

Nylander, C.
1970   *Ionians in Pasargadae: Studies in Old Persian Architecture.* Boreas; Uppsala Studies in Ancient Mediterranean and Near Eastern Civilizations, 1. Uppsala: Uppsala University.

Ramage, N. H., and Ramage, A.
1976

Ratté, C.
1989   *Lydian Masonry and Monumental Architecture at Sardis.* Ph.D. Dissertation, University of California at Berkeley.

1992   The 'Pyramid Tomb' at Sardis. *Istanbuler Mitteilungen* 42: 135–61.

In press   Not the tomb of Gyges. *Journal of Hellenic Studies.*

Scheibler, L.
1976   *Griechische Lampen.* Kerameikos; Ergebnisse der Ausgrabungen XI. Berlin: De Gruyter.

Stronach, D. B.
1978   *Pasargadae: A Report on the Excavations Conducted by the British Institute of Persian Studies from 1961 to 1963.* Oxford: Clarendon.

Gold, Granite, and Water:
The Bir Umm Fawakhir Survey Project 1992

CAROL MEYER

Oriental Institute
University of Chicago
Chicago, Illinois 60637

In January 1992 the Oriental Institute of the University of Chicago carried out a brief season of survey work at Bir Umm Fawakhir in the central Eastern Desert of Egypt. Long believed to be a Roman way-station on the route between the Nile and the Red Sea, the site can now be identified as a fifth–seventh century A.D. Byzantine gold-mining town. The main part consists of over 200 buildings, of which 55 were mapped in detail, ranging from one-room huts to multi-family houses of 16 or more rooms. Specialists' studies of the geology of the area, the pottery, and some first–second century A.D. graffiti in a nearby cave were undertaken as well.

INTRODUCTION

The Oriental Institute of the University of Chicago carried out an archaeological survey project in the Eastern Desert of Egypt at Bir Umm Fawakhir between January 11 and 23, 1992. The site lies half way between the Nile and the Red Sea coast, about 5 km northeast of the Wadi Hammamat, famous for its quarries and graffiti. Bir Umm Fawakhir is usually discussed along with the other ruins on the Quft (Coptos) to Quseir road, the most striking remains being a series of intervisible watch towers and fortified way stations (also called *hydreumata*) marking the Roman route. Depending on how one counts and dates the stations, Bir Umm Fawakhir is about the sixth in line after Matula, Laqeita (ancient Phoenicon), Qasr Banat, Wadi Mweh, and Bir Hammamat (fig. 1). Although the Roman route has been surveyed and the hydreumata planned (see Meredith 1952, 1953; Reddé and Golvin 1987; Zitterkopf and Sidebotham 1989), none of them has ever been excavated.[1]

The modern settlement at Bir Umm Fawakhir consists of a guard post, two tea houses, a few residential houses, and a mosque still under construction. The settlement lies in a fairly wide, flat, sandy area (ca. 7.5 km²) surrounded by jagged mountains dissected by numerous wadis. The western end of the open area is sharply defined by a ridge of mountains; the main road passes through a natural gap here (fig. 2). In the mountainside are a number of ancient gold mines, and at its foot are the wells, all-important in the desert. The mountains close in again as the road continues southeast towards Quseir and the Red Sea. The main group of ancient ruins is in a long, narrow wadi hidden from the road by a spur of hills (fig. 3). Other, smaller clusters of ruins are found closer to the modern settlement, near the main granite quarry, around an angle in a mountain as the road turns southeast, and in other places nearby that have been reported but not yet investigated.

It is quite a remarkable experience to walk through the main settlement at Bir Umm Fawakhir. The ancient town consists of several hundred buildings strung out on either side of a sandy wadi bottom that served as the main street. The buildings are all dry stone masonry but are well enough preserved that doors, niches, benches, trash heaps, and other features are readily visible. Steep granite cliffs enclose the settlement as though walled. The best views, in fact, are those from the tops of the cliffs; then the irregular, independent character of the house units becomes clearer. Our expectation was that a map would make the site still more comprehensible, and mapping and documentation of the surface remains were our major goals. Bir

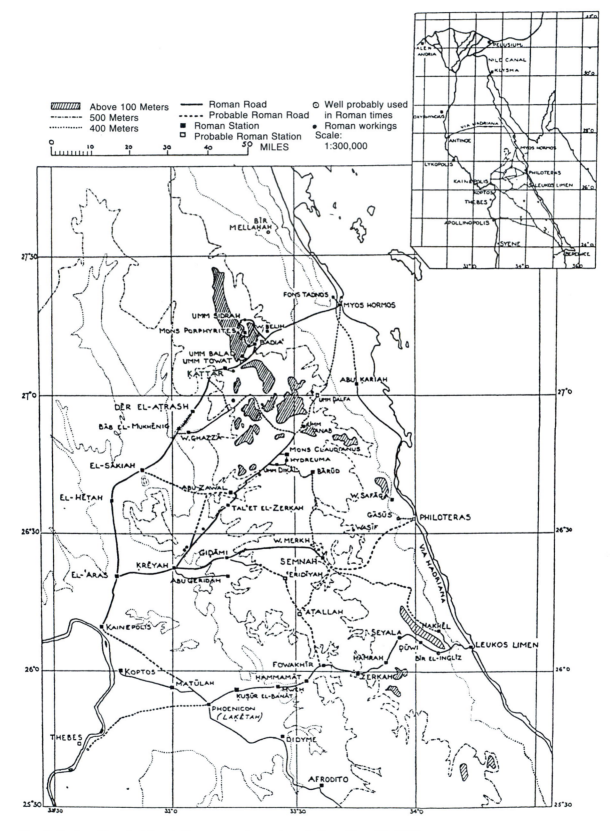

Fig. 1. Eastern Desert of Egypt: Roman remains and roads (from Meredith 1952).

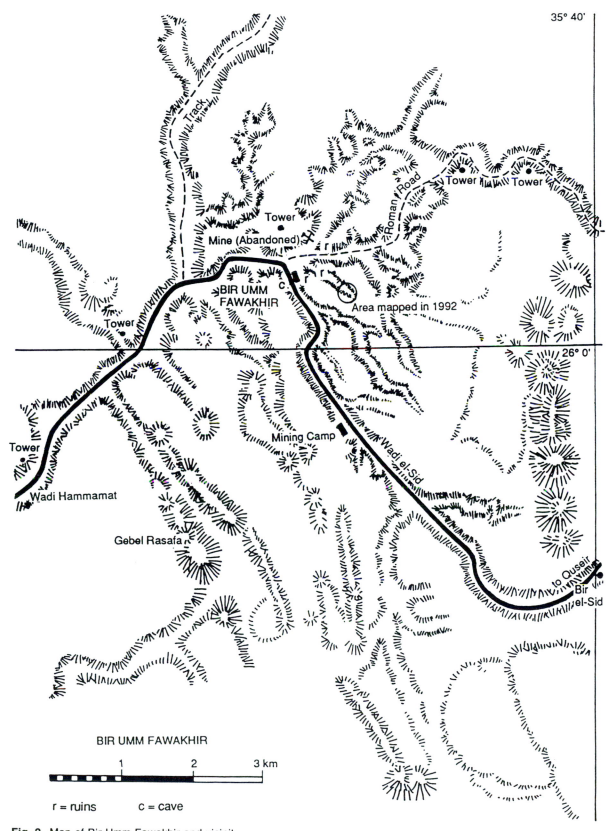

35° 40'

Track

Roman Road

Tower   Tower

Tower

Mine (Abandoned)

Tower

c.

BIR UMM
FAWAKHIR

Area mapped in 1992

26° 0'

Tower

Wadi el-Sid

Mining Camp

Tower

Wadi Hammamat

Gebel Rasafa

to Quseir

Bir
el-Sid

BIR UMM FAWAKHIR

| | 1 | 2 | 3 km |

r = ruins   c = cave

Fig. 2. Map of Bir Umm Fawakhir and vicinity.

Fig. 3. View of Bir Umm Fawakhir from the Roman watch tower. Left of center, one of the outlying settlements may be seen on the bottom of the broad wadi that also served as the ancient Roman road. Right of center, the narrow wadi enclosed by hills contains the main settlement of Bir Umm Fawakhir. The white patches to the far right are fine surface silts deposited by a recent flash flood. The modern road and tea houses are just out of sight to the right.

Umm Fawakhir is an opportunity to study an entire ancient community without excavation. Urgency to study the site now stems from the fact that it is being looted, and from the increased traffic on the Red Sea road, and hence from visitors who can too easily tumble the dry stone masonry.

PREVIOUS ACCOUNTS OF
BIR UMM FAWAKHIR

No systematic archaeological survey or excavations had been carried out at Bir Umm Fawakhir prior to 1992, but the site is mentioned in a number of travelers' accounts. Bir Umm Fawakhir was accessible only by camel caravan at the beginning of the 20th century, and even the construction of a paved road did not drastically increase traffic. The few vehicles that traveled the road primarily served mining operations and the quiet port of Quseir. At times the road was restricted by the army. Thus few visitors lingered at Bir Umm Fawakhir, none of them long enough to explore all the ruins and their outliers. That, as well as a certain slippage in geographical names, occasionally makes it difficult to reconcile the old reports. Some of them do, however, preserve information about parts of the site now lost.

Wilkinson knew the Wadee Foakheér for its masses of pottery, the settlement ruins, and a temple, which he attributed to Ptolemy I. His estimate of the size of the settlement was very large, "reckoning the different isolated portions of it, will have contained upwards of a thousand houses or huts of the miners" (Wilkinson 1835: 421–22). His slightly later travel guide notes the "huts of ancient miners, breccia quarries, and hieroglyphic inscriptions on the rocks" (Wilkinson 1843: 50), apparently conflating the Wadi Hammamat and Bir Umm Fawakhir.

One of the earliest visitors was Arthur E. P. Weigall, who followed many of the major camel routes and published a popular account in *Travels in the Upper Egyptian Deserts* (1909). He refers to the Bir Hammamat by name, but then names everything from there to Bir Umm Fawakhir as Wady Fowakhîeh, including the bekhen-stone quarries in the Wadi Hammamat and the ruins at Bir Umm Fawakhir. Weigall refers to a long graffito of Vizier Amenemhet of the 11th Dynasty that mentions gold workers, and from it he seems to infer that the gold mines at Bir Umm Fawakhir go back to Pharaonic times (Weigall 1909: 41–43). By far his most valuable contribution to the documentation of the site was his description of the Ptolemaic temple:

In the reign of Ptolemy III, B.C. 240, a little temple was built near the Bir Fowakhîeh at the east end of the valley of the quarries. Wandering over this amphitheatre amidst the hills we came upon the remains of the little building, which had been constructed of rough stones augmented by well-made basalt columns. It was dedicated to the god Min, the patron of the Eastern Desert; but as it was only about 12 feet by 22 in area the priests of the god could not have commanded the devotion of more than a few of the quarrymen (Weigall 1909: 49–50).

He made the only known copy of the inscription in the temple (Weigall 1909: pl. 10). He also referred to groups of workmen's huts nearby, the gold mines, and the "very fine pink granite [that] began to be quarried just to the east of this well in Roman days" (Weigall 1909: 50). The book unfortunately has no maps, although the 1932 Qena-Quseir Road map published by the Survey of Egypt shows the temple directly south of the Roman tower, in effect flanking the western entrance to the Bir Umm Fawakhir area.

Couyat called Bir Umm Fawakhir "une véritable ville" with a temple, quarries, and almost 10,000m³ of crushed quartz from mining. Most interesting, he reports a papyrus, now lost, and two statues found in the quarries. Battered, headless, and almost armless, the statues are nonetheless in a Classical style and were identified by Couyat as a nude Apollo and a semidraped Venus (Couyat 1910: 533–36).

Reinach (1910: 130) noted the ruins of the temple and the abundant sherds, and he repeated the estimate of 1000 houses. He remarked on the absence of a military post, suggesting that it might have been buried by repeated well-cleaning. Murray (1925: 146) added nothing to earlier accounts, noting only the existence of the Ptolemy III temple and gold mines, but no way-station. His photograph seems to show the outlying cluster of ruins between the mine adits and one of the granite quarries. Englebach (1931: 134) suggested taking the "basalt" columns from the Ptolemaic temple to the Egyptian Museum, but he mainly commented on the mines and quarries.

Some of the early geological surveys made valuable observations on the Bedouin, flora, fauna, and antiquities as well as on the regional geology. Barron and Hume (1902: 49, 261) mentioned miners' huts, the temple, and granite quarries of Bir Umm Fawakhir, and they estimated the gold yield as 2 to 5 dwts (3 to 7.7 grams) per ton, not commercially viable. A later book briefly notes the "extensive ancient mines in which the quartz veins (up to ten inches in width) are most irregular in direction and size" (Hume 1937: 732). Most important of all, Hume reprinted Alford's 1900 sketch map of Fowakhir Gold Mine (Hume 1937: pl. 171), reproduced here as fig. 4. Rough as it is, the map seems to show the temple on the *east* side of the road, in the group of ruins closest to the modern settlement.

When Guéraud published the Bir Umm Fawakhir ostraca, he gave some background information on the site, noting the abundance of sherds, the

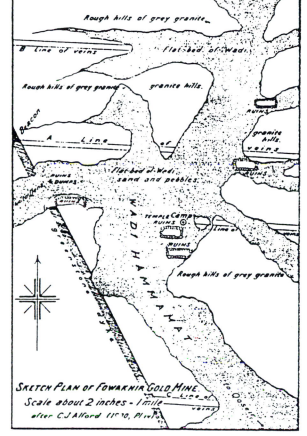

Fig. 4. From Hume 1937, reprint of Alford 1900.

Ptolemy III temple, and the mines and their tailings, although it is not clear whether he ever visited the site himself. For one thing, the well is not at the center of the settlement but at the far western end. He also seemed to accept the estimate of a thousand or more huts (Guéraud 1942: 141–42). He did, however, describe a little of the renewed mining activity in 1940 and 1941 and the discovery of antiquities in the ancient debris, namely grinding stones, pottery vessels, lamps, beads, a few coins, and above all 60 or so ostraca (Guéraud 1942: 143). Unfortunately none of the artifacts have been published, though the ostraca are said to have come from both mine tailings and the group of houses closest to the mines (Guéraud 1942: 148). Palaeographically dated to the late first and second centuries A.D., seven ostraca are in Latin and all the rest in Greek. Almost all of them pertain to military activity in the Eastern Desert, either at Bir Umm Fawakhir or elsewhere; none of the professions named were necessarily connected with mining (Guéraud 1942: 147). Almost all of the ostraca are letters concerned with provisions sent or desired; one badly damaged text may be a list of tools (Guéraud 1942: 196), though again none of them has to pertain to mining. There are several puzzling features about this corpus. If the ostraca were found in ancient mine tailings, then the mines must have been worked after the letters were discarded, perhaps even a very long time after. In other words, some of the mining activity must be late second century or later. Secondly, some of the ostraca are said to have come from the group of houses closest to the mines, but the nearest surviving cluster of houses is in fact associated with the same fifth to sixth century pottery as the buildings in the main wadi. Perhaps there was another group of huts closer still to the mines but destroyed by the 1940–1941 mining activity. There is simply no way to recheck the context of the ostraca. Finally, no military installation or hydreuma has been certainly identified at Bir Umm Fawakhir, although a line of cut stones near the modern mosque looks promising (see below).

Debono's expedition through the Wadi Hammamat remarked in general on the huts near the gold mines and the abundant grinding stones. On the basis of potsherds (six illustrated), he dates the mining activity as far back as the Pharaonic era (Debono 1951: 80–81, pl. 14). No map is provided and no mention is made of the well or of Fawakhir, so it is unclear exactly which gold mine he means. Later in the article he notes "un grand cimetière et d'autres plus petits, datant tous de l'époque grecque ou romaine, . . . sur une hauteur dominant les villages d'ouvriers des mines d'or. . . . Ils [the cemeteries] ont été malheureusement dévastés à fond par les voleurs" (Debono 1951: 82). None of the cemeteries were found by the Bir Umm Fawakhir Project in 1992.

Meredith's study of the Eastern Desert includes no new information specific to Bir Umm Fawakhir, although by his time the Ptolemaic temple had been destroyed (Meredith 1953: 98). In regard to the exploitation of the gold mines, however, he concluded that in general "in the central area both the Ptolemies and the Ancient Egyptians worked the gold mines, but not, apparently, the Romans" (Meredith 1953: 97). His concise and useful list of criteria for identifying ancient gold mining sites includes:

(a) ancient workings (both open-cast on auriferous dykes and underground to considerable depths

vouched for by modern engineers. . .); (b) abundant reciprocatory rubbing-stones everywhere (each pair consisting of a two-lugged upper stone, slightly convex with roughly parallel striations, rubbed against a rectangular, concave nether stone similarly striated); (c) upper and lower rotating hand-mills, like those of the fellahin today . . . ; (d) rubbing stones, usually the two-lugged upper stones, built into walls . . . : (3) the later use of rubbing stones as anvils or pounding stones (their old striations partly worn away and pock-marked with small pits); (g) banks of gold-crushing tailings . . . ; (i) underground water level (apparently, in places, visibly higher in ancient times than today). (Meredith 1953: 95).

All the criteria are relevant to finds at Bir Umm Fawakhir, although none specify a date.

A survey of the major routes and ruins in the Eastern Desert by Reddé and Golvin has this to say about Bir Umm Fawakhir:

Au kilomètre 89, près d'un poste de police moderne, apparaissent d'assez nombreuse ruines, d'époque ptolémaïque et romaine, soit un temple de Ptolémée III, et un ensemble de cabanes antiques . . . , probablement romaines, près d'une série de fronts de taille dans des carrières de granit. Quatre kilomètres plus loin sont connues d'anciennes mines d'or encore exploitées au debut de ce siècle. Dans les déblais d'une de ces exploitations a été trouvé un lot d'ostraca grecs et latins qui attestent la présence, en ces lieux, de militaires chargés de surveiller l'exploitation des mines et des carrières à la fois dans le défilé et dans une série de petits postes alentour. Le fortin n'a malheureusement pas été retrouvé (Reddé and Golvin 1987: 9–10).

The reference to a gold mine 4 km away is a little confusing. Are the authors referring to the gold mines at the modern mining camp (fig. 2), the cluster of ruins between them and Bir Umm Fawakhir, or some other mine outside the zone of the Bir Umm Fawakhir Project? If a gold mine other than that at Bir Umm Fawakhir is the source of Guéraud's ostraca, then some of the oddities about those ostraca might be explained. On the other hand, it is difficult to see why the Roman military would have by-passed the good water source at Bir Umm Fawakhir and the main Roman route, as marked by the intervisible towers. As for the statement that the soldiers were overseeing mining and quarrying, there is as yet no proof from the ostraca themselves that that is what they were doing.

Zitterkopf and Sidebotham (1989: 177), in their detailed survey of the Coptos to Quseir route, note the lack of any fortification at Bir Umm Fawakhir but feel that the sizable population alone would have afforded protection. The large population is deduced quite reasonably from the hundreds of huts and outlying groups of buildings. The problem is that the buildings are associated with fifth–seventh century A.D. pottery (Zitterkopf and Sidebotham 1989: 166). The authors are the first to assign a Byzantine date to the sherds, and we agree, but that still leaves no evidence of a Roman station, fortified or not, and certainly no larger a Roman population there than at any of the other hydreumata along the route. The extensive gold mining and granite quarrying are noted, and Zitterkopf and Sidebotham state that most of the mining on the Coptos to Quseir route centered on gold (as opposed to, say, the important stone quarries at Mons Claudianus or Mons Porphyrites), primarily in the el-Fawakhir vicinity (Zitterkopf and Sidebotham 1989: 160, 177). This suggests that they accept a Roman date for the gold mining at Bir Umm Fawakhir.

A final observation on the site comes from Henry Wright (personal communication), who did in fact find the possible remains of a Roman station. It now consists of a row of cut blocks barely visible at ground level near the modern mosque; everything else at the site is built of uncut stones. Wright reports Roman-period sherds, and the ones collected by the Bir Umm Fawakhir Project seem to confirm his observation (fig. 27). If the wall represents part of the Roman way station, then it is not immediately adjacent to the modern wells nor directly on the ancient road, which took a northerly loop marked by watchtowers rather than the modern southerly loop past Bir es-Sid. All the other way stations on the Quft-Quseir road have wells or storage tanks *inside* rather than 200–300 m away, and in fact the hydreumata could be described as fortified wells. The area of the possible Roman building is in direct line for some of the heaviest wadi wash from flash floods, not to mention modern mining and road building activity; so it may well have been tumbled and obscured. It deserves to be investigated more closely.

Clearly, the published accounts of the site are fragmentary and sometimes conflicting, and without good maps either of the region or of the site itself it is difficult to resolve the problems. Some parts of the site have been destroyed, such as the Ptolemaic temple, and others remain unpublished, such as the artifacts found at the same time as the ostraca. Perhaps most seriously, the main body of ruins was mistakenly called Roman for at least 150 years, until Zitterkopf and Sidebotham inspected the pottery and found it Byzantine.

Part of the reason for the misidentification may be the long-held belief that the Byzantine presence in the desert was minimal or nonexistent. The Roman and pre-Roman periods back as far as Predynastic times are far better documented and studied. Many works concerning Byzantine Egypt ignore the Eastern Desert altogether; and Alexandria indeed dominated the cultural, economic, military, political, and religious scenes. One person who at least considered the Byzantine presence in the Eastern Desert was Maspero (1912: 10–11). He noted the wealth of minerals and the important ancient trade routes to India, but stated that the rather inconvenient port at Clysma was the only Red Sea port utilized under the Byzantine rulers (in fact, Berenice was also in use; see below). Literary references to the Eastern Desert are almost totally lacking, barring one seventh-century source that adds no information to the Roman writers. Maspero suggested that when the Blemmyes were defeated[2] they fled to the Eastern Desert and finished off whatever was left of the old routes and stations. He concluded, "et ainsi, peu à peu, sans qu'on puisse fixer une date précise, la domination romano-byzantine cessa d'être effective dans ces paysages: ce qui explique le silence total qui les enveloppe à notre époque" (Maspero 1912: 11).

Johnson and West do not directly deal with the Eastern Desert at all. They do mention the ports at Clysma (Suez), Aela, Ocelis near the Bab el-Mandeb, and Adulis, the chief port for the kingdom of Axum (Johnson and West 1949: 137). More specific data can be gleaned from the list of ships seized by the king of Axum in A.D. 524/525 for war: 20 from Clysma, 15 from Aela, 9 from India, 7 each from Berenice and Farsan Island, and two from Jotabe (Johnson and West 1949: 138), a mention, at least, of Berenice. The authors noted in passing that "the caravan route from Myos Hormos to Antinoopolis [well north of the Wadi Hammamat route] was important enough for the alabarch [a customs official] to maintain an office in the latter city in the sixth century" (Johnson and West 1949: 106), but they felt that after Justinian the eastern trade via the Red Sea and Indian Ocean dwindled in favor of overland routes to Persia (Johnson and West 1949: 138).

Certainly Constantinople knew of Axum, a major kingdom centered in the north Ethiopian highlands with a Red Sea port at Adulis (near Massawa in Eritrea). Diplomatic exchanges occurred in the time of Constantius II, and Justinian in particular tried to strengthen trade relations (Munro-Hay 1991: 8, 57). Above all we have the sixth century work of Cosmas Indicopleustes, whose section on the Axumite port at Adulis includes a description of a monumental throne with a long Greek inscription dedicated by a Ptolemaic ruler. Cosmas also mentioned merchants from Alexandria and Aila (Aqaba) at Adulis (II.54) as well as the Axumite silent gold trade with the Sasu (II.51).

In light of new evidence from sites such as ᵓAbu Shaᵓar (Sidebotham et al. 1989), Wadi Nakheil (Prickett 1979: 297–303), and Bir Umm Fawakhir, and what can be gleaned from old accounts concerning Berenice (Floyer 1893; Meredith 1957; Sidebotham 1986: 53), the idea of Byzantine neglect of the Eastern Desert needs to be re-examined.

GEOLOGY OF THE BIR UMM
FAWAKHIR AREA

We place the geologist's report at the beginning of the section on the work accomplished by the 1992 Bir Umm Fawakhir survey because the geology explains a great deal about the site's layout and about its reasons for existence. The only resources are mineral. A series of faults and contact zones meet at the western end of the Bir Umm Fawakhir area, explaining both its high western ridge of mountains and the gap that permits the road to pass through. The Fawakhir granite to the east is the aquifer, the water being carried in fine cracks in the rock until it meets the dense ultramafic rocks at the western end of the area, and the wells are in fact dug near the contact zone. The pinkish granite was quarried at one time, probably the Roman period. The extensively worked gold mines follow the quartz veins in the Fawakhir granite. The main group of ruins lies in a narrow wadi whose steep sides serve as a boundary and almost as a town wall; the east end is defined by a high dyke of tough felsite rock with a natural gate in it.

A BRIEF GEOLOGICAL REPORT ABOUT
THE BIR UMM FAWAKHIR AREA
BY MOHAMED B. E. OMAR MOSTAFA

Introduction

The Eastern Desert extends from the Nile Valley east to the Red Sea, and consists essentially of a backbone of high, rugged mountains running parallel to the coast. These mountains of the Precambrian Basement Complex are flanked to the north, east, and west by intensively dissected sedimentary plateaux. The Precambrian Basement Complex forms part of the western segment of the extensive Late Proterozoic Arabian-Nubian Shield. Recent studies show that the evolution of the complex is better interpreted in terms of plate tectonic models. A complex of ensimatic terranes are considered to have evolved through the process of volcanic arc accretion, ophiolite obduction and granitoid magmatic crustal thickening between ca. 950–580 Ma. The Precambrian Basement Complex of the Eastern Desert consists of sequences of volcanic and volcano-sedimentary rocks that have been metamorphosed to lower greenschist facies and intruded by a variety of granitic and basic rocks. Structurally, it is generally accepted to subdivide the Eastern Desert into three major segments: northern, central, and southern. Each segment is characterized by differences in gross lithological constitution and differently enhanced structural styles.

Egypt has a long history of gold mining dating back to Pharaonic times. The Romans and later peoples produced gold. Weather-worn waste piles and ruins at old mines vary in character, suggesting multiple periods of operation. There are more than 95 known gold deposits and occurrences in Egypt, mainly associated with the Precambrian Basement Complex of the Eastern Desert; and the last mine (Fawakhir) closed in 1958. An estimated 1,710 tons of gold has been produced from alluvial/colluvial and hard rock deposits. Hard-rock mining was concentrated on the oxidized portions of gold-quartz veins, where simply mining techniques could be employed and gold could be won by unsophisticated hand-milling and leaching. Evidence of firesetting is seen, and many sites are marked by discarded grinding stones and hand-held stone hammers. The region was prospected in detail by the ancients, and abandoned workings such as small trenches, shafts, and quarries are common sights in the desert. Any site explored today will almost certainly contain ancient workings.

Local Geology

The investigated area predominantly comprises an elongate stock of heterogeneous hybrid granitoids referred to as "Fawakhir granite," emplaced into serpentinite rocks. Structurally, the western side of Bir Umm Fawakhir (above the water well)

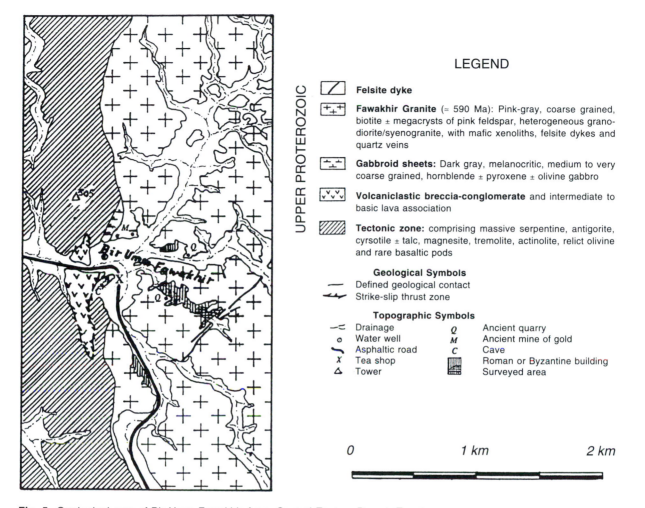

LEGEND

UPPER PROTEROZOIC

◢ **Felsite dyke**

◩ **Fawakhir Granite** (≈ 590 Ma): Pink-gray, coarse grained, biotite ± megacrysts of pink feldspar, heterogeneous grano-diorite/syenogranite, with mafic xenoliths, felsite dykes and quartz veins

▱ **Gabbroid sheets:** Dark gray, melanocritic, medium to very coarse grained, hornblende ± pyroxene ± olivine gabbro

▣ **Volcaniclastic breccia-conglomerate** and intermediate to basic lava association

▨ **Tectonic zone:** comprising massive serpentine, antigorite, cyrsotile ± talc, magnesite, tremolite, actinolite, relict olivine and rare basaltic pods

Geological Symbols
— Defined geological contact
◄◄ Strike-slip thrust zone

Topographic Symbols

⌒ Drainage		Q	Ancient quarry
⊙ Water well		M	Ancient mine of gold
⌐ Asphaltic road		C	Cave
X Tea shop		▦	Roman or Byzantine building
△ Tower			Surveyed area

0   1 km   2 km

Fig. 5. Geological map of Bir Umm Fawakhir Area, Central Eastern Desert, Egypt.

represents an intensive, narrow, tectonized zone of serpentinite rocks associated with gabbroid sheets, volcaniclastic sediments, and intermediate to basic lava associations (fig. 5).

Structure and Lithology

Fawakhir Granite. The Fawakhir granite is for the most part a coarse to very coarse crystalline rock, mottled gray to pink in color, comprising crystals of quartz clusters, feldspar (plagioclase), variably distributed pink feldspar (orthoclase), and tiny spots of black biotite and stained-opaque mineral hematite. In many localities the pink feldspar crystals are large, up to 1.5 cm long, giving the rock a porphyritic character. In addition, there are still younger dykes of pink felsite, pegmatite (respectively fine-grained and coarse-grained acidic

rocks), and numerous quartz stringers and veins invading the granite.

Fawakhir granite is variably heterogeneous and consists of a wide range of composition between gray granodiorite to pink alkali feldspar granite with mafic xenoliths derived from the pre-existing rocks. It is jointed (fig. 20) and exfoliated (fig. 21), resulting in the normal rectangular pattern and in spheroidal masses of granite respectively. In addition, this causes a breakdown of feldspar crystals into kaolin in some places. There are three main sets of joints as shown in Table 1. As a result, Fawakhir granite is easily cut for blocks.

North–northeast of Bir Umm Fawakhir are some remains of mining activities by the ancient prospecting for the noble metal and its extraction from surface pits, trenches, and shafts and primitive underground mines. Gold occurs in veins made up of massive, milky quartz with disseminated gold and sulphide minerals (galena, pyrite, chalcopyrite, pyrrhotite, and sphalerite). The mineralized veins are structurally controlled, being fissure fillings or confined to zones of intensive fracturing that have approximately east-west trends, moderately dipping to the south. The veins may be arranged as a series of en echelon veins (up to 1 to 2 m width) with pinches and swells and parallel veinlets and stringers of considerable thickness as well.

Serpentinite Rocks. The serpentinite rocks occupy the western part of the investigated area. The color ranges from grayish green, green, to black, or earthy (khaki) for the altered rocks. The serpentinite rocks may be medium to coarse grained, locally banded, massive, with dull, waxy texture and a smooth to a splintery fracture. They are crisscrossed by veins of fibrous chrysotile serpentine, joint fillings of magnesium carbonate, and granitoid offshoots as well (Hussein 1990). These rocks are intensively altered and sheared in places, and are associated with well-developed actinolite-tremolite, chlorite, talc schist, relict olivine, and rare basaltic pods.

Gabbroid Sheets. The gabbroid sheets are dark gray, medium to coarse grained, melanocratic, composed mainly of hornblende amphibole, a few interstitial feldspars (ophitic, subophitic texture), and relicts of olivine and pyroxene.

Volcaniclastic Sediments and Intermediate to Basic Lava Association. These are reworked pyroclastics and volcaniclastic deposits, mainly volcaniclastic breccia conglomerate associated with intermediate to basic volcanic lava. These volcanics are both pillowed and non-pillowed and are predominantly aphyric in texture. Vesicles and amygdaloidal structures developed in these lavas; the cavities are filled with an aphanitic cement.

PHARAONIC, PTOLEMAIC, AND ROMAN REMAINS

Actual Pharaonic remains at Bir Umm Fawakhir are so far limited to Debono's six sherds (Debono 1951: pl. 14). The most remarkable piece of evidence, however, for the ancient Egyptians' knowledge of the Bir Umm Fawakhir area is the Turin Papyrus. One plausible reading takes it as a map of the bekhen-stone quarries in the Wadi

TABLE 1.
Joint Alignments at Bir Umm Fawakhir

Trend	Dipping Toward	Range of Angle
Northeast–southwest	Southeast	40–65
	Northeast	40–65
		90=
Northeast–southeast	Northeast	50–70
		90=
Subhorizontal Joints		

Hammamat and the gold mines a little farther east at Bir Umm Fawakhir. The papyrus was found at Deir el-Medina, across the Nile from Luxor (ancient Thebes) and may be attributed to one of the bekhen-stone quarrying expeditions carried out during the reign of Ramses IV of the 20th Dynasty. The Turin Papyrus shows mountains labeled as gold mines, a small miners' camp, a well, a sizeable Amun temple, and two roads to the sea running off the map (Harrell and Brown 1992).[3]

Evidence for a Ptolemaic presence is limited to the now-lost Ptolemy III Euergetes temple, though most of the early travelers discussed above made observations on it, most notably Weigall (1909: 49–50). Ptolemy III, however, is known to have promoted energetically the trade with Africa, specifically for war elephants, and this entailed establishing ports along the Red Sea coast and routes through the desert. The Roman system of hydreumata and watch towers probably followed the Ptolemaic route, and it has even been suggested that the latter were built then (Zitterkopf and Sidebotham 1989: 180).

The Roman remains are far more sparse than when the whole complex of house ruins in the main wadi and the outliers was attributed to them. Still, we definitely have the watch tower over the western gap leading into Bir Umm Fawakhir, some sherds, a few bits of faience, the graffiti in the cave (see next section), the quarries, and perhaps one wall remnant of a large building or way station. The granite quarries are tentatively taken to be Roman in date because the Romans are the ones who most avidly sought out the granites, porphyries, breccia verde antique, and other handsome Eastern Desert stones. The ancient Egyptians seem to have relied mainly on the more accessible Aswan granites, and apart from Mons Porphyrites the Byzantine rulers do not seem to have worked the stone quarries as zealously as their predecessors. Also, the quarrying techniques and chisel marks appear to match those observed at Mons Claudianus, an important granite quarry exploited mainly in the first and second centuries. It has long been presumed that Bir Umm Fawakhir was one of the series of hydreumata on the Quft to Quseir road, and the absence of the expected fortified way station was consistently noted. The area around the modern wells has been thoroughly clawed up by modern mining activity, but none of the 19th century travelers noted any ruins there. Still, it seems unlikely that the Romans ignored a good water source in the desert, and the fact that their road did pass this way is proven by the string of intervisible towers. The remnant of a wall made of cut stones near the new mosque needs to be investigated as a possible Roman building.

THE GRAFFITI
BY TERENCE WILFONG

Inscriptional material from the 1992 Bir Umm Fawakhir Survey was limited to a number of graffiti found in a cave west of the Byzantine settlement, across the modern road (fig. 6). Preliminary records of these graffiti were made on the morning of January 19. The cave, apparently a natural, shallow one, is located in a fairly sheer cliff face and was the site of occasional mining attempts. There was no sign of recent human activity in the cave, although there was considerable evidence that it was frequently used by animals. The back wall of the cave bears many gouges made by chisels, including a sort of sunburst design that apparently was cut preparatory to carving out a hole. There are three manmade holes in the floor, apparently quite old. A few small potsherds were found in the cave, ribbed pottery of the sort found in the settlement site.

The main interest of the cave is the graffiti it contains: 11 separate inscriptions. All of the graffiti were either written in a reddish-brown paint or carved (fig. 7). The painted graffiti have suffered from the elements and are generally faint. Two are painted pictorial representations of a boat (fig. 7:3) and an animal (fig. 7:6). The boat graffito is a drawing of a boat with a square sail, several oars, and apparently a steering rudder of some sort; the drawing is done in reddish-brown paint with a heavy brush; it is damaged and very faint.[4] The animal graffito, showing the upper part of a lion(?), is done with a fine brush in a practiced hand. Fig-

Fig. 6. Cave with graffiti.

ure 7:5 is a single marking in reddish paint, which may be a quarry-mark of some sort. Three of the graffiti are apparently texts, but they are so faint and damaged as to make the script unidentifiable at present. Figure 7:1 is a series of very faint scratches into the rock face; the light in the cave made it impossible to copy accurately or identify it. Figure 7:7 is also very faint and uncertain; it appears to be in the same paint and brush-type as the lion drawing (fig. 7:6), which is immediately below. It is likely that fig. 7:7 may even be a part of the drawing. Figure 7:10 is a series of extremely faint marks in red paint that may not even be an inscription. Of the identifiable scripts, fig. 7:9, a seven-line painted inscription in Epigraphic South Arabian, is of great interest. The text is highly damaged, but it has been very tentatively dated to the first or second century A.D.[5]

The remaining four graffiti, all in Greek, are completely legible. Two are of the common "good luck" type (*eutuchê* or some variant thereof), written in reddish paint by Salês (fig. 7:8) and Dorkôn (fig. 7:4). The name "Dorkôn" makes up another of

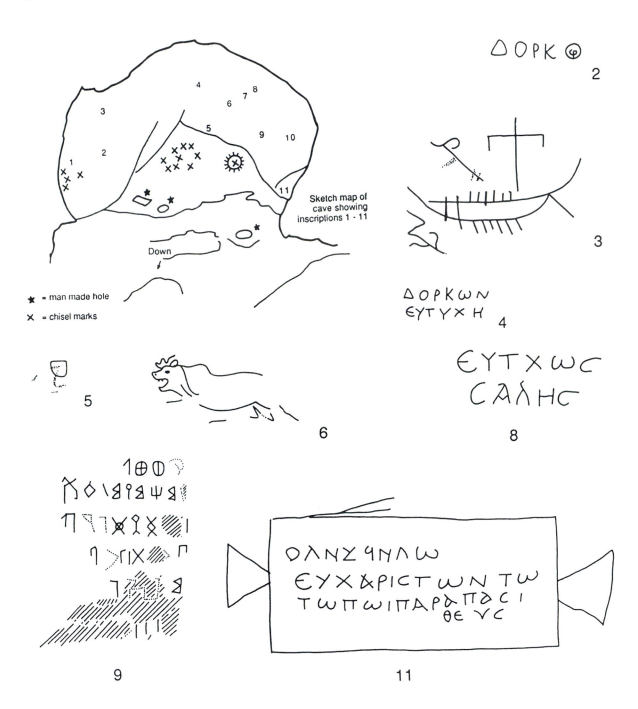

Fig. 7. Graffiti from Bir Umm Fawakhir. **1.** Unreadable, scratched in, 34 cm long, 21 cm high. **2.** "Dorkôn," carved, ca. 14 cm across. **3.** Ship, red paint, ca. 39 cm across, 31 cm high. **4.** "Dorkôn. Good luck!" red paint, 18 cm across, 8.5 cm high. **5.** Unidentifiable, red paint. **6.** Lion, red paint, ca. 36 cm across. **7.** Unreadable, possibly same hand as #6 directly above, red paint, ca. 34 cm across. **8.** "Good luck! Salês." red paint, ca. 33 cm across. **9.** Epigraphic South Arabic, one word in second line is legible "mhmym," perhaps "protected place," such as a shrine. Red paint. **10.** Very faint, red paint. **11.** "Longinos gives thanks to all the gods in this place," name written cryptographically, carved 53 cm across, 15 cm high.

the graffiti (fig. 7:2), this time carved, so it is not possible to know if it is by the same man. Dorkôn was a common name in Roman Egypt; other graffiti by men of the same name are known from else-

where in the Eastern Desert. The remaining graffito (fig. 7:11) is the most elaborate: a carved four-line inscription enclosed in a *tabula ansata* design. The first line is written cryptographically, the rest in the

Fig. 8. View of felsite dyke at the southeast end of the main settlement. Clusters of houses may be seen to the left, and the empty wadi bottom to the right.

normal script. It is the inscription of a man named Longinus, who gives thanks "to all the gods in this place." Figures 7:4 and 7:11 have been previously published (Letronne 1848),[6] although both were incorrectly copied and the cryptogram in 11 completely misunderstood.

Unfortunately, none of the Greek graffiti contain dates, and none have distinctive enough forms to be dated epigraphically. The names—Dorkôn, Salês, and Longinus—are all common and all attested for the first three centuries A.D. The mention of "all the gods" in fig. 7:11 makes it likely that the text dates to before the "Christianization" of Upper Egypt in the third and fourth centuries but does not permit a more definite date. It is clear that the Greek graffiti (and the South Arabian text as well) predate the Byzantine settlement by at least a few centuries, and that they are probably roughly contemporary with the 60-plus Greek and Latin ostraca found in the vicinity of Fawakhir at the turn of the century.

THE BYZANTINE SETTLEMENT

The goals of the Bir Umm Fawakhir Survey were to map the main group of ruins and to take a sample of surface pottery, thus preserving at least some record of the site. With 12 working days only, we mapped 55 buildings and some of the topography, copied the graffiti, and took seven sherd collections. Mapping began at the southeast end of the main wadi because a natural "gate" in a high felsite dyke there defines the eastern limit of the

site (fig. 8), and because the houses are better preserved (if looted) and easier to understand than the more ruined buildings closer to the modern road. The orientation off of magnetic north comes about because we followed the natural alignment of the settlement, strung out along its main street, the wadi bottom. In all, approximately one quarter of the buildings in the main wadi were plotted.

Two datum points were established on large granite boulders in the wadi bed and marked with rectangles in black enamel. Datum 101 is close to Building 54 and Datum 102 is near Building 5. A third datum point was shot in and marked on the granite knob overlooking Building 45. No artificial grid was imposed on the site because the buildings are still visible and could be treated as units in their own right. We were fortunate in borrowing the Oriental Institute's Lietz Set 3 Total Instrument Station (TIS), which greatly facilitated the work. The TIS bounces an infrared beam off a prism held over the point being shot and reads slope distance, horizontal distance, elevation, and much other information. It also gives north and east coordinates automatically, which permitted us to plot all points each evening.

The survey procedure first called for Heidorn, Meyer, or Wilfong to sketch a building or group of buildings in a field notebook. In the accompanying field notes, comments could be written on features such as benches, niche measurements, bonding, looters' holes, grinding stones, small finds if any, ash, bones, and anything else of interest. One person acted as instrumentman to shoot the points selected by the sketcher. All points were numbered

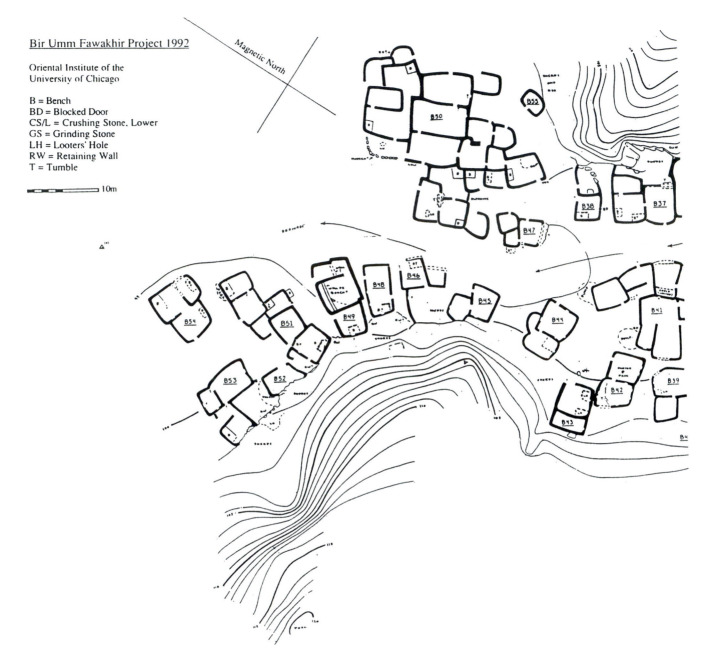

Fig. 9a. Map of Bir Umm Fawakhir.

on the sketches, in the surveyor's notebook, and on the data collector. A "B" prefaced a building point, a "T" a topography shot. The third person sketched the next buildings. As an added benefit, the sketches could be photocopied each evening for the photographer, who could tape the copies in his notebook and mark film roll numbers, shot number, and general direction on each sketch and thus eliminate possible confusion. All buildings shot on a given day were plotted the same evening on

graph paper at a scale of 1:200, the sketches being used as guides for connecting the plotted dots. The buildings were numbered 1 to 55 starting at the "East Gate," down a south side wadi, up a north side wadi, and then down the wadi bed toward the west. All contiguous rooms in a unit received one number, as Building 1 (a one-room outbuilding) or Building 50 (a 19-room agglomeration). No attempt was made to distinguish houses and outbuildings initially, and indeed the pattern was not

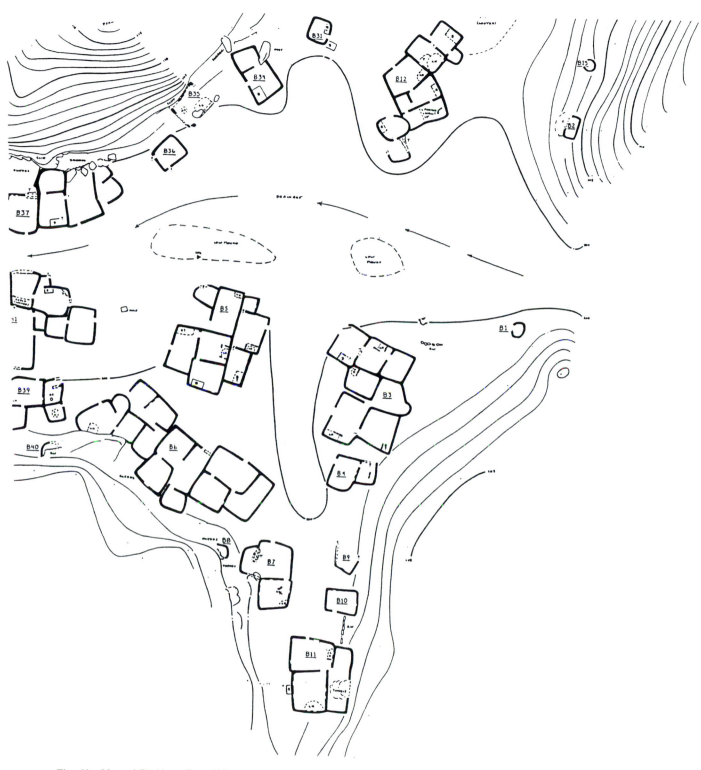

Fig. 9b. Map of Bir Umm Fawakhir.

clear until the remains were mapped. No attempt was made to letter or number rooms or features within a building, because we thought that premature; but if any house be more intensively studied or excavated, more detailed labels could easily be added then.

The map produced (fig. 9) is one of the most important results of the project. The wadi bottom plus

Fig. 9c. Map of Bir Umm Fawakhir.

some small side branches are the main streets of the site, quite broad in places and narrow in others. Rain is so rare that drainage was probably not a major problem for the ancient inhabitants, but floods since then have damaged parts of several buildings, notably Buildings 12, 3, 5, 41, 47, 45, and 54. A high felsite dyke runs behind Buildings 21, 15, 2, 1, and 11, and a natural gate between Buildings 1 and 2 marks the southeast end of the site. Clearly there was no attempt at a Classical town plan laid out on a grid system.

The houses, too, are irregular. They have a pattern but nothing like the nearly contemporary houses of Jême (Medinet Habu). Houses typically consist of two or three rooms with one entrance from the street (Buildings 4, 7, 11, 14, 19, 24, 29, 34, 38, 39, 42, 43, 44, 45, 47, 53, and 54). Two or more of the two- or three-room houses may be agglomerated into a larger unit (Buildings 3, 5, 6, 12, 17, 27, 37, 41, 51, and above all 50). The remains of Buildings 21, 28, and 46 are badly tumbled. The plans of Buildings 48 and 49 and not yet clear; they seem to have been partly reworked. Scattered on the slopes behind the houses or in the empty spaces between them are a number of one-room outbuildings, either rounded or subrectangular in plan (Buildings 1, 2, 8, 9, 10, 13, 15, 16, 18, 20, 22, 23, 25, 26, 30, 31, 32, 33?, 35, 36, 40, 52, and 55). Some are quite small, irregular constructions like Building 26, but some are fairly large like Building 18. Building 10 has two carefully made wall niches. Building 13 has a bench, and perhaps Buildings 31 and 35 as well; benches and niches are generally associated with houses. We cannot yet ascertain the function of the outbuildings—storage, animal shelter, workshops, or latrines. In addition there are some low walls, usually only one stone high, in places where sliding rocks or sand wash were likely to be problems. We have labeled them as "retaining walls." Finally, there are a few rectangular, stone-built features that might have been benches or hearths; one lies between Buildings 1 and 3, one between Buildings 14 and 16, and another between Buildings 27 and 28.

Thus, although we mapped 55 buildings, only 16 to 21 are houses, 10 or 11 are large, agglomerated houses, and the remaining 22 or 23 are outbuildings. The separateness of the houses and the lack of crowding are also noteworthy. When population estimates are made for the ancient community, this will have to be taken into account.

All of the buildings appear to have been built of dry stone masonry. There is virtually no evidence of mortar or plastering, although if excavation be undertaken and now buried portions of walls be uncovered, the picture could change abruptly. Although the building stones are carefully selected and laid with skill, we have as yet found no cut masonry. Most of the building stones are granite cobbles or felsite chunks, and the granite is now badly weathered and crumbly. One question is whether the stone was already weathered when the builders selected it, or whether the decay has occurred since then. The walls are typically built with neat inner and outer faces, the space between being filled with smaller stones, often felsite, and sometimes potsherds. All of the sherds observed *in situ* in wall fill were body sherds, but they do deserve closer attention because they are clearly older than the wall construction. The walls are sufficiently rough that it is difficult to get an exact measurement of their widths, but they are generally about 0.5 m wide. Especially thick walls or double walls, however, were noted and drawn in. Wherever possible we recorded nonbonded walls and blocked doors, although neither feature is common. Building 50 seems to have added on at least six one-room units, but apart from that there is not as much evidence of adding on and expanding as one might find in long-inhabited homes. Herein lies one reason for suggesting that the community was fairly short-lived.

Enclosed courtyards or work areas are common features of most Middle Eastern architecture, but as yet few "rooms" can be identified as possible courtyards at Bir Umm Fawakhir. The only clues come from the circulation pattern, areas too large to be roofed easily, or perhaps from wider than usual doorways.

The houses typically are provided with wall niches for storage, though the number of niches varies widely. The large, well-preserved Building 27 has only one, and sprawling Building 50 has only two preserved, whereas the much more modest Buildings 11 and 42 have at least eight niches each. Niches show no pattern of arrangement and need not even be on the same level in the same wall (fig. 24, Building 42). Sometimes only half a niche is preserved, and in badly ruined walls the niches may of course be totally lost.

Benches are another characteristic built-in feature. They are generally made of a row of slabs set upright and apparently filled with sand and small stones. The benches are either backed up against a wall or built into a corner. A large, smooth boulder was used as a bench in Building 38, and several buildings have outside benches as well. Looters have consistently clawed into the interior benches, and sometimes the shape of a looter's hole is the only indication that a bench once existed there (note Building 17). The features are called "benches" because they are characteristic features of Egyptian houses of all ages, from Deir al-Medina to Mons Claudianus and the Esna hermitages, up to the present day. They could, of course, have served other functions as well, such as holding water jars, but until it is demonstrated otherwise we are using the provisional label of "bench."

Hearths are so far surprisingly uncommon, even though it gets cold in the desert in the winter. Building 27 has a stone-rimmed corner in one room with some ash, and circles of stones in Buildings 12 and 17 might have been other hearths. Some of the smaller benches also might have served as hearths, but without any ash that is difficult to prove. Apart from dung, fuel was probably scarce in the desert, and winds have blown away most of the surface ash; nonetheless, hearths are a domestic feature that may be expected should excavation be initiated.

Building 14 has a stone-lined basin or trough of unknown function; the west wall of the house is so destroyed that it cannot be determined whether the area was enclosed or only partly enclosed. The grinding stones and mortars found in the houses may or may not pertain to domestic use; they generally are considered to be ore crushing stones re-used as building material. In any case, only one crushing stone so far as been found *in situ*, a threshold block in Building 17.

One outstanding feature of the site is the trash heaps immediately adjacent to each house or group of houses or else dumped up on the slopes behind them. The trash heaps provide an opportunity to investigate deposition patterns of a specific house or group of houses without much, if any, of the reworking, pitting, clearance, or redeposition usual on long-lived sites. Sherds or other artifacts can with some security be attributed to the closest house or houses, although more caution must be exercised with surface material.

We have no floors or remains of door panels or roofing material yet, and only two or three doubtful windows. Judging from a few intact thresholds and the looters' holes, floors in this part of the site lie 30–50 cm or less below the surface of the sand that has drifted in. If excavation be undertaken, floor levels should be reached quickly. Doors, at least those opening onto the streets, presumably would have been made of wood; at least one stone

door socket is still visible. Door jambs generally are constructed of fairly large, carefully laid stones, often long, thin ones (fig. 18, Building 27). Walls might have been plastered, though water is a prime commodity in the desert and we have as yet very little evidence of plastering. The walls were probably well chinked, however, as the desert winter wind is penetrating and cold. All of the niches have been labeled "niches" even when the thin back walls have fallen away so that the features now look like windows. Generally there is enough rough rubble behind a damaged niche to show that no finished sill ran through the wall. The modern houses at Bir Umm Fawakhir tend to have small, shuttered or shaded windows, often high in the wall. The two most problematic cases are the window/door in Building 27 (see below) and the two westernmost niches in Building 11; they do go through the wall and do seem more finished than the usual broken niches. Of roofs, we have not a scrap. The rooms presumably were spanned by palm logs, stringers, and some sort of roofing material. It had to be solid enough to stand the *hamsin* winds, but not necessarily waterproof. Even today in the Valley, people mostly just get miserable and wet when a rare heavy rain falls and drips through the ceiling. Wood for doors, roofs, and anything else is valuable in the desert and was probably one of the first things stripped away.

Overall, the houses are quite idiosyncratic and certainly had some leeway for expansion. Building 41 grew in a particularly ungainly fashion. The houses seem reasonably spacious and fitted out with comforts such as niches for storage and benches for resting or sleeping. There is, at this point, no sign of central planning or regimented, military orderliness, much less of cramped, mean, slave quarters. Administration there must have been, but so far it cannot be seen to have affected residents' house plans in any obvious fashion.

What we do not have at Bir Umm Fawakhir is almost as interesting as what we do have. First and foremost there are no defenses, even though security was always a concern in the desert. A gold miners' camp would be rather tempting to raiders, as would a caravan marching to or from the Red Sea ports with trade goods. If the site were a military post, then one would by definition expect fortifications. The Byzantine fort at ꜣAbu Shaᶜar, also long identified as Roman, does in fact have a defensive wall, towers, fortified gate, regular streets, barracks, and a central building (probably a *principia* or a church; Sidebotham et al. 1989: 130,

143). Even most of the monasteries of the period had some defenses. It was suggested that Buildings 1 and 2 might have been guard posts at Bir Umm Fawakhir's southeast "gate," but there is as yet nothing to distinguish them from any of the other outbuildings. The steep ridges overlooking the settlement have numerous pot drops and sherds, but so far no guard posts, much less fortifications. The old Roman tower overlooking the road to Bir Umm Fawakhir might have served Byzantine sentries as well, but again there is no evidence for much use—no accumulation of potsherds for instance. It is conceivable that there were some defenses or guard posts at the northwest entrance to the main settlement, or perhaps some out on the broad open area toward the wells, but nothing has been found there yet. Should work be resumed at Bir Umm Fawakhir, the problem of defenses would be explored further.

None of the buildings mapped so far looks like a warehouse, although there must have been some facility for storing food and supplies. Almost everything had to be hauled from the Nile Valley, and hence there must have been some central point for loading and unloading, distributing, and storing goods, even if only temporarily.

What a Byzantine administrative building in the desert may have looked like we do not know, but there must have been some administration for a settlement of this size. If Bir Umm Fawakhir was in fact a gold mining camp, it is difficult to believe that the Byzantine government could have kept its hand out of a pot so potentially lucrative. Until modern times, all expeditions to or settlements in the Eastern Desert were wholly or partially supported by the current regime, whether the ruler was pharaoh, emperor, or sultan. We will return to this question later, but given the Byzantine government's direction (or misdirection) of its citizens' taxes and lives, it may be assumed that some representative kept track of activities at Bir Umm Fawakhir. At the very least, we would expect ostraca.

That some of the inhabitants of Bir Umm Fawakhir were Christians is indicated by bowls with stamped crosses (fig. 10), but there is no church. It has been suggested that the Ptolemaic temple might have been converted, but the temple is long destroyed and none of the 19th century travelers mentioned any sign of Christian reuse.

Animal lines or shelters are not in evidence, although animals must have carried supplies to the people of Bir Umm Fawakhir. The Roman hydreumata on the Wadi Hammamat route do not, it is

Fig. 10. Interior of bowl stamped with Coptic cross from Building 8. Max. Dimension 4.7 cm.

true, have any of the animal lines characteristic of the northern Wadi Qena route or quarry towns like Mons Claudianus. Camels, which do not need much shelter, probably bore most of the traffic, but a few donkeys, sheep, or goats might have been tended, as they are by the present-day Bedouin. Given a hike of a kilometer from Building 3 to the modern wells, a donkey or so to carry water would have been desirable. Some of the outbuildings, or perhaps the irregular, open(?) space in Building 41, might have sheltered animals, but it remains to be demonstrated. A study of the bones from the trash heaps next to the houses might answer some of the questions about animals.

If baked bread were brought from the Valley,[7] it would have reached the hardtack stage by the time it got to the settlers, but it could have been done. Fuel for baking or heating would always have been at a premium, but as mentioned hearths are uncommon and ovens are totally undocumented so far.

Mining tools also had to come from the Valley, but there must have been an on-site smithy to resharpen and mend them. Such a facility, however,

Fig. 11. Rotary grinding stone and three anvil stones.

would most logically have been located near the mines, a part of the site much disrupted by modern activity.

Finally, we expect cemeteries. Debono's (1951) mention of thoroughly looted graves on the ridges overlooking the settlement is the only hint so far as to where they might have been. The 1992 project encountered no graves, but the work was concentrated on the town proper. One would expect no grave goods at all for Christians, but at places like Jeme (Medinet Habu) there seems to have been some variability in burial practices.

ARTIFACTS

By far the most abundant surface finds at Bir Umm Fawakhir are potsherds, which Heidorn discusses (below). There is also some splintery bone on some of the trash heaps or in the spoil from looters' holes. Other finds are meager, mainly crushing or pounding stones, three glass sherds, a sandstone trough, a ceramic lamp fragment, and one mud brick.

The crushing stones are made of granite, one piece being a handsome porphyry. One type of crushing stone consists of a heavy, lower stone and a smaller upper handstone for rubbing back and forth. Most of the examples are the heavy, concave lower part (see fig. 18, Building 27); the upper handstones have not been found so far. The other type of crushing stones is a rotary mill; both upper and lower stones have been recorded on site (fig.

11). Unfortunately, neither the dating of the crushing stones, whether Ptolemaic, Roman, or Byzantine, nor the gold extraction techniques used in the Byzantine period have received much attention. The oldest relevant source is Diodorus Siculus who, following Agatharchides' second century B.C. account, describes the extreme misery of the Egyptian gold miners. To extract the gold from the ore, workers

> take this quarried stone . . . and with iron pestles pound a specified amount of it in stone mortars, until they have worked it down to the size of a vetch. Thereupon the women and older men receive from them the rock of this size and cast it into mills of which a number stand there in a row, and taking their places in groups of two or three at the spoke or handle of each mill they grind it until they have worked down the amount given them to the consistency of the finest flour (Diodorus of Sicily III.13).

The rotary mills found at Bir Umm Fawakhir fit this picture, but the mortars do not; the one from Building 42 is a limestone too soft for crushing quartz. No trace of iron tools has yet been detected. Lucas (1962: 228) basically followed Diodorus' description. Recently Klemm and Klemm (1991) restudied the question of gold ore milling techniques. According to their description, the raw ore was first crushed on rather small anvil stones (ca. 30 × 30 cm) by means of rounded stone hammers weighing about a 0.5 to 1.0 kilo. In the Ptolemaic period, large concave grinding stones with a heavy, crescent-shaped upper stone were used to pulverize the ore, versus the flat stones used by the ancient Egyptians. The rotary mill or quern was a Roman innovation, though surprisingly enough the Roman anvil stones were smaller, ca. 15 × 15 cm (Klemm and Klemm 1991).

The quartz pounders from Bir Umm Fawakhir come close to this description of the hammer stones. Are the concave crushing stones Ptolemaic and the rotary mills Roman or later? Or were the concave stones used in the first stage of ore reduction and the rotary mills for the fine grinding? Closer inspection of the wear marks on the concave stones might answer this question, but further research on Byzantine gold extraction techniques is needed as well.

The finds are also noted with their buildings, but are listed together here. All items were left in place on site.

> Building 7. A rectangular, concave lower crushing stone.
>
> Building 14. Two round, bashed pounders made of quartz. Diameters 6.3 and at least 9 cm respectively.
>
>   Glass lamp stem (fig. 12b). The fragment is of bubbly, olive-colored glass without weathering or pontil scar. Stemmed glass lamps shaped something like a flaring champagne glass with no foot were common in Byzantine times (Meyer 1989: 240). Such lamps rested in holders, usually large metal disks with circles cut out to hold the lamps. The whole could be suspended by chains.
>
> Dump behind Buildings 12, 13, 14. A subrectangular granite grinding stone, measuring ca. 27 × 17 × 9 cm.
>
>   One cobalt blue glass sherd, thin, no weathering.
>
>   One glass jar or beaker neck, light olive, bubbly, no weathering.
>
> Building 17. One rectangular, concave lower crushing stone.
>
>   One rotary crushing stone made of porphyry, broken in half and reused as a threshold.
>
> (Outside Building 17) One rectangular, concave lower crushing stone.
>
> Building 27. Two rectangular, concave lower crushing stones.
>
>   One sandstone trough fragment, 27 cm wide × 12 cm high × 19 cm long before break. The interior is pecked. Sandstone is not native to Bir Umm Fawakhir, although the Nubian sandstones begin not far west of Bir Hammamat.
>
> Building 37. One rounded quartz pounding stone.
>
> Building 39. Fragment of a grinding stone.
>
> Building 40. Ceramic lamp fragment (fig. 12a), buff ware, now crumbly. The design is faint.

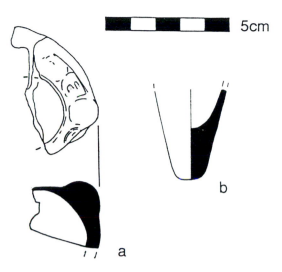

Fig. 12. Fragment of ceramic lamp (a) and glass lamp (b).

> Building 42. Fragment of a mortar made of limestone.
>   One mud brick.
>
> Building 43. (Outside) Rectangular, concave lower crushing stone.
>
> Building 51. Fragment of a mortar.

Again, what we do *not* have is interesting. There are yet no textile fragments, no metal, and no wood fragments, although the latter two materials probably were scavenged almost immediately after abandonment of a building or the site.

THE SHERD SAMPLE

Potsherds are easily the most abundant find at the site, so much so that the project could easily have spent the entire field season on them alone. Given that they are all surface finds and subject to displacement and that priority was given to mapping the settlement, we had to find some means of controlling the sheer numbers of sherds to be processed. The requirement that all sherds be tallied, drawn, and left on site at the collection point further restricted the number that we could handle.

We therefore took samples from three areas of particular interest and then a sample of one in ten of the different structures and features in the main settlement. We were particularly interested in: the wall remnant near the modern mosque as being the possible locus of a Roman structure; the mine tailings across the road as possibly clarifying Guéraud's statements about the ostraca; and the area of the wells, probably the most continuously utilized part of the site. The technique was to find some point that could be identified again on these littered and reworked surfaces and to lay out a circle with reference to that point. A nail was sunk into the ground and a circle with a 1 m radius described (the "dog-leash" technique); all sherds within the circle were collected during a five-minute period. This at least ensured that the areas sampled were comparable in size.

In the main settlement it soon became clear that there were three predominant kinds of features: houses or agglomerated houses, one-room out-buildings, and trash heaps. Eliminating all those disturbed by looting, we randomly selected one in ten of the remaining features. For houses we could not use this selection procedure because only one, Building 27, was relatively undisturbed. Here, sherds were so sparse that we collected from all rooms not contaminated by the dump on the slope behind the building. One trash heap was randomly selected, the dump behind Building 6; not surprisingly, it proved to be the largest sherd collection. For the one-room outbuildings, we selected Buildings 13 and 40; the Building 33 collection had to be abandoned because the building is almost completely buried in rock fall. Nonetheless, it did yield some interesting sherds and may be counted as the eighth sample. We used the dog-leash technique for the dump behind Building 6 but collected everything within the walls of Buildings 13 and 40 within the time limit.

The pottery corpus gathered by this sampling method differs somewhat from a collection of attractive sherds that one tends to spot when walking over the site. Amphorae and cooking pots are much better represented in the sampled corpus, and some kinds of sherds were collected that would have been overlooked otherwise, such as the burnished sherd (fig. 29j) or the lamp (fig. 12). On the other hand, the "X-Group" painted cups and bowls and the polished and rouletted orange bowls and dishes are more sparsely represented.

The pottery corpus from the 1992 season makes no claim whatsoever to being comprehensive, though it should be considerably expanded by another sample in the next season. These sherd collections together will provide at least some record of the surface material, and if excavation ever be undertaken, the surface collections should complement the excavated sherds.

THE POTTERY
BY LISA A. HEIDORN

One of the goals of the initial survey season at the ancient encampment, wells, and mine tailings at Bir Umm Fawakhir was to collect surface samples of sherds to date such features. Whitcomb and Meyer had drawn a number of surface sherds during brief visits to the site in 1978 and 1991 respectively. Their sketches formed a preliminary classification of pottery types which we used where applicable during the 1992 season. The sampling of eight small areas in 1992 resulted in the analysis and drawing in the field of 371 sherds. Half of the areas were sampled using the "dog leash" method (above). The diagnostic and body sherds collected within in each circle during a five minute period were sorted, tallied, and left on site. The body sherds were counted on sherd sheets that noted wares and surface treatments. In most cases the surface color of the sherds was determined from the *Munsell Soil Color Charts*, and the readings are listed in the notes. Diagnostic pieces were drawn and described.

The sampled sites, and the pottery collected from them, are discussed below. Some comparisons with types from other sites in Egypt are given in Appendix B accompanying the descriptions of sherds. Both the ceramic analysis and the dating indicated by the ceramic remains should be considered preliminary.

Northwest of Modern Mosque: Southeast Edge of Preserved Ancient (?) Walls

The collection of sherds from this site consisted of the surface sherds within a circular area measuring 2 m across. The center of the circle was on the northeast corner of a stone embedded in the earth. The stone was one of a number that appear to be lined up just below the surface, perhaps indicating the presence of an ancient wall. The sunken area north of the sample area—presently a convenient place for trash disposal—may be the interior of a building, and the earth mounded around the sunken trash dump may rest upon ancient walls. However, the site is close to the modern settlement and the road linking the towns of Quft on the Nile and Quseir on the Red Sea coast; only excavation could produce sherds from a less seriously disturbed context.

The diagnostic sherds in this sample consisted of a reddish-brown amphora handle (fig. 27c), an amphora stump-base of the same reddish-brown fabric (fig. 27e), and two amphora rim sherds (fig. 27a, b). A sherd from a wide-mouthed jar with everted rim (fig. 27d) was also found.

Thirty-three reddish-brown ware body sherds came from unidentifiable forms. However, other body sherds were from silt amphorae, including three neck fragments and one body fragment with ridged exterior. Two reddish-brown sherds had white-slipped exteriors(?).

Area of Ancient (and Modern) Wells

This collection consisted of surface sherds found near the western edge of the rock debris near the numerous ancient wells. The sherds were found on the level ground on the western side of one of the rubble mounds. This area has been reused throughout the millennia because it has easily attainable water, and the sherds amidst the debris around the ancient well heads undoubtedly represent more than one time period. Due to the great amount of rock tumble in the area, it is difficult to discern the ground plans of any of the ancient constructions that might have been located there.

The diagnostic sherds on the surface in this area were numerous. They included the following: a reddish-brown amphora stump base (fig. 27q); a small knob base (fig. 27s); a reddish-brown amphora handle (with traces of red slip?) (fig. 27r); an amphora rim with bulbous lip (fig. 27f); a marl handle with ridges on the exterior (fig. 27t); three silt bowl rims (fig. 27j–l); a rim from a small jar (fig. 27g); a jar or bottle rim with light-colored surfaces (fig. 27i); a wide-mouthed silt jar rim with red slip (fig. 27m); two wide-mouthed jar rims with interior ledges (fig. 27n–o); a light brown globular jar rim with a cream exterior (fig. 27p); and a reddish-brown channeled jar rim with light-colored slip partially preserved on exterior (fig. 27h); a sherd from a wide-mouth vat (fig. 28a); and a ring-base fragment (fig. 28b).

Also collected during the survey were 27 reddish-brown body sherds (two with ribbed exteriors), five sherds with red slips, seven reddish-brown silt sherds with light-colored slips, and one sherd made from a light-colored (marl?) clay.

Mine Tailings South of Modern Road (Sites A and B)

Two small sherd samples were collected in the dumps sloping down in front of the ancient mine

entrances to the south of the Quft to Quseir road. Surface sherds were collected from a small area (Site A) on the northern slope of hill above the road. The sherds from the area, however, were chosen for their diagnostic value, and no body sherds were collected from the spot. The surface sherds of the main sample area (Site B) were gathered from within a 2 m circle on the western face of the eastern arm of the small bay. Site B was located on the arm of the bay opposite from and facing Site A. Numerous mine entrances, paths, and probable wall remains are visible amidst the thick deposits of rock and debris covering the steep northern slope of this escarpment and the ground at its base.

Only four rim sherds were collected from Site A. One neck and shoulder fragment belonged to a small globular jar with a neck ridge (fig. 28d); its fabric had some small chaff pieces and a few white particles added as temper. The other three sherds belonged to various reddish-brown silt bowl forms. The bowl shown in fig. 28f may in fact be a lid. The bowl sherds shown in fig. 28c and 28e have red slips on their interior and exterior surfaces.

The diagnostic sherds from Site B included an amphora toe with a slight concave depression in base (fig. 28k); an amphora rim and neck (fig. 28g); a small lid or base fragment (fig. 28m); a reddish-brown cooking-pot rim with a handle scar and red slip on the exterior (fig. 28h). A small bowl with single channel on the exterior below rim (fig. 28i) and a marl bowl with an incised line below the rim on the exterior (fig. 28j) were also collected. The double-barreled jar handle with a thick red slip (fig. 28l) may be the only imported sherd in this group. Also found at Site B were 29 reddish-brown body sherds, 1 coarse light-ware jar handle, and 6 reddish-brown sherds with light-colored slips on their exteriors.

Dump Behind Building 6

Sherd debris was concentrated on a narrow area behind, and up the slope from, Building 6. The sample area chosen was behind this agglomerative building and within the sherd scatter of the trash dump. The housing complex and the dump were located at the base of a cliff.

Numerous diagnostic sherds were collected from the site. They included the following: an amphora rim and neck with dark orange- to buff-colored surfaces (not illustrated, but see fig. 29g);[8] two reddish-brown amphorae stump-bases (fig. 29n–o);

a reddish-brown cooking pot with a "piecrust" rim (fig. 29a); a cup or bowl with orange slip and burnished surfaces (fig. 29b); a flanged silt bowl of reddish-brown ware with slip (fig. 29e); a carinated silt bowl with black spots atop the thickened rim (fig. 29c); two rim sherds from a (the same?) reddish-orange wide-mouthed jar (fig. 29h); a wide-mouthed, light-colored (marl?) jar rim and neck (fig. 29f); one reddish-brown and one light-colored ware jar handle (the latter shown in fig. 29l); one light-colored shoulder and neck fragment with part of a handle preserved and ribbed profile (fig. 29g); a fine reddish-brown shoulder and body sherd with a few exterior ridges (fig. 29i); a silt bowl rim with burnished exterior (fig. 29d); a base fragment with remnants of a bright orange exterior slip (fig. 29k); and a buff ware ring-base (with greenish core) like the example shown in fig. 29m.

There were also 21 reddish-brown body sherds, 16 light-colored body sherds (mostly ribbed ones), and 1 pink sherd with a burnished orange surface. A number of body sherds in this group merit separate description. Decorated sherds include an orange sherd with red exterior (slipped?) and black painted decoration (fig. 29p), a reddish-brown sherd with black decoration (fig. 29q), and one incised orange bowl fragment with a purple-gray burnished exterior and black burnished interior (fig. 29j). Other body sherds include 20 light orange (around 2.5 YR 6/8 in surface color) fragments, some with exterior ribbing; two light pink (lighter than 2.5 YR 6/6) sherds with ribbed profiles, and two others of the same surface color but with a lot of black and sandy temper; 21 orange-brown sherds (ranging from 2.5 YR 5/6 to 6/8) some with exterior ribbing; and a ribbed pink sherd (5 YR 7/3) with an orange exterior surface. It is unclear which of the sherds were manufactured of typical Egyptian clay and which may have been imported.

Building 13

This sample consisted of all surface sherds within a small square outbuilding. The sherds were collected from the middle of the hut in an attempt to lessen contamination from sherds falling out of wall crevices where they had been placed as chinking during the construction of the hut. It is, of course, not certain which of the disturbed surface sherds are contemporary with the occupation or construction of this building.

The diagnostic sherds included a carinated shoulder and rim sherd of a buff-colored jar (fig.

30e); a silt vat with white and black decoration (fig. 30a); a dark reddish-gray jar rim with combed bands on the exterior of the body (fig. 30c) and a reddish-brown sherd with a portion of a handle from the same jar (?) (fig. 30b); and two cooking-pot rims (fig. 30d). There were also 14 reddish-brown body sherds. Most of these silt sherds had ribbed exteriors, and one had cord marks on its exterior. Also collected from Building 13 were six light-colored ("buff") body sherds with ribbed exteriors, two coarse marl sherds whose greenish exteriors bore two bands of combed lines, and one reddish-brown body sherd with combing on its exterior surface.

Slope Below Building 33

This sample consisted of two sherds from the surface of the slope below a circular structure designated Building 33, located at the base of an escarpment. The sherds were retained because of their unique shapes and wares. One is probably a base fragment of a small jar (fig. 30g), and the other was from a handmade jar with incised decoration (fig. 30f).

Building 37

This sample area consisted of a rectilinear building of six rooms. All surface sherds found in the middles of the rooms were collected. The sherds adjacent to the walls were once again avoided to lessen contamination from sherds that might have fallen from wall chinking. The only diagnostic sherd was an orange, flanged bowl with red slip and exterior rouletting (fig. 30h). A sign had been scratched on the interior, perhaps a simplified Chi-Rho.

The other reddish brown sherds from this building consisted of 14 body sherds, 4 sherds with light-colored slip, 2 sherds with a red slip, and 1 light brown fragment with red slip (possibly manufactured of a marl and silt clay mixture). Six sherds of fine marl clay were also collected here.

Building 40

The sherd sample was collected from within a circular outbuilding on the hillside. The hut was ruinous, and the sample may be considered a continuation of the trash mounds located up the steep slope from this building. The diagnostic sherds included a reddish-brown amphora handle with part of the neck; a carinated bowl (fig. 30i); a small marl cooking-pot with horizontal handles, incised rim and corrugated exterior (fig. 30k); a bowl with a thickened rim and corrugation on the exterior below the carinated mid-section (fig. 30n); a rim from a wide-mouthed vat like that shown in fig. 30a;[9] a wide-mouthed marl jar (fig. 30m); a red-slipped bowl or jar rim (fig. 30j); and a fragment from a carinated silt bowl (fig. 30l). Two marl ring-bases like the base illustrated in fig. 29m,[10] and a base of a globular cup or small jar (fig. 30o) were also found.

In addition, there were 29 reddish-brown body sherds (some of these were ribbed amphorae sherds), 1 reddish-brown sherd with light-colored coating on the exterior, 3 reddish-brown sherds with red slip on the interiors and/or exteriors (one is a ribbed jar sherd), and 15 marl body sherds.

Surface Sample

Three interesting sherds were noted from areas not systematically collected. A handle and rim fragment was picked up from the surface near the western approach to the main settlement (fig. 30p). The handle is made of clay fired to a pink color and has an orange exterior surface or slip. It may be part of a cooking pothandle and rim. The other two surface sherds are described with "Slope below Building 33."

The Pottery Dating

The analysis of the sherds from the 1992 season at Bir Umm Fawakhir has established tentative dates for some of the sherds and surveyed areas. The sherd scatter in the area northwest of the modern mosque included fragments of amphorae which clearly date to the first and second centuries A.D. when compared with excavated materials from other sites in Egypt. But the sherd sample was small, and it was collected from an area greatly disturbed by modern activity. The sampled sites around the wells and downslope from the mine entrances were also areas much disturbed by human activity. The materials collected in the survey of the sites included sherds ranging in date from the early Roman to the Coptic periods (and later?) in Egypt. Most of the sherds collected within the main settlement, however, can be roughly dated between A.D. 400 and 600. The comparative materials used in dating the types do not allow us at this time to date the ancient settlement more narrowly.

SUMMARY OF RESULTS OF THE 1992 SURVEY

The goal of the Bir Umm Fawakhir Survey was to document the surface remains of the site and thus preserve a record of it, and to investigate more thoroughly the nature of the site, which to date has almost always been called Roman rather than Byzantine. In 12 days we mapped approximately one quarter of the community in the main wadi, sampled the sherds, and clarified some questions about the different periods of occupation. The Ptolemaic presence remains elusive, although it definitely was documented in early travelers' accounts and perhaps was attested by the concave crushing stones. The Roman remains are far more skimpy than formerly believed; we do have the Roman tower, the first–second century graffiti, some sherds, and probably the granite quarries, but no obvious, fortified way station like Wekalat Zarka or others on the Quft-Quseir road. The mysterious cut stone wall near the modern mosque may be Roman, judging from the sherds collected in its vicinity.

The geological study explains many features of the site, why it exists and why it is laid out the way it is. The title of this article, "Gold, Granite, and Water," summarizes the most important resources of the site. Precambrian granite is the aquifer feeding the wells that made it possible to use this caravan route through the desert and to build a settlement the size of Bir Umm Fawakhir. Perhaps the most important geological features, however, are the gold quartz veins in the granite. We also know that granite blocks were cut from two rather modest quarries, but we do not know why those spots were chosen rather than any of the other masses of granite all around. Small granite blocks and cobbles were the building material for the houses. Standing at the wells, we can see where erosion has dissected, deeply, the Fawakhir granite into numerous wadis, some broad, some narrow. The broad ones permitted passage of the caravans between the Nile and the Red Sea, and one of the long, narrow, steep-sided wadis enclosed the main Byzantine settlement, which is further constricted by a series of fault structures and the felsite dyke running nearly at right angles to the wadi axis. These are the points at which the wadi narrows or nearly closes, the final constriction forming a natural gate at the southeast end of the site.

We can begin to see the pattern of the ancient community with buildings strung along either side of the sandy wadi bottom. There was no formal town planning; the landform determined the layout of the settlement. From the maze of walls and doors and rooms we can now discern three main kinds of buildings: a two- or three-room house, an agglomerated unit made up of two or more connected houses, and one-room outbuildings. All are constructed of unworked native granite, apparently unmortared but well chinked with small stones or sherds. Some of the houses were altered, enlarged, or even annexed by a neighboring house, although each building unit nonetheless preserved some space separating it from the next. Trash was dumped outside the houses or at the foot of the cliffs behind them, a practice that has a great deal of potential for archaeological investigation. There is no compelling reason to consider the occupants slaves or prisoners as described in Diodorus' much earlier account. The buildings sprawl along the wadi, and although the houses fall into an identifiable pattern of several rooms and a generally similar amount of space, the specific layout of any one house seems quite idiosyncratic. Most houses even have modest built-in comforts such as benches or storage niches. In short, there is no sign of the regimented quarters or tight control expected for slaves or prisoners.

The rest of our conclusions are more questions than answers. Who were the ancient inhabitants? What was their relation to the Nile valley? Does the presence of a rather considerable amount of Nubian style pottery suggest a connection to Nubia? The clear layout of the community will permit a useful estimate of the number of residents, though we postponed this until the next season's mapping is completed. What of the means of supply and support? This must have come from the Valley, and the large amphorae could have contained any of a variety of victuals, but so far we lack storehouses, animal lines, and even ovens. A study of the bones and bone splinters from the trash heaps should provide information about the kinds of animals present.

We still do not know, for certain, what ancient Bir Umm Fawakhir was doing there; the four most probable functions seem to be gold mining, granite quarrying, serving the Nile-Red Sea long distance trade, or military.

Although we know that gold was extracted from Bir Umm Fawakhir in antiquity, it is not clear whether mining occurred in the Byzantine, Roman, Ptolemaic, or earlier periods, or at several different times. We could look to both the mines and their vicinity and to the main group of ruins for evidence. If Byzantine Bir Umm Fawakhir was primarily a gold mining camp, then we have the following expectations:

(1) We expect mining tools and debris both from hacking out the gold-bearing veins in the mountainsides and from crushing and washing the gold quartz.

The area at the foot of the mines has been thoroughly disturbed by modern mining activity. Washing tables, if any, are no longer in evidence (see Vercoutter 1959 for gold washing tables). The only information pertaining to ore extraction so far comes from the concave crushing stones, pounders, and the rotary mills. The crushing stones need reinspection and closer dating, and Byzantine mining techniques in general need further research.

(2) We also expect smithies for repairing metal implements. We might also find some construction near the adits, if only because some of the shafts are vertical or nearly so and some sort of platform for hauling men and ore out would be needed.

As mentioned, there are no surviving indications of mining-related buildings at the foot of the mines, although there are some dry stone platforms and hut circles near some of the adits. Is there enough associated pottery to suggest a date?

(3) We expect a mining camp to be fairly short-lived. When the ore is mined out, the miners leave, especially in an environment as harsh as the Eastern Desert.

There is little evidence that Byzantine Bir Umm Fawakhir grew slowly from the northwest end to the southeast or vice versa. All of the buildings inspected so far have the same kind of construction and general layout pattern. The same holds for at least two of the outliers as well. Some of the houses have been altered but so far as can now be determined, no more than might be expected in several decades. There is no layering of building upon building; enough of the looters' holes reach bedrock to demonstrate this. Against this expectation of a short life span of the community we have an amazing amount of pottery. The duration of the site could be investigated by: (a) test excavations in the trash heaps to investigate the stratigraphy and to see what differences there may be in sherds from top to bottom; (b) statistical comparison of excavated (non-migrated) sherds from either end of the site. The basic repertoire of sherds is the same from one end of the site to another, but quantitative differences might be detected. It will be critical to distinguish chronological differences from functional ones; (c) further study of the non-bonded walls, blocked doorways, and alterations to the houses.

(4) If Bir Umm Fawakhir is in fact short-lived, we should be able to narrow the rather broad fifth–seventh century range of preliminary pottery dates. The best evidence is likely to come from ostraca or coins, but that would require excavation. Pottery comparisons to Valley sites are not likely to be as useful, given that most Valley sites are quite long-lived and the Byzantine pottery broadly dated, if treated at all. In fact, as a one-period site Bir Umm Fawakhir is more likely to assist in dating other sites than vice versa.

(5) In a mining camp we expect working class goods. High status or costly goods should be at a minimum. On the one hand, we have no indication of slave or prisoners' quarters, but on the other, the houses are all fairly modest and reasonably similar in size and facilities. It will be important to define "costly" in terms of fine ceramics, manufactured goods, or the elegant Coptic textiles.

(6) For a gold mine, we expect a fairly high level of administrative control of the workforce, supplies, and above all, the product. All major ventures in the Eastern Desert were, until the present day, supported to some degree by the current government. The pharaonic mining expeditions often were carried out by high officials. Most of the Roman merchants traveling through the desert may have represented private consortia, but the government built and maintained the roads, wells, and way stations, provided protection, and collected a 25 percent tax. In the Mamluk period, a group of extremely wealthy merchants, the *karim*, handled most of the India trade via the Red Sea, but they too were aided and protected by the government (Meyer 1992). In the Byzantine period, we have as yet no evidence that any private individual or consortium could have financed a venture such as the Bir Umm Fawakhir mines, and in fact we have virtually no literary evidence for Byzantine exploitation of the Eastern Desert. Whatever the case, the Byzantine government exercised, or tried to exercise, such rigid control over the lives of the populace in the Valley that it seems unlikely that they ignored something as potentially lucrative as a gold mine. We would expect some sort of administrative headquarters, a governor's residence, a warehouse for provisions, a strong room perhaps, and above all accounts and ostraca.

(7) We expect some degree of protection for the gold produced, both at the site and for the jour-

ney to the capital. Guardposts to warn of raids and some armed guards would be expected, but not a full military installation. The tops of the ridges overlooking the site do have numerous pot drops and should be inspected more closely for watch stations.

We also know that granite was quarried at Bir Umm Fawakhir, one quarry lying near the northern outlier by the Roman road (see fig. 3), and the second, smaller quarry in the main group of ruins.

The first problem, however, is to determine whether the quarries themselves are Roman or Byzantine, and the earlier date seems the likelier. The tool marks match the ones at Roman Mons Claudianus, the Romans were more avid collectors of exotic luxury stones than the Byzantine rulers, and the fifth to seventh century settlement is far too large for the modest quarries in question. There are, nonetheless, several lines of inquiry that could help date the granite quarries.

(1) The best dating evidence is likely to be the tool marks. As noted, they seem to match Roman cutting marks from other granite quarries in the Eastern Desert, but on the other hand, Byzantine granite quarrying techniques are unstudied as yet.

(2) The second, small quarry lies in the main group of ruins quite close to the houses. Inspection of the area might provide some clues as to the quarrying/building sequence here.

(3) If the granite quarries were Roman, we would expect traces of housing, sherds, and tools. To date, none have been found and sherds (apart from amphorae) may never have been abundant at an actual working site. Furthermore, the Byzantine sherds now predominate over the whole site.

A second possibility is that granite quarrying was a sideline for the Byzantine town. If such were the case, we would look for features a little different from a gold mining camp.

(1) We expect a workmen's camp, though not necessarily a short-lived one, as granite is unlikely ever to be worked out. Granite quarrying will instead depend on the ability to organize and provision the workmen, the capacity to transport the blocks, and especially on the demand for exotic luxury stones.

(2) A quarrymen's camp would be no more luxurious than a gold miners', so again we would expect few if any costly goods.

(3) Above all, we expect signs of the transport used for hauling the blocks to the Nile, which means animal traction. Camels are attested as draft animals hauling stones from Mons Porphyrites

(Raschke 1978: 884), but oxen were far more commonly employed. We would look for several features: animal lines or shelter, water troughs, and a track improved sufficiently for oxen and heavy blocks and carts.

Such features may never be found because the modern asphalt road has long since obliterated the old camel and cart tracks. Also, none of the Wadi Hammamat hydreumata have animal lines such as those found at the ancient stations on the Qena road.

(4) Protection for a quarry would be limited to the men themselves and the animals. Raiders do not want multi-ton granite blocks.

We know that an important Roman trade route, as marked by the intervisible towers, passed by Bir Umm Fawakhir, and we suspect that it and its wells served as a way station on the Nile-Red Sea road, though it seems to lack a fortified way station such as the one at Wekalat Zarka. If the Byzantine settlement also acted as a way station for the desert caravans, we have yet another set of expectations.

(1) We would look for facilities for traveling caravans, primarily water, shelter, and protection from raids. The Roman and Mamluk caravans may have counted hundreds of animals, as estimated from the tonnage needed to fill a middle-sized Red Sea vessel (Meyer 1992). Unfortunately we have almost no information on the Byzantine desert caravans or Red Sea ships. We would expect watering troughs, animal lines, some protection for the caravan's bundles and bales of valuable goods, and perhaps a caravanserai. None of these is in evidence, though the area closest to the wells is thoroughly disturbed.

(2) There would be relatively few permanent residents at a desert way station.

(3) We would expect some evidence of the import and export goods, which were mostly items of considerable value. A few items might have been consumed on site, and somewhat more broken or abandoned in transit. The meager evidence for Byzantine trade on the Red Sea and Indian Ocean coasts has been reviewed above, namely Justinian's treaty with Axum and the routes through Clysma, Antinoopolis, and Berenice.

(4) We would expect some protection of the resting place and of the caravans en route, perhaps no more than a stout walled enclosure for the one and armed guards for the other.

We know from the first–second century ostraca that Bir Umm Fawakhir had a military function in the Roman period and that security against desert tribes or raiders was always a concern. The possibility that Bir Umm Fawakhir functioned primarily as a military base, however, is not seriously considered. The site lacks any major fortifications or defenses except what was given by its natural, sheltered location. Small guard posts on the tops of the ridges may be expected, but have not yet been located. Bir Umm Fawakhir has no resemblance to the Byzantine fort at ʾAbu Shaʿar, which has a rectangular defensive wall, corner towers, a towered gate, a regular street plan, barracks, and a focal, main building (Sidebotham et al. 1989: 130). Byzantine military control of the Eastern Desert seems to have been sporadic at best.

In sum, Bir Umm Fawakhir represents a special opportunity to study an entire ancient community from its reason for existence down to its very trash heaps, with or without excavation. Our brief project in 1992 not only rendered the site much more comprehensible but made it one of the best-studied Byzantine settlements in the Eastern Desert. Along with sites such as ʾAbu Shaʿar, Bir Nakheil, and what can be gleaned concerning Berenice, we can begin to ask questions about the Byzantine exploitation of the Eastern Desert. We hope in the future to continue mapping the site and to pursue some of these questions about the region, the function of Bir Umm Fawakhir itself, and the people who lived there.

APPENDIX A
DESCRIPTIONS OF INDIVIDUAL BUILDINGS

Building 1. A small, nearly circular outbuilding near the southeast "gate." Although Building 1 is in a good position for a guard post, it looks toward the settlement not out from it.

Building 2 (see Building 12). A small, rectangular outbuilding near the southeast "gate." The northwest wall is partly collapsed, but the door seems to have been at the north corner. The large amount of tumbled rock in front suggests the possibility of a small terrace there.

Building 3. A seven-room house consisting of one three-room and one four-room unit. The room without a door probably had one in its northeast wall; it is badly tumbled whereas the other three rooms are fairly well preserved. The northernmost corner of the building has

Fig. 13. Building 5 in right foreground, B12 *et seq.* upper right section, Building 31 isolated, Buildings 34, 35, 36 with tripod and prism pole. Wilfong standing by datum point 102.

Fig. 14. Building 6.

been washed away by wadi floods. The apse-like feature, which is backed into the talus slope from the felsite dyke, may represent part of a circular outbuilding "captured" by Building 3. The very narrow passage between the two house units is not yet explained, although other, unmapped houses have similar features. Building 3 has five benches, of which three are looted; it has no preserved niches, but none of the walls now stand very high.

Building 4. A partly destroyed two-room house that nonetheless has two niches and remnants of a bench.

Building 5 (fig. 13). An eight-room, three-unit house. Two of the doors are questionable, though given the preservation of the walls it is difficult to see where else they could have been. The northernmost rounded room is ruined down to the height of a single stone. The best-preserved doorway shows clearly in fig. 13. Four of the five benches have been looted, and the fifth looters' hole

may mark the location of another bench. There are only two preserved niches, the southernmost one of which has no back and so resembles a window.

Building 6 (fig. 14). A rambling, thirteen-room house with units of two, four, four, and three rooms. Building 6 is backed against a cliff and granite boulders on the southwest; the larger looters' hole reaches granite bedrock. Two sets of walls are double thick, one set on the cliff side, the other on the northeast front, suggesting that the rooms so enclosed were added later. The whole cliff slope behind Buildings 39, 6, and 7 is dense with potsherds, probably representing debris from those buildings. Building 6 had at least six niches, and two upright stones by the looter's hole seem to indicate that it was once a bench.

Building 7 (fig. 15). A three-room house. The backmost room is built against the cliff, and only the line of

Fig. 15. Building 7 at lower left, Buildings 9, 10, 11 at foot of talus slope.

boulders suggests the original position of part of the back wall. Apart from a piece of the door jamb, the partition wall is almost totally lose in stone tumble. Building 7 is noteworthy mainly for one room that has an especially large number of niches, five. Starting at the door and running counterclockwise, their maximum dimensions are: 30 cm wide × 33 (top gone); 30 × 28 × ca. 38 deep; 29 × ca. 30 × ca. 34 deep; 29 × 30; 35 × 30 × ca. 30 deep. A rectangular, concave grinding stone rests in the room with the niches, and a small looters' hole has been grubbed in the south corner. Note the jointed granite in the foreground.

Building 8. One-room outbuilding. Only two walls and a bit of a third are preserved. The back wall, on the cliff side, is lost and most of the structure filled with rocks and sherds. Here we found the best specimen of a Coptic stamped bowl (fig. 10).

Building 9 (fig. 15). Building 9 now consists of two walls and a remnant which is reduced to a single face of stones running towards Building 4. If anything more existed between them, it is now lost in the litter of small stones falling off the felsite dyke. The west wall of Building 4 is curiously bowed inside.

Building 10 (fig. 15). Building 10 is an exceptionally well constructed one-room outbuilding. The doorway is made of carefully stacked large stones surviving 90 cm high, and the room has two built-in niches. This of all the outbuildings has the most resemblance to a small house, and the single row of stones in the retaining wall gives the illusion of linking Building 10 to Building 11.

Building 11 (fig. 15). A fairly large three- (or four?-) room house at the southwest end of the side wadi. Parts of this building are badly damaged. Wall collapse and rock fall from the slope of the felsite dyke have obliterated a possible cross wall and filled the cliffside room or rooms. Looters have dug one hole in the bench in the front room, and an exceptionally deep hole in the back room. It is roughly 0.5 m deep (it is hard to measure because of the debris piled around it) and seems to go through wadi cobbles to bedrock. On the other hand, the remnants of the outside bench are as yet untouched. The front room has four niches; running clockwise from the door their maximum dimensions are: 43 cm wide × 42 (top gone) × 35 deep; (damaged) 28 × 22 high × 30 deep; 31 × 24 (top gone) × 22 deep; (damaged) at least 32 cm high. In the southwest room four niches could not be reached for accurate measurement because of the looters' hole inside and the rock fall outside; we did not wish to climb the walls and so topple more stones. The other two niches were badly broken. We did note, however, that the two southwest niches look more like windows than niches. The sill on one seems to run through to the outside wall, and in this case the possibility of a real window or windows must be considered.

Building 12 (fig. 13, 16). Probably two house units plus two attached rooms. Of the latter, the round one has a bench and two doors, but the southwest room is reduced to a rim of single stones. Unfortunately it is impossible to determine whether or not the walls are bonded without moving a considerable amount of wall fall. The larger of the two house units now has four rooms, although at one time the back room may have been partitioned into two. The unit has at least one bench and a circle of stones that might mark a hearth. The smaller, three-room house unit has one bench and may have had a second in the room with the niches. The niche above the looters' hole measures 30 cm wide × (top and bottom gone) × 35 deep; the second niche is mostly destroyed. Wall fall and the large looter's hole plus its debris fill almost half the room. The small room at the south end of the unit may have been added, but the bonding or lack of it is not visible.

Fig. 16. Building 12 at center, Building 13 to left, Buildings 2 and 15 on slope behind.

Building 13 (fig. 16). A one-room outbuilding with a bench. It is unusual in that it has two doors.

Building 14. A two- or three-room house. The westernmost wall is destroyed to the level of the face of one line of stones, and the door is completely lost. It is not even clear whether this area was completely walled or roofed; its main feature is the stone-lined feature tentatively called a basin or trough. If lined and sealed it could have held water for domestic or craft purposes, or perhaps even for animals. If roofed, it might have served for storage like the small cellar in the "Roman Villa" at Quseir al-Qadim (Meyer 1982: 203). There are several small looters' pits around Building 14, but the largest is in the former bench inside. Two niches and an exterior bench have survived, however. The niches in the room with the looted bench measures 22 cm × 20 × 20 deep; the one in the south room is ca. 20 cm wide × 25 high. Artifacts found in Building 14 include the base fragment of a glass lamp (fig. 12) and two bashed and broken quartz pounding stones, ca. 6.3 cm and 9 cm in diameter respectively.

A broad dump area runs behind Buildings 12, 13, and 14. The surface has been fairly thoroughly dug into by looters, but a few surface finds may be noted: a roughly rectangular granite crushing stone measuring ca. 27 × 17 × 9 cm, a cobalt blue glass fragment, and what seems to be the neck of a jar or beaker of light olive green glass.

Building 15 (fig. 16). A small, circular, one-room outbuilding built into the slope behind Buildings 12 and 13.

Building 16. A small, one-room outbuilding, nearly triangular in shape. Built into the slope behind Building 14.

Building 17. One of the most regular of the houses, yet with some unusual features. It seems to consist of a four- and a three-room unit, plus a large central room. The door to this room is an unusually broad 93 cm, so the "room" could conceivably have been a courtyard. It is graced by a small looters' hole and a large one that

yielded some fragments of bone. Close to the door is a rectangular, concave crushing stone; another lies just outside the house. The four-room southwest house unit has one looters' hole, possibly representing a former bench. The northeast three-room house has two looted benches and a circle of stones, possibly a hearth. The threshold to the back room, however, consists of a piece of porphyry, apparently the upper part of a rotary crushing stone broken in half.

Building 18. One-room outbuilding with two doors.

Building 19. A badly tumbled two-room house with three doors, a bench, and a niche, 37 cm wide × (top missing) × 34 deep. A partial row of stones appears to connect Building 19 to Building 18.

Building 20. One-room outbuilding scarcely preserved more than one stone high. The northwest corner has been completely washed away. A rim of stones in front of it in the wadi may represent another outbuilding. Sherds are abundant behind Buildings 19 and 20.

Building 21. One room with a bench is detectable, plus a possible rectangular feature outside. Building 21 is so badly destroyed that the plan became clear only when the wall remnants were mapped. The fragmentary walls upstream in the wadi bed may be retaining walls. This end of the wadi has been particularly eroded and filled with sand by wadi wash.

Building 22. A small, one-room outbuilding, two walls of which consist of an angle in the cliff behind it. A low retaining wall may have formed a step or platform up to Building 22.

Building 23. Very meager remains, scarcely projecting above ground surface. There is no clear doorway. A line of stones between Buildings 23 and 22 forms a low retaining wall below the cliff.

Building 24. A three-room house. It has two benches outside the front door and two interior niches, one ca. 20

Fig. 17. Building 27 at center, Building 28 behind.

× 15 cm, and the other, in the rounded room, 50 cm wide. Building 24 is fairly well preserved, and the door jambs to the rounded back room still stand over a meter high. The puzzling feature is the possible niche on the outside.

Fig. 18. Building 27, doorway with concave grinding stone.

Building 25. Appears to be a one-room outbuilding built against the cliff face. The remains are badly damaged and confusing. Although the area to the east now is littered with sherds and debris, there may have been another room there on a higher level. The "retaining wall" no longer preserves enough evidence to prove that it was once a real wall, though there is enough rock tumble to the south to account for one. We did detect the remnant of a wall, possibly with a door, that might have connected Buildings 24 and 25 at one time. The easiest path up to Building 26 runs uphill from the sherd dump behind Building 25.

Building 26. A tiny, one-room outbuilding set against a cliff face above Buildings 25 and 27.

Building 27 (fig. 17, 18). Appears to consist of two (or three) two-room house units plus later modifications and additions to the east and south. This is one of the best preserved buildings mapped in 1992. The western unit has a small rounded back room and a trapezoidal front room; the wall between is so badly tumbled that only one possible door jamb can be seen. Near the looters' hole in the front room rests part of a sandstone trough. What remains is a rectangular piece 12 cm high, 26 long, and 19 wide before the break. The interior is pecked. Sandstone is not native to the area, though the nearest outcrops of Nubian sandstone are not far west of Bir Hammamat. The main entrance to the rest of the house from the wadi "street" leads into a large room, perhaps even a courtyard, that in turn opens north into a large, irregular room and east into another set of four rooms. If divided, the irregular room would make a normal two-room house, but unfortunately there is no sign of a partition wall. Alternatively, the irregular room may be a later enclosure; its south wall abuts rather than joins the wall on the east, and its west wall seems to be a double wall with the rounded room; it is not known whether the third wall angle abuts another room. What

Fig. 19. Building 29.

the room does have, however, is a stone-rimmed feature in one corner with ash in it, and more ash in another corner. The features presumably represent one or two hearths. The eastern set of four rooms has one small looters' hole, one niche (half preserved), and one window. The window sill is now 58 cm above the floor but flush with the path on the east side of Building 27, so it might have served for secondary access. A piece of a rectangular, concave crushing stone lies on the floor of this room, and a similar crushing stone may be seen in a doorway leading north. Figure 16 shows the stone and two doorways, the nearer preserved almost 2 m high. Just inside and to the right of the door with the crushing stone is another looted bench. The last room in the unit is built against the cliff face, actually on granite boulders for part of the east wall. The boulders project like a handy shelf. Behind Building 27 is a row of large boulders that encloses the third side of a small space between the cliff and the back of the house. One curved and two straight walls or retaining walls further up the slope are too poorly preserved to determine their function. Finally, a large looters' hole has been dug behind Building 27.

Building 28 (fig. 17). Probably a two-room house. Only the back part of two rounded rooms of Building 28 survive, with one niche. The rectangular feature in front is made of granite cobbles and chinked. Some of the cobbles seem burnt. The whole of the sandy bay behind Building 28 and up the slope is littered with potsherds.

Building 29 (fig. 19). A two-room house with two rooms (or courtyards?) added on. The walls of the east and south rooms abut the house proper where they meet. The two wadi-side doors and the possible bench are badly ruined. Part of the house's interior wall is tumbled; the niche measures 17 cm wide × 20 cm high. The area between Building 29 and the cliff delimited by two retaining walls is dense with sherds.

Building 30. One-room outbuilding, roughly rectangular. The corner between it and the cliff is part of the Building 29 sherd dump.

Building 31. One-room outbuilding with one exterior and one possible interior bench. If there ever was another room to the south, it has been washed away by the wadi.

Building 32. One-room, rounded outbuilding. The back wall is built up against the boulders of the cliff; the front is lost in rock fall.

Building 33. One-room, rounded outbuilding, now consisting of a low circle of stones built up against some granite boulders.

Building 34 (fig. 13). Two-room house. This house was built close to a steep cliff face, and the east wall incorporated a large boulder. The front room has a large bench. Eastward, towards Building 30 or Building 31, is an ashy area that may be a dump, a working area, or remains of a modern fire. Between Building 34 and the cliff is a row of rocks that may have served as a retaining wall; the area immediately west is a sherd dump.

Building 35 (fig. 13). Probably a one-room outbuilding now marked chiefly by a line of stones against the cliff face and a large looters' hole. The line of the other three walls can barely be traced.

Building 36 (fig. 13, with tripod and prism pole leaning against a wall). One-room outbuilding. Although the walls are thick and relatively well preserved, wall fall obscures the possible door locations.

Building 37 (fig. 20, 21, 22). A large, agglomerated house consisting of two three-room units and two added-on rooms. The latter might be interpreted as another two-room house, but given their small size and peripheral location we are, for now, calling them subsidiary rooms. Neither is bonded to the other or to the main house; the back room utilizes the cliff face. The middle unit of three rooms seems to consist of a two-room

Fig. 20. Building 37 at center, Building 38 to left. Note jointed granite.

Fig. 21. Building 37 from above. Note jointed granite to the right and exfoliated granite to the left.

house with a bench and a niche and a possible courtyard. The southeast courtyard wall changes angle abruptly at an abutted joint. Its back wall is built over large boulders and now forms a sort of terrace between the room and the cliff, the terrace being littered with sherds. The final three-room house, judging from the double walls and the abutting front wall, seems to have been modified at some time, though the sequence is not yet clear. The front room had at least two niches (left, 30 cm wide × 36 × 33 deep; right ca. 24 wide × 30 × 28) though more may have been destroyed when the rest of the wall collapsed. The southwest room had two benches, now mostly hidden by wall fall. A rounded quartz pounding stone also was found here. The space behind this house and the cliff is another sherd dump; the odd walls that mark it off

on the northwest and southeast are actually taking advantage of granite ledges.

Building 38 (fig. 20). A two-room house built against the cliff face. One wall seems to have been founded on a line of boulders, and another boulder was used as a bench. The front room, however, had no good door, although it does have a normal bench and a blocked doorway. For a house, it is unusual in having no communication between the two rooms.

Building 39 (fig. 23). Apparently a two-room house with two attached rooms. The main room of Building 39 has one looters' hole and three niches; running clockwise from the door they measure 30 cm wide × 35 high; not measured; 30 cm wide × (top damaged) × 35 deep. The north corner of the room is broken up. Of the two at-

Fig. 22. Building 37 showing wall construction over boulders at the foot of the cliff.

Fig. 23. Building 41 in foreground. Left to right, corner of Building 6, Buildings 39, 42, 43, corner of Building 44.

tached rooms, one has a large looters' hole, and one has a fragment of a grinding stone. The room with the grinding stone is damaged and the front wall(s) unclear.

Building 40 (fig. 23). One-room outbuilding constructed against a retaining wall on the cliff slope. The area between Buildings 39 and 40 is dense with sherds. The sole fragment of a ceramic lamp was collected here.

Building 41 (fig. 23). A large agglomeration of at least two, perhaps as many as four house units. The northeast face of Building 41 has been damaged by wadi wash and the whole complex appears to have been added on to or reworked several times. Reference to the plan is crucial to following the description of this building. The southernmost two-room "house" seems to consist of a fairly large room added on to a back room that, in turn,

may be contiguous with the eastern unit of three rooms. This unit has been damaged, but it does seem to have two large rooms with a bench, another looted shelf or bench, and a small corner room. The northwest one-room unit looks like an outbuilding "captured" by Building 41, though whether the room or rooms in between constituted another house is unclear. Neither the possible door on the wadi side nor the possible cross wall (which would enclose a back room) at the rear are certain. Finally, the westernmost unit defies interpretation at this stage. There is a large sandy area from which two rooms are separated or partly separated. The partly separated room has a wall niche measuring 27 cm wide × 22 high. A blocked door facing northwest does nothing to simplify the picture. Three sherd dumps are associated with Building 41.

Fig. 24. Building 42. Niches on two levels.

Fig. 25. Building 49 on left, Building 48 on right.

Building 42 (fig. 23, 24). A two-room house. This well-preserved house had eight niches, and perhaps two more in the tumbled west and east walls of the back room. The two in the front room (clockwise) measure 22 cm wide × 24 to sand (no back; it now looks like a cat door), and 34 cm wide × 22 to sand × 38 deep. The niches in the second room (clockwise) measure ca. 32 cm wide × 25 (top gone) × 38 deep; 34 cm wide (top, bottom, back gone); damaged; 49 cm wide × 37 × 44 deep; 35 cm × 30 high × 30 deep; 34 wide × ca. 37 high × 32 cm. A piece of a mortar was found in the front room. It appears to be made of a white nummultic limestone, not a native rock at Bir Umm Fawakhir. Limestone is not useful for crushing gold quartz either. The second room produced the sole mud brick noted so far.

Building 43 (fig. 23). A two-room house. Two sides are built into the cliff slopes, so the exceptionally thick walls may have been necessary to hold back rock fall. The front door is obscured by tumbled stones. The larger room has two benches, looted, and one damaged niche. The wall between the rooms seems very thick, and wall fall has obliterated the door. The back room is on a higher level than the front room. Its niche measures 34 cm wide × 30 × 36 deep; the back wall might have had one or two niches as well. A rectangular, concave crushing stone lay on the slope down from the front door.

Building 44 (fig. 26). A three-room house with a possible bench and six niches. Counting clockwise from the front door, the niches measure 33 cm wide × 32 × 37 deep; 26 × 32 high × 33 deep; damaged; 52 wide × (top

Fig. 26. Building 50 in foreground, Building 55 in the angle with cliff, wadi street.

damaged) × 31 deep. The ones in the back room (clockwise) measure 36 cm across × 42 high × 33; and 39 cm × (bottom damaged) × 24 deep. The slope behind Building 44 toward Building 43 is a sherd dump.

Building 45. A two-room house built against the cliff face. The walls are now tumbled, but there is some indication that each of the rooms had a niche.

Building 46. Badly ruined on the wadi side. Only one door is well preserved, but Building 46 did have two rooms and probably a bench. The wall running to the cliff seems to enclose a courtyard or working area, now littered with sherds. The niche is dubious.

Building 47. A three-room house. Two rooms connect, the third being reached by its own door. Wadi wash has tumbled walls and damaged a possible exterior bench.

Building 48 (fig. 25). An unusual one-room building. It has two or three niches and a possible bench, and it is as large as some of the two-room houses such as Building 4 or Building 38, but there is no sign of an interior wall. The two doors are also unusual, and the one unbonded corner suggests that the building might have been modified. A low retaining wall runs towards Building 46, and the slope behind Building 48 is another sherd dump, partly looted. Another rectangular stone feature might have been constructed on the slope behind Building 48 but the remnants were so sparse that only one point could be plotted.

Building 49 (fig. 25). A three- or four-room house. The large central room has an odd double wall on its west side that may be a built-in shelf, a remnant of an earlier wall, or some other architectural feature. The northeast room might have been subdivided into two but the rock fall is not very coherent. The southwest room has its own door, a bench, and perhaps a niche. Two retaining walls run to Buildings 48 and 51 on either side.

Building 50 (fig. 26). The largest of the agglomerated buildings, consisting of four fairly large house units, a courtyard, and six "hooked on" rooms. The large "room" marked by one low wall and no less than four doorways is taken to be a courtyard. The two rooms behind the courtyard are exceptionally large for a house, but they are provided with niches. The well-preserved west niche measures 37 cm wide × 51 high × 39; the damaged east niche is 40 cm wide and ca. 30 deep. A single room has been added outside this unit and would be most accessible to it. The northern house unit consists of three fairly large rooms, two of which are provided with benches, and two "hooked on" rooms. One is quite irregular in shape, and the outermost room, with a blocked door, is actually handier to the two-room house unit just described. Opening southeast from the courtyard is five-room unit, which has two further outside doors, one looking northeast and one facing the wadi. The apse-like feature and the double thick wall next to it may be relics of some rebuilding operation. The large room, at the south end of Building 50, has a bench and a remnant of a circle of stones, looted, that might have been a hearth. The five-room unit, two added-on rooms with benches, and one more attached room now form, with Building 47, a slightly retired open or working area. In other words, turning in from the wadi street around Building 47 one would find an open area with six doors opening off it, three leading to one-room annexes and three to either Building 47 or Building 50. That the configuration may not be original is indicated by the last three-room unit of Building 50, the one closest to the wadi street. It seems to have been a two-room house "captured" by Building 50; the blocking wall is clearly secondary. This, plus another short wall joined to the Building 50 courtyard, gave the unit a third, irregular room. The front room has been looted, and each of the back rooms has a niche.

Building 51. An agglomeration of two two-room houses plus two attached rooms. Building 51 may originally have been two separate two-room houses. The northern unit is still intact with two niches in the front room measuring (clockwise from the front door) 28 cm wide × 30 high, and 60 cm wide (rest damaged). The second room contains the remains of a bench. The second two-room house is backed up against the cliff. One room has a bench and possibly a niche; a now-blocked door once connected the two rooms. A short, L-shaped bit of wall together with the east wall of Building 52 now screens the entrance to the back room of Building 51. The narrow entrance space is further littered with sherds and debris. At some time, a short wall was constructed to link the front and back of Building 51, and two one-room additions were built in the angles between the house units. One added-on room has easy access to the Building 51 and Building 52 area, but the other, with both an interior (looted) and an exterior bench, looks towards Building 49. A mortar fragment was found in the doorway of the latter room.

Building 52. One-room outbuilding. The back wall is built against the cliff; the west wall has a semicircular bulge in it, and the east wall was built in two segments. The unusually wide door, 1.05 m, suggests a non-domestic use, perhaps shelter for animals. The open area west of Building 52, in the angle behind Building 53, also seems to function with Buildings 51 and 52. But the open area and the slopes behind Buildings 52 and 53 are sherd dumps, partly looted.

Building 53. A three-room house. One room, with a bench, is backed up against the cliff and a retaining wall. The two-room section nearer the wadi has remnants of three niches. A short wall segment between the two parts of the house added a little privacy to the entranceway.

Building 54. A three-room house. It opens not onto the wadi street but toward the open, sandy area bordered by Buildings 51 and 53. Each room of Building 54 probably had one bench, and one room had one niche, perhaps more. One of the interior doors seems exceptionally wide, but that may be due to wall fall.

Building 55 (fig. 26). One-room, rectangular outbuilding. The looters' hole in the south third of the interior might mark a former bench. Sherds, debris, and ash have been dumped at the foot of the cliff behind Building 55.

APPENDIX B
THE POTTERY
BY LISA HEIDORN

Northwest of Modern Mosque: Southeast Edge of Preserved Ancient(?) Walls

Fig. No.	Description	Munsell Color	Notes	Comparanda
27a	Amphora rim sherd	Exterior surface colors range from 7.5 YR 6/6 to 10 YR 6/3.	The clay had been tempered with a medium amount of chaff, small white particles, and perhaps some sand. A handle scar is visible immediately below the rim.	Parallels for this rim type are found in W. R. Johnson 1979: pls. 21z, 22e, 23q, 25p, 28k, 29m and q, 30b and m, 31f, 32m and o–q (first–second centuries A.D.); Prickett 1979: pl. 86a. and e (QRS-51); and Whitcomb and Johnson 1982: pl. 14f and g. See also Riley in Sidebotham, Zitterkopf, and Riley 1991: 609, fig. 31:48 (from Umm Balad trash dump; dated first–second centuries A.D. by parallels with Quseir al-Qadim material). Riley notes also the parallels from Khasm el-Menih (Herbert and Wright 1988–1989: 4, fig. 7a).
27b	Amphora rim	"	Same, minus the handle scar.	"
27c	Amphora handle	Fired surface color 2.5 YR 4/4.	A few white particles and sand temper were visible in the breaks.	
27d	Wide-mouthed jar with everted rim	The exterior surface was red (10 YR 5/6) and the core was tan.	It is unclear whether this vessel had been manufactured of silt or marl, or perhaps a	For similar forms, see, for example, W. R. Johnson 1979: pl. 29c (fine red sandy fabric; first–second centuries A.D.), and Whitcomb 1982: pl. 10n (red ware with moderate amount

Fig. No.	Description	Munsell Color	Notes	Comparanda
			mixture of clays. A few small white bits were noticeable in the broken section.	of sand temper); and Sidebotham, Zitterkopf, and Riley 1991: 611, fig. 34:86 (Qattar Station; materials date from first–fourth centuries A.D.). Some of the later, fine ware cooking pots from Hermopolis are also quite similar to this form; see Spencer and Bailey 1982: 50, fig. 11 (C 28–30) and p. 30 (first half of the fifth–first half of seventh centuries A.D.). See also the cooking pots from Nazlet Tuna in Tyldesley and Snape 1988, especially pp. 30–33 and figs. 3.1–3.2 (ca. A.D. 350–650).
27e	Amphora stump base	Exterior surface color 7.5 YR 5/4.	A few shite particles may have been added to the clay as a tempering agent.	

Area of Ancient (and Modern) Wells

Fig. No.	Description	Munsell Color	Notes	Comparanda
27f	Amphora rim with bulbous lip		The light reddish-brown silt ware had a moderate amount of sand temper.	Similar rims from the first and second centuries A.D. were found at Quseir al-Qadim and nearby sites; see W. R. Johnson 1979: pl. 241 (fine red ware with cream slip), and Prickett 1979: pl. 88b (tan with sand temper).
27g	Rim from a small jar	The surface color was 5 YR 6/4.		
27h	Channelled jar rim		The traces of slip preserved in the exterior channel were "cream-colored" (no Munsell reading was taken in the field).	The rim may be part of a handled jar like that shown in B. Johnson 1981: pl. 54:410 (fine red ware with pink slip; second half of the second to early third centuries A.D.).
27i	Jar or bottle rim with light-colored surfaces	The (marl?) clay had been fired to a 7.5 YR 6/4 color in the section and had 5 Y 8/2 surfaces.	The temper included sand and some small dark particles.	A similar rim (with a thicker lip) was found in Roman levels at Quseir al-Qadim; see Whitcomb 1982: pl. 28e (buff-cream with sand temper; resin on interior and rim).
27j	Bowl rim	The surface colors ranged from 2.5 YR 6/4 to 6/6.	Surfaces blackened, but the interior surface still displayed a light burnish.	The form is like an example from Quseir al-Qadim; see Whitcomb 1982: pl. 11k (first–second centuries A.D.). See also Sidebotham, Zitterkopf, and Riley 1991: 611–12 and fig. 33:75 (Umm Balad trash dump; mostly first–second centuries A.D., some first–fourth centuries A.D.).
27k	Bowl rim	"	Some smali bits of chaff added to the clay.	
271	Bowl rim	"		

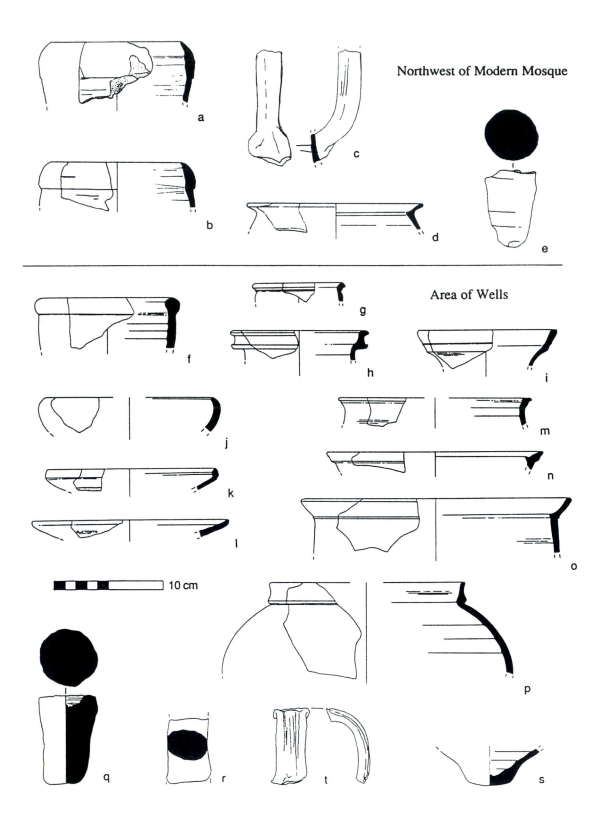

Fig. 27. Sherds from northwest of modern mosque and area of wells.

Fig. No.	Description	Munsell Color	Notes	Comparanda
27m	Wide-mouth jar rim	There was a 2.5 YR 6/6 slip on the interior and exterior of this sherd.	Some sand had been added as temper.	
27n	Wide-mouthed jar rim with interior ledge	Red slip on the exterior (10 YR 5/8)	The vessel in fig. 27n (perhaps a bowl?) is manufactured of silt clay with a red slip on the exterior.	It is similar to a rim from Quseir al-Qadim; see W. R. Johnson 1979: pl. (fine brown ware). See also Sidebotham, Zitterkopf, and Riley 1991: 611–12 and fig. 33:68 (Umm Balad trash dump; mostly first–second century A.D., some first–fourth century A.D.); and *ibid.*, 617 fig. 38:130 (el-Heita; first–second century A.D. evidence, plus some fifth–seventh century A.D. material).
27o	Wide-mouthed jar rim with interior ledge	2.5 YR 6/4 surfaces.	A small amount of small white particles may have been added as temper.	It is similar to types of cooking vessels found throughout the first millennium A.D. There are numerous close—but not precise—parallels from the Roman levels at Quseir al-Qadim. For a few parallels, see W. R. Johnson 1979: pl. 25b (fine red ware); Whitcomb 1982: pl. 28j (red with moderate amount of sand temper); and Sidebotham, Zitterkopf, and Riley 1991: 613 fig. 34:86 (Qattar Station; materials date from the first–fourth centuries A.D.). See also, Spencer and Bailey 1982: fig. 11 (Type C: first half of the fifth century to the first half of the seventh century A.D.); and Tyldesley and Snape 1988: figs. 3.2:5, 3.3:5 (ca. A.D. 350–50).
27p	Rim of globular jar	The surface color was 10 YR 8/3 (from firing and not a slip?) and the interior surface color was 2.5 YR 5/6.	The clay had some small chaff particles added as temper.	Close parallels are found in Mysliwiec 1987: 152, no. 1922–24 (early Byzantine; see p. 153). For somewhat similar pots of various date ranges, see (slightly different) Late Roman examples in Prickett 1979: pl. 85q (rust-brown ware with sand temper; purple exterior slip); Jones 1991: 138, fig. 3:1 (dated to the third through mid-seventh centuries A.D.; note the slightly different rim and presence of rilling on the exterior of this unslipped, red ware pot); and Spencer and Bailey 1982: fig. 6–7 (first half of fifth to first half of seventh century A.D.).
27q	Amphora stump base	The surface color was 5 YR 5/4, and it had a gray core.	Sand and a few white particles were noticeable in the break.	
27r	Amphora handle		Reddish-brown (with traces of a red slip?).	
27s	Amphora handle	The exterior surface color was 5 YR 6/4.	The fragment was either manufactured of a fine silt clay or perhaps a marl and silt clay mixture.	It may be the base of an amphora type (North African or Spanish?) like the example illustrated in Whitcomb 1982: pl. 16f (first–second centuries A.D.).

Fig. No.	Description	Munsell Color	Notes	Comparanda
27t	Handle	The color of the surfaces was 2.5 YR 7/4.	Small dark particles and perhaps some sand had been added as temper.	
28a	Wide-mouthed vat	The interior and exterior surface color was 2.5 YR 5/6.		See references to fig. 30a for a few parallels to similar vessels. It is unclear whether this form should be dated earlier or later in the series of this vessel type.
28b	Ring base	10 R 5/8 slip on exterior and interior.	The sherd was manufactured of reddish-brown ware.	

Mine Tailings South of Modern Road (Sites A and B)

Fig. No.	Description	Munsell Color	Notes	Comparanda
28c	Bowl	The slip color is 2.5 YR 6/8.	There is a small amount of chaff and some small white particles which were added to the clay as temper. The interior has many slight rills on the surface (which may be evidence for spiral burnishing that has worn away?).	For early Roman period parallels, see W. R. Johnson 1979: pl. 30k (gray-brown with sand temper and covered with bitumen); Prickett 1979: pl. 87i (orange-brown core with purple-brown slip on interior); Whitcomb 1982: pl. 25e (brown with red slip); Holladay 1982: 135 pl. 29:8 ("last half of the second century A.D."; brown fabric with exterior rim burnish). Parallels for this bowl form—but from later periods—are found in Hayes 1972: 170, fig. 33:109; 172 (slip over interior and rim; spiral burnishing on interior, ca. A.D. 580/600-mid seventh century); Jacquet-Gordon 1972: pl. 221:16 (bowl type E with orange slip, A.D. 500–750); and perhaps also Mysliwiec 1987: 117, no. 1310 (brown fabric with a thick red slip; A.D. 395–640).
28d	Gobular jar with neck ridge		The fabric had some small chaff pieces and a few white particles added as temper.	
28e	Bowl	The color of the red slip was 10 R 5/6.		Similar types of vessels may be found in, for instance, Hayes 1972: 112–18 and figs. 19 and 20 (forms 67–71; dated ca. 360–470 A.D.); Egloff 1977: 69–71 and pl. 36:6–10 (types 6–11; especially similar to type 7 which is dated to the end of the fourth into the fifth centuries A.D. [see p. 34]); and B. Johnson 1981: pl. 33:214 (African Red Slip Ware; undated). See also the Egyptian Red Slip bowl(s) in Spencer, Bailey, and Burnett 1983: fig. 46:81.5 (A.D. 400–550).

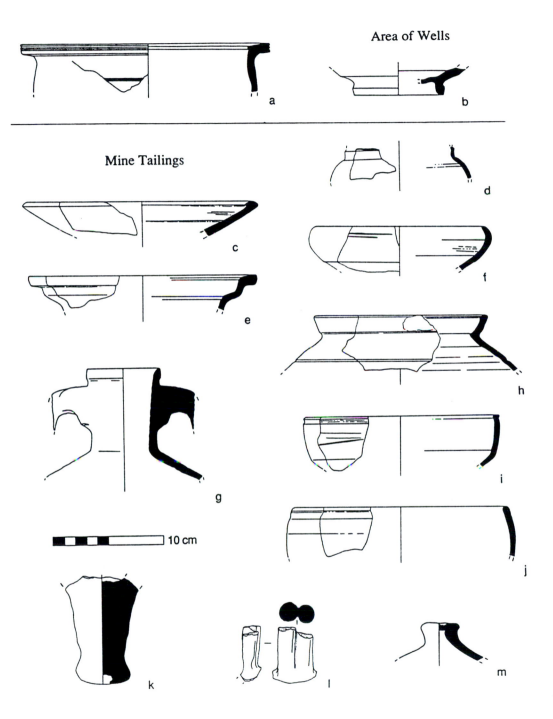

Fig. 28. Sherds from area of wells and mine tailings.

Fig. No.	Description	Munsell Color	Notes	Comparanda
28f	Bowl		Possibly a lid?	For comparable types see Mysliwiec 1987: 118, no. 1378–88 (5th–8th centuries A.D.; p. 119); Spencer, Bailey, and Burnett 1983: fig. 8:8 (probably second century A.D.). Spencer, Bailey, and Davies 1984: 50–52, fig. 31:4 (ca. A.D. 350–525), p. 40, fig. 48:T 18 (second–fourth centuries A.D.). See also Sidebotham, Zitterkopf, and Riley 1991: 604 fig. 27:6 (Mons Porphyrites: castellum and trash dumps southeast of castellum; first–second and third–fourth centuries A.D.) and 611 fig. 33:75 (?) (Umm Balad trash dump; mostly first–second centuries A.D., some first–fourth centuries A.D.); Rodziewicz 1976: pl. 17:K6 (but with burnishing on the interior; perhaps to be dated between the mid-third and the mid-fifth centuries A.D. [see pp. 28–29, and 52]); Hayes 1972: 325 fig. 65:1 (Late Roman C Ware; late fourth–early fifth centuries A.D.).
28g	Amphora rim and neck		The silt fabric had chaff (and sand?) added as temper.	For similar forms from other sites, see references to fig. 29g.
28h	Cooking pot rim with handle scar	The color of the fabric in the section was 7.5 YR 6/4, while the slip was 2.5 YR 5/8.	A medium amount of sand and a few white particles were visible in the break.	The form is similar to types from Quseir al-Qadim; see Whitcomb 1982: pls. 10k, n–o and 22m (first–second centuries A.D.). See also Tyldesley and Snape 1988: especially 30–35 and figs. 3.1–3.3 (ca. A.D. 350–640); Sidebotham, Zitterkopf, and Riley 1991: 610, fig. 32:53 (Umm Balad trash dump; mostly first–second centuries A.D., some first–fourth centuries A.D.) and 613, fig. 34:86 (Qattar Station; materials dated from first to fourth centuries A.D.).
28i	Small bowl with single channel on exterior below rim	It is fired to a 10 YR 7/3 color on the interior and 2.5 Y 8/2 on the exterior (slip?).	The marl (?) fabric is tempered with sand and includes a few white particles.	For a similar bowl see Rodziewicz 1976: 61–62 and pl. 32:W8 (light-colored fabric with light-colored slip). Rodziewicz notes that the ceramics of his Group W are Upper Egyptian products and that these marls do not appear until the seventh century A.D.; they disappear in the remains at Kom el-Dikka before the beginning of the ninth century A.D. He compares this bowl to a pottery form found at Thebes in the latter sixth to early seventh(?) century A.D.; see Winlock 1926: 86, fig. 37C (fine red fabric with red slip). (However, see a discussion of the dating of the archaeological materials from the monastery by Bailey in Spencer, Bailey, and Burnett 1983: 43. Hayes dates the pottery from between A.D. 475 and 500 and up to around A.D. 625. Bailey would date the materials to the late fifth–sixth centuries A.D.). See also the Mysliwiec 1987: 78:822 (marl and silt mix[?] with painted decoration). These sherds were excavated immediately below Coptic levels and Mysliwiec (1987: 73) includes them under a

Fig. No.	Description	Munsell Color	Notes	Comparanda
				heading of "Spätzeit bis zur Byzantinischen Periode." See also the similar shape in Mysliwiec 1987: 114, no. 1297 (however, it is an Egyptian Red Slip Ware A vessel with a painted decoration).
28j	Bowl with incised line below rim	The section color is 5 YR 6/4 and the exterior surface is 2.5 Y 8/2.	Sand and some dark particles were added as temper.	This bowl type may be comparable to a slightly heavier and more closed form illustrated in Mysliwiec 1987: 158, no. 1959a (silt ware; A.D. 395–640).
28k	Amphora toe	The exterior surface color was 5 YR 6/4.	Sand had been added to temper the clay.	
28l	Double-barreled jar handle	The color of the core was 5 YR 6/4 and the surfaces were covered with a red slip (10 R 5/8).	The handle may belong to an amphora.	See, for example, the references in Sidebotham, Zitterkopf, and Riley 1991: 603 (Mediterranean types dated from the later first century B.C. until the mid-second century A.D.).
28m	Lid or base fragment	The surface color was 2.5 YR 5/8.	Sand temper was visible in the break.	If this fragment is part of a lid, it is comparable to an undated type illustrated in Barbara Johnson 1981: pl. 75:606 (fine red fabric with a few white inclusions). However, it is possible that it is a base fragment, and perhaps the base of a bowl like the examples illustrated in Tyldesley and Snape 1988: figs. 3.14:6 and 3.24:4–6 (ca. A.D. 350–650).

Dump Behind Building 6

Fig. No.	Description	Munsell Color	Notes	Comparanda
29a	Cooking pot with "pie-crust" rim	The surface color is 2.5 YR 5/4.		Similar shapes are found in Spencer, Bailey, and Burnett 1983: fig. 61:8.2 (A.D. 400–600); Jones 1991: fig. 3:5 (A.D. 400–600; following the dating of the Hermopolite examples); Mysliwiec 1987: 125, no. 1509, 150, no. 1840–43 (A.D. 395–640); Jacquet-Gordon 1972: pl. 220:C18 (A.D. 500–750); Egloff 1977: pl. 81:6 (type 289, but without exterior ridges of Bir Umm Fawakhir example; this group of vessels [types 284–98] are dated between the first half of the fifth and the beginning of the seventh centuries A.D.).
29b	Cup or bowl with orange slip			
29c	Carinated bowl with black spots on rim			For similar types, see Jacquet-Gordon 1972: pl. 219:A15 (A.D. 500–750); and Mysliwiec 1987: 130, nos. 1547–49 and 156, nos. 1951–52, 1959 (slightly different types made from marl clay and with no painted decoration; A.D. 595–640). Note that this bowl type seems quite

Fig. No.	*Description*	*Munsell Color*	*Notes*	*Comparanda*
				similar in ware and decoration to the "Nubian-influenced" (X-Group) pottery presented in Mysliwiec 1987: 120, 122, nos. 1464–88. See also a similar type, although with a much wider diameter, in Sidebotham, Zitterkopf, and Riley 1991: 618 fig. 39:143 (El-ʾAras; ceramics dated from the first–fourth centuries A.D. However, no. 143 is dated by Riley to the first–second centuries A.D.).
29d	Bowl rim		Silt fabric, burnished exterior.	
29e	Flanged bowl			Comparable bowls are found in Mysliwiec 1987: 109, nos. 1190–93, 1201, 1202–3 (brown fabric with red slip; A.D. 395–640). Mysliwiec compares these bowls with examples from Epiphanius, Kellia, and Alexandria (although the Bir Umm Fawakhir example does not have the rounded body profile). See Winlock 1926: 86 fig. 37:Q and U (ca. late fifth–sixth centuries A.D.); Egloff 1977: pl. 40:7 (especially type 38; first half of the fifth century A.D.); and Rodziewicz 1976: pl. 18:K15b (same time as Groups C and D = end of the fifth–beginning of the seventh centuries A.D.?) and pl. 25:O21a and b especially (last phase of Group C = sixth and seventh centuries A.D.). Another parallel comes from Amarna; see Jones 1991: fig. 1:6 (Egyptian Red Slip Ware A). Jones notes that vessels of this type of ware at Amarna range in date from the third/fourth to the mid-seventh centuries A.D. (p. 140). See also Hayes 1972: 142–44 and fig. 26 (form 91 [types C and D]; early sixth through ca. seventh century A.D.); Jacquet-Gordon 1972: pl. 222:E33 especially (A.D. 500–750); Spencer, Bailey, and Burnett 1983: fig. 41:53.1, 54.7, and 55.1 (type E; A.D. 400–550); B. Johnson 1981: pl. 3:25 (Egyptian Red Slip Ware A; fourth century A.D.) and pl. 36:230–31 (African Red Slip Ware of the late third–fourth centuries A.D. [no. 230] and the fourth to mid-fifth century A.D. [no. 231]); Tyldesley and Snape 1988: fig. 3.44.3–4 (ca. A.D. 350–650); and Kaiser et al. 1975: 74:11k (early in second half of fifth century A.D.), 76:13f (mid-sixth century A.D.). An example from Mons Porphyrites is earlier in date; see Sidebotham, Zitterkopf, and Riley 1991: 605 fig. 28:15 (Lycabettos Village; well-dated pottery and objects from the site belong to the first–second centuries A.D.).
29f	Wide-mouth jar rim and neck			Similar types are illustrated in, for instance, W. R. Johnson 1979: pl. 85r (light brown to grey with chaff and a buff to brown slip; from the Late Roman materials at site QRS-18);

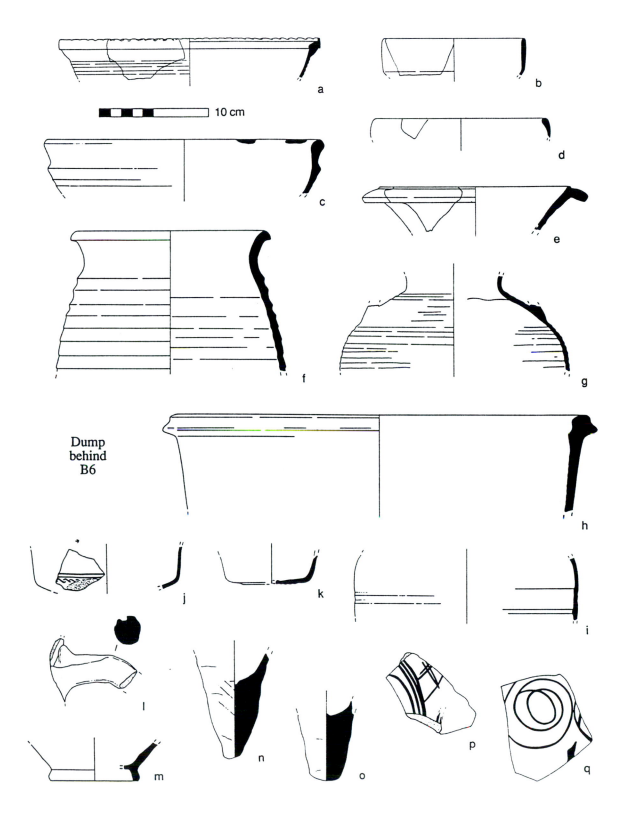

Fig. 29. Sherds from dump behind Building 6.

Fig. No.	*Description*	*Munsell Color*	*Notes*	*Comparanda*
				Winlock 1926: 84 fig. 36 (similar to a *qadus* but no knob base; made of reddish-brown ware; ca. late fifth–sixth centuries A.D.); Egloff 1977: pl. 73:13 (type 248 of red fabric; A.D. 650–730) and pl. 74:7 (type 249 of reddish-brown fabric; end of fourth to beginning of fifth centuries A.D.); Mysliwiec 1987: 165, no. 2029 and 166, no. 2041 (A.D. 395–640; and see his references on p. 167, footnote 267); Spencer, Bailey, and Burnett 1983: fig. 64 (J1–4; *saqiya* pots of about A.D. 550–700); Spencer, Bailey, and Davies 1984: fig. 30:3 (cooking pot type C3; ca. A.D. 400–550); and Jacquet-Gordon 1972: pls. 225:L3 and 228:R2 (A.D. 500–750).
29g	Shoulder and neck fragment with part of handle		There is a dark stain on the interior of the neck.	For similar jar forms, see Mysliwiec 1987: 164, nos. 2019–21 (silt wares; A.D. 395–640) and Sidebotham, Zitterkopf, and Riley 1991: 610–12 and fig. 32:54, 56, 62 (Umm Balad trash dump; mostly first–second centuries A.D., some first–fourth centuries A.D.).
29h	Wide-mouthed jar			The sherd is somewhat similar to a type illustrated in Mysliwiec 1987: 159, no. 1977 (ca. A.D. 395–640).
29i	Shoulder and body sherd		A few exterior ridges.	
29j	Bowl fragment		Orange ware with purple-gray burnished exterior and black burnished interior.	
29k	Base fragment			For a similar base, see the base on a cup of "Aswan pink" ware in Pierrat 1991: 189, fig. 60d (and 60e; both R Ware vessels manufactured around Aswan). These examples from Tod, however, appear to date to a later period (from level +75: "vers 1000"; see p. 199).
29l	Jar handle	The surface color is 5 Y 7/2.	Silt fabric.	The handle may belong to jar types like those illustrated in Mysliwiec 1987: 164, nos. 2019–22 and note references in footnotes on p. 163 ("Coptic amphorae" manufactured of Nile silt clay; A.D. 395–640).
29m	Ring base		Buff ware with greenish core.	
29n	Amphora stump base		Reddish-brown	
29o	Amphora stump base		Reddish-brown	
29p	Painted sherd			See 29q.
29q	Painted sherd			These decorated sherds may come from painted jars like those in Spencer, Bailey, and Burnett 1983: 47 and fig. 71.

Building 13

Fig. No.	Description	Munsell Color	Notes	Comparanda
30a	Vat with white and black decoration	The surface of the sherd was 10R 4/6. A 10 R 2.5/1 black decoration is painted atop a pinkish-white (7.5 YR 8/2) painted band.		See similar vat forms in Spencer, Bailey, and Burnett 1983: figs. 50:F18 (Egyptian Painted Red Slip Ware; A.D. 400–500 [?]). Bailey compares this unstratified example with one from Elephantine that may be dated to the second half of the fifth century; see Kaiser et al. 1976: 110, fig. 9e. See also Spencer, Bailey, and Burnett 1983: fig. 74:O6.4 (A.D. 400–500); Jacquet-Gordon 1972: pls. 223:G15 (no decoration) and 225: L9 and M21, 228:S3 (A.D. 500–750); Winlock 1926: fig. 41J (ca. late fifth–sixth centuries A.D.); Mysliwiec 1987: 134, especially nos. 1588–89 and 142, nos. 1706 (A.D. 395–640); and Tyldesley and Snape 1988: fig. 3.27:5 (simpler profile and no painted decoration; ca. A.D. 350–650). A number of other "large jars/bowls" in the latter publication are also quite similar to the Bir Umm Fawakhir e example, although none have painted decoration.
30b	Rim with handle	The surface color of 30b and 30c ranged from 10 R 4/3 to 5 YR 4/2 on the interior.	30b and 30c did not join.	For a few similar cooking vessels, see Winlock 1926: 92, fig. 47 (painted decoration on cream-slipped exteriors; ca. late fifth–sixth centuries A.D.); Jacquet-Gordon 1972: pls. 224:K1–2 and 225:L6 (coarse red-orange ware; A.D. 500–750).
30c	Jar rim		Dark reddish-gray with combed bands on the exterior of the body.	See 30b.
30d	Cooking pot (two sherds)	The surface color of these sherds was 10 R 4/4.	Although the sherds did not join, they may be the same pot.	For similar vessels, see Prickett 1979: pl. 85q (Late Roman); Mysliwiec 1987: 145, no. 1794 and 1804 (A.D. 395–640); Jacquet-Gordon 1972: pl. 225:L6 (A.D. 500–750); Sidebotham, Zitterkopf, and Riley 1991: 607–8 and fig. 30:39 (Badia⊃; pottery from the first–fourth centuries A.D. and later); Sidebotham et al. 1989: 15, fig. 17:28–30 (slightly different; third/fourth–seventh centuries A.D.).
30e	Jar rim and shoulder	The surface color of the sherd is 10 YR 8/3.	Sand and some white particles are visible in the break.	For a similar marl jar, see Pierrat 1991: 171–72 and fig. 37d (from levels -35 to -10: "après 650, jusqu'à 750 ou plus tard"; see p. 199).

Slope Below Building 33

Fig. No.	Description	Munsell Color	Notes	Comparanda
30f	Handmade jar with incised decoration	The interior surface was brown (7.5 YR 5/2), and the exterior was predominantly red (2.5 YR 4/6) with brown to gray firing discolorations.	The fabric had a medium amount of chaff temper.	No precise parallels are known, although the Sudanese/Nubian tradition is clear in form, fabric, and incised decoration. See, for example, the similar (earlier?) handmade jars in Williams 1991: 211 fig. 18c and 376 fig. 214e. Although the two tombs with these examples perhaps date to the last century B.C.–first century A.D., this pottery tradition was an enduring one.

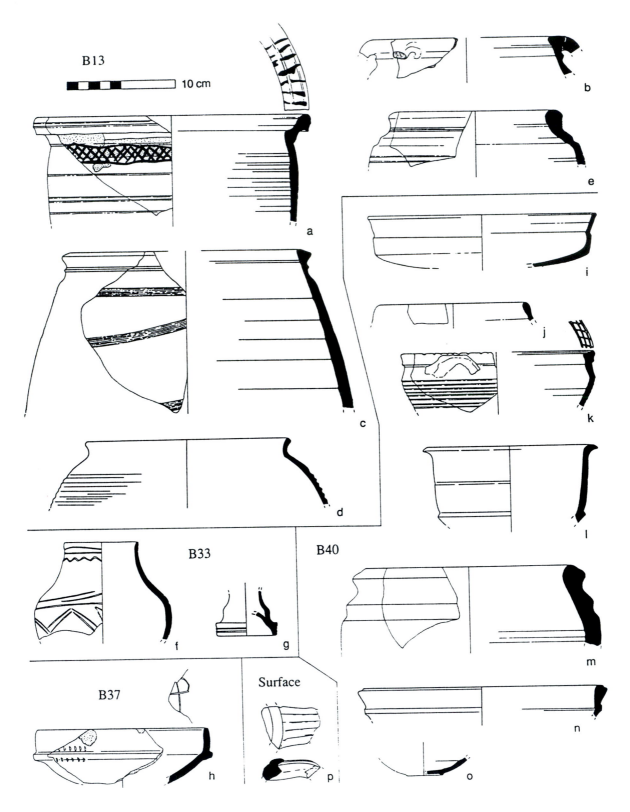

Fig. 30. Sherds from Buildings 13, 33, 37, 40, and from the surface.

Fig. No.	Description	Munsell Color	Notes	Comparanda
30g	Base of small jar	The sherd had a light red-brown section (5 YR 6/4), and a thick red, burnished slip covered the exterior (10 R 4/8).	The fabric was fired hard and no temper was visible.	For a similar pitcher base, see, for instance, Spencer and Bailey 1985: fig. 32:M5.15 (orange-pink fabric with white-buff surface; probably ca. 400–550).

Building 37

Fig. No.	Description	Munsell Color	Notes	Comparanda
30h	Flanged bowl		There is rouletting above and below the waist, and grog is visible in the break.	For similar bowls, see the Late Roman example in Prickett 1979: pl. 85e (QRS-18; Late Egyptian Red Slip A ware); Spencer, Bailey, and Burnett 1983: fig. 41:E52.2 (Egyptian Red Slip; A.D. 600–700+) and fig. 57:H12.2 (Egyptian Fine Ware; A.D. 550–700+); Tyldesley and Snape 1988: fig. 3.54:4 (ca. A.D. 350–650); Egloff 1977: fig. 40:6 and 11 (type 37). This type of bowl was dated to the second half of sixth through the beginning eighth centuries A.D. The type was not present in the fifth century levels at Kellia. See also Mysliwiec 1987: 106, nos. 1100–16 (various rim diameters; Egyptian Red Slip A) and 109, no. 1176 (A.D. 395–640); Winlock 1926: 86 fig. 37V (ca. late fifth–sixth centuries A.D.); Jacquet-Gordon 1972: pl. 221:E19 (A.D. 500–750); Rodziewicz 1976: pl. 26:O24 (Group O, second quarter of third century and later?; see p. 58); and Kaiser et al. 1975: especially 76:13a (mid-sixth century A.D.), but also 78:15b (late sixth–early seventh centuries A.D.). See also Sidebotham et al. 1989: 153 fig. 16:1 (Egyptian Red Slip A; seventh century A.D.). Hayes (1972: 387–401) discusses Egyptian Red Slip Ware A. He notes that type V from the monastery of Epiphanius is a late version of the flanged bowl series (seventh century A.D.?; Hayes 1972: 392–93).

Building 40

Fig. No.	Description	Munsell Color	Notes	Comparanda
30i	Carinated bowl		The sherd was described as having a flaky, red surface ("amphora ware").	For some parallel forms, see Mysliwiec 1987: nos. 1435–45 (especially no. 1441; A.D. 395–640); Jacquet-Gordon 1972: pl. 219:A16 and 220:C7 (larger example; Egyptian Red Slip Ware; A.D. 500–750); Egloff 1977: pl. 44:3 (type 86; A.D. 390–450); Winlock 1926: 90, fig. 42:D–E (somewhat different; ca. later fifth–sixth centuries A.D.); and Sidebotham,

Fig. No.	Description	Munsell Color	Notes	Comparanda
				Zitterkopf, and Riley 1991: 613 fig. 34:88 (reddish-brown fabric with cream coating on exterior, from Qattar Station, first–fourth centuries A.D. and later).
30j	Bowl or jar rim	The unslipped surface of this sherd is 5 YR 6/4, and the red slip is 10 R 4/6.		
30k	Small cooking pot with horizontal handles	The exterior surface color is 10 YR 8/3.		For similar silt vessels, see Egloff 1977: pl. 81:3 (type 287 is dated to the beginning of the fifth century A.D.) and Mysliwiec 1987: 150, nos. 1856–68 and 151, nos 1901–7 (vessels from the first group have no rilled rims, and neither group has evidence for handles; A.D. 395–640). See also Jacquet-Gordon 1979: pl. 220:C5–7 (A.D. 500–750), and Spencer, Bailey, and Burnett 1983: fig. 63 ("frying pans" with slightly different rims; A.D. 400–550).
30l	Carinated bowl	The surface color was 10 R 4/6.		For similar types and some useful references, see Spencer, Bailey, and Burnett 1983: 37–38 and figs. 53–55 (wider diameters; Egyptian Red Slip H—some unslipped—dated to about A.D. 400–550, and Egyptian Red Slip B types dated to about A.D. 500–600) and Mysliwiec 1987: 130, nos. 1551–61 and 132, nos. 1562–68 (A.D. 395–640). See also Prickett 1979: pl. 85g (QRS-18; Late Roman); and Egloff 1977: pls. 45:6–10 and 46:1–3 (the various types date from the seventh–eighth centuries A.D.). The closest parallel is pl. 46:2 (type 100; parallels date to the fourth–fifth centuries A.D. and this type at Kellia is dated to the end of the fifth century). Similar vessels are also found in Jacquet-Gordon 1972: pl. 221:E11–13 (A.D. 500–750); Winlock 1926: 89, fig. 41H (ca. late fifth–sixth centuries A.D.); Tyldesley and Snape 1988: 58–63 and figs. 3.15–3.17 ("tripods" with wider diameters than the example from Bir Umm Fawakhir; see especially fig. 3.17:2; ca. A.D. 350–650); and perhaps also Sidebotham, Zitterkopf, and Riley 1991: 614–15 and fig. 35:105 (site two kilometers northwest of Deir el-Atrash; evidence perhaps of fourth–fifth century A.D. date).
30m	Wide-mouthed jar		The surfaces of this coarse marl sherd were described in the field notes as greenish-buff, and although no Munsell readings were taken, the color is about 2.5 Y 7/4 or 5 Y 7/3.	Although its diameter is slightly wider, the jar form is reminiscent of the example from B13 in fig. 30e; see also references for fig. 30e.

Fig. No.	Description	Munsell Color	Notes	Comparanda
30n	Bowl with thickened rim	The red-brown surface color is 10 R 4/6.		This bowl is like an example with black spots atop the rim from the "Dump behind B6"; see fig. 29c and references. Also see a similar marl bowl form in Sidebotham et al. 1989: 158, fig. 18:37 (third/fourth–seventh centuries A.D.).
30o	Base of a globular cup	The exterior surface color was 7.5 YR 7/4 and the exterior was 10 YR 8/3.	Marl fabric.	

Surface Sample

Fig. No.	Description	Munsell Color	Notes	Comparanda
30p	Handle and rim			See, for instance, Tyldesley and Snape 1988: fig. 3.37:2 (10 R 4/6 fabric; ca. A.D. 350–650); Whitcomb 1982: pl. 22:1 (orange with red slip; first–second centuries A.D.); perhaps it could also belong to examples illustrated in Egloff 1977: pl. 49:4, 6 (type 125; beginning of the fifth century A.D.), pl. 51:1–5 (types 134–37; also beginning fifth century A.D.). Egloff (1977: 102) notes, however, that this cooking pot form scarcely changes from the first and second centuries A.D. and later.

NOTES

[1] The team consisted of Carol Meyer, Field Director; Henry Cowherd, photographer; Lisa Heidorn, archaeologist; Abdel Regal A. Mohammed, Inspector; Mohamed B. E. Omar Mostafa, geologist; and Terence Wilfong, Egyptologist. Omar contributed the section on the geological setting of the site; Wilfong wrote the report on the graffiti; Heidorn prepared the report on the pottery corpus; and all photographs were taken by Cowherd unless otherwise noted. Thanks are due to Dr. William Sumner, Director of the Oriental Institute which funded the project; to Dr. Peter Dorman, Director of Chicago House which served as our base of operations; to Dr. Mohammed Bakr, Dr. Ahmed Moussa, and Dr. Mutawiya Balboush of the Egyptian Antiquities Organization; to Amira Khattab of ARCE, who saw the project through too many snarls; to Dr. Henri Riad for invaluable advice; to Dr. Mohammed Sughair, Director of Antiquities of Southern Egypt; and to Rabia Hamdan and the inspectorates at Qena and Quft.

[2] The Romans defeated the Blemmyes in A.D. 452 and imposed a hundred years' peace. In A.D. 535 the Blemmyes were again defeated, this time by the Nobades, more or less definitively.

[3] The article also has a useful bibliography of previous publications about the Turin Papyrus.

[4] The squiggle in front of the mainsail may represent a foresail or artemon. The square rigging suggests that the ship is Roman rather than a Medieval lateener. The combination of sails and oars is unusual; merchantmen relied on sail power, and triremes, like the one represented in the Wadi Hammamat (Bernand 1972: pl. 60), relied on oars, with supplementary sail that could easily be dismantled for fighting. There were, however, some merchant galleys; the larger ones might carry an artemon, and the oars could be employed for approaching or leaving harbor (Casson 1971: 157, Fig. 140).

[5] Walter W. Müller, of the Philipps-Universität in Marburg, replied to an inquiry about the reading of the text that only one word mhmym was clearly legible. In Sabean it means a "field irrigated by a dam-canal," hardly an appropriate word in the middle of a desert, nor is it attested as a proper name. Another possibility is that

it is related to an Arabic word for a protected place, perhaps referring to an ancient shrine. In light of the reference to "all the gods in this place" in inscription fig. 7, 11, this is so far the most plausible reading, though it would be more satisfying if more of text were clearer.

[6]Figure 7:4 is published as Letronne's number CDXCVII (1848. 452) and fig. 7:11 as CDXC (vol. 2: 448). From Letronne's publication, the graffiti were subsequently republished in Franz 1853: 4716 d[50] and 4716 d[45], respectively, and from thence in Bernand 1972, numbers 138 and 134 respectively. None of these editions were made from the original.

[7]Some of the long Pharaonic graffiti in the Wadi Hammamat describe the organization and provisioning of quarrying expeditions. They specify water, loaves of bread, meat, cakes, and offerings of wine, beer, incense, and slaughtered cattle (Weigall 1909: 41, 48; Couyat and Montet 1912: 19, 29).

[8]Similar amphorae rims are published in Egloff 1977: 109–12 (for dating of various types) and pl. 57:4, 6, and 7 (type 164: beginning of sixth–end of seventh centuries A.D.; type 166: A.D. 450–550; and 167: A.D. 650–730). See also the discussion of the dating and areas of manufacture of amphora type 164 in Ballet and Picon 1987: 21–26 (the type may have been manufactured from the fourth up to the seventh centuries A.D.). See also, Jacquet-Gordon 1972: pl. 227:P4 (A.D. 600–750 [p. 89]), P5, P8; Mysliwiec 1987: 164, nos. 2019–22; Spencer and Bailey 1982: fig. 5:B17 (with more exterior surface ridges). This type is also found at Hermopolis in contexts dated to the early fifth–seventh centuries A.D. See also the discussion and references on pp. 16–19, and note that a later publication of the remains from this site date the Type B amphorae from Hermopolis to about A.D. 400 and on. Note also the similar amphorae illustrated in Spencer, Bailey, and Burnett 1983: fig. 12:3 (?) (seventh century A.D. or later; see p. 3); Prickett 1979: pl. 85a (QRS-18; Late Roman); and Riley in Sidebotham et al. 1989: 153–54 and fig. 16:13 (buff fabric with creamy exterior). Riley notes that this type may have originated in Cyprus or the Antioch region; he dates it to the early fifth–mid-seventh centuries A.D.

[9]The surface color of the sherd from Building 40 is 10 R 5/6. See fig. 29c and its references.

[10]The bases from Building 40 measured seven to eight centimeters in diameter.

BIBLIOGRAPHY

Ballet, P.; and Picon, M.
1987   Recherches préliminaires sur les origines de la céramique des Kellia (Égypte): importations et productions égyptiennes. *Cahiers de la céramique égyptienne* 1: 17–48.

Barron, T.; and Hume, W. F.
1902   *Topography and Geology of the Eastern Desert of Egypt.* Cairo: National Printing Department.

Bernand, A.
1972   *De Koptos à Kosseir.* Leiden: Brill.

Casson, L.
1971   *Ships and Seamanship in the Ancient World.* Princeton: Princeton University.

Cosmas Indicopleustes
1968,   *Topographie chrétienne*, vols. 1, 3, trans. by
1973   Wanda Wolska-Conus. Paris: Éditions du Cerf.

Couyat, M.
1910   Ports gréco-romains de la Mer Rouge et grandes routes du désert arabique. Pp. 525–42. *Comptes Rendus des Séances de l'Année 1910.* Académie des Inscriptions et Belles-Lettres. Paris: Picard et Fils.

Couyat, M.; and Montet, P.
1912   *Inscriptions hiéroglyphiques et hiératiques du Ouâdi Hammâmât.* Mémoires de l'Institut Français d'Archéologie Orientale 34. Cairo: Institut Français.

Debono, F.
1951   Expédition archéologique royale au désert oriental (Keft-Kosseir). *Annales du Service des Antiquités de l'Égypte* 51: 1–33.

Diodorus Siculus
1967   *Diodorus of Sicily*, trans. by C. H. Oldfather. Cambridge, Massachusetts: Harvard University.

Egloff, M.
1977   *Kellia: La poterie copte, quatre siècles d'artisanant et d'échanges en basse-Égypte.* Recherches Suisse d'Archéologie Copte, vol. 3. Geneva: Librarie de l'Universite.

Englebach, R.
1931   Notes of Inspection. *Annales du Service des Antiquités de l'Égypte* 31: 132–37.

Floyer, E. A.
1893   *Étude sur le Nord-Etbai.* Cairo: Imprimerie Nationale.

Franz, J., ed.
1853   *Corpus Inscriptionum Graecarum*, vol. 3. Berlin. (Material collected by Augustus Boeckh.). Repr. New York: Olms, 1977.

Guéraud, O.
1942   Ostraca grecs et latins de l'Wâdi Fawâkhir. *Bulletin de l'Institut Français d'Archéologie Orientale* 41: 141–96.

Harrell, J. A.; and Brown, V. M.
1992   The World's Oldest Surviving Geological Map: The 1150 B.C. Turin Papyrus from Egypt. *Journal of Geology* 100: 3–18.

Hayes, J. W.
1972　*Late Roman Pottery*. London: British School at Rome.

Herbert, S.; and Wright, H. T.
1988– Report on the 1987 University of Michigan/
1989　University of Assiut Expedition to Coptos and the Eastern Desert. *Newsletter of the American Research Center in Egypt* 143/144 (1988/1989): 1–4.

Holladay, P. G.
1982　Introduction to the Pottery Plates. Pp. 74–76. In *Cities of the Delta, III: Tell El-Maskhuta*, ed. John S. Holladay. American Research Center in Egypt Reports 6. Malibu, California: Undena.

Hume, W. F.
1937　*Geology of Egypt*, vol. 2, part 3. Cairo: Government Press.

Hussein, A. A.
1990　Mineral Deposits. Pp. 511–66. In *The Geology of Egypt*, by R. Said. Brookfield, VT: A. A. Balkema.

Jacquet-Gordon, H.
1972　*Les ermitages chrétiens du désert d'Esna*, vol. 3: *Ceramique et objects*. Fouilles de l'Institut Française d'Archéologie Orientale du Caire 29/3. Cairo: Institut Française d'Archéologie Orientale.

Johnson, A. C.; and West, L. C.
1949　*Byzantine Egypt: Economic Studies*. Princeton: Princeton University.

Johnson, B.
1981　*Pottery from Karanis: Excavations of the University of Michigan*. Kelsey Museum of Archaeology Studies 7. Ann Arbor: University of Michigan.

Johnson, W. R.
1979　Roman Pottery. Pp. 67–103. In *Quseir al-Qadim 1978: Preliminary Report*, by Donald S. Whitcomb and Janet H. Johnson. Cairo: American Research Center in Egypt.

Jones, M.
1991　The Early Christian Sites at Tell El-Amarna and Sheikh Said. *Journal of Egyptian Archaeology* 77: 129–44.

Kaiser, W.; Dreyer, G.; Gempeler, R.; Grossman, P.; Haeny, G.; Jaritz, H.; and Junge, F.
1976　Stadt und Tempel von Elephantine, Sechster Grabungsbericht. *Mitteilungen des Deutschen Archäologischen Instituts Abteilung Kairo* 32: 67–112.

Kaiser, W.; Dreyer, G.; Grimm, G.; Haeny, G.; Jaritz, H.; and Müller, C.
1975　Stadt und Tempel von Elephantine: Fünfter Grabungsbericht. *Mitteilung des Deutschen Archäologischen Instituts Abteilung Kairo* 31: 39–84.

Klemm, R.; and Klemm, D.
1991　The Development of Gold Ore Milling Technique from Predynastic to Arabic Time in Egypt. *Archaeological Stone Abstracts: Conference at the British Museum 14–16 November 1991* (Abstract).

Letronne, M.
1848　*Recueil des inscriptions grecques et latines de l'Égypte*. Paris: Imprimerie Royale.

Lucas, A.
1962　*Ancient Egyptian Materials and Industries*, 4th ed., rev. by J. R. Harris. London: Arnold.

Maspero, M.
1912　*Organisation militaire de l'Égypte byzantine*. Paris: Champion.

Meredith, D.
1952　The Roman Remains in the Eastern Desert of Egypt. *Journal of Egyptian Archaeology* 38: 94–111.
1953　The Roman Remains in the Eastern Desert of Egypt. *Journal of Egyptian Archaeology* 39: 95–106.
1957　Berenice Troglodytica. *Journal of Egyptian Archaeology* 43: 56–70.

Meyer, C.
1982　Large and Small Storerooms in the Roman Villa. Pp. 201–13. In *Quseir al-Qadim 1980: Preliminary Report*, by Donald S. Whitcomb and Janet H. Johnson. Malibu: Undena.
1989　Byzantine and Umayyad Glass from Jerash: Battleship Curves. *Annual of the Department of Antiquities of Jordan* 33: 235–43.
1992　*Glass from Quseir al-Qadim and the Indian Ocean Trade*. Studies in Ancient Oriental Civilization 53. Chicago: University of Chicago.

Munro-Hay, S.
1991　*Axum: An African Civilisation of Late Antiquity*. Edinburgh: Edinburgh University.

Murray, G. W.
1925　The Roman Roads and Stations in the Eastern Desert of Egypt. *Journal of Egyptian Archaeology* 11: 138–50.

Mysliwiec, K.
1987　*Keramik und Kleinfunde aus der Grabung im Tempel Sethos' I in Gurna*. Deutsches Archäologisches Institut, Abteilung Kairo, Archäologischer Veröffentlichungen 57. Mainz: von Zabern.

Pierrat, G.
1991　Essai de classification de la céramique de Tod: de la fin du VIIe siècle au début du XIIIe siècle ap. J.-C. *Cahiers de la céramique égyptienne* 2: 145–204.

Prickett, M.
1979　Quseir Regional Survey. Pp. 257–352. In *Quseir al-Qadim 1978: Preliminary Report*, by Donald S. Whitcomb and Janet H.

Johnson. Cairo: American Research Center in Egypt.

Raschke, M. G.
1978 New Studies in Roman Commerce with the East. Pp. 604–1361. In *Aufstieg und Niedergang der Römischen Welt*, vol. 2, part 9:2, ed. Hildegard Temporini. New York: de Gruyter.

Reddé, M.; and Golvin, J.-C.
1987 Du Nil à la Mer Rouge: Documents anciens et nouveaux sur les routes du désert oriental d'Égypte. *Karthago* 21: 5–64.

Reinach, A. J.
1910 Voyageurs et pèlerins. *Bulletin de la Société Archéologique d'Alexandrie* 13: 111–44.

Rodziewicz, M.
1976 *Alexandria I: La céramique romaine tardive d'Alexandrie.* Warsaw: Editions Scientifiques de Pologne.

Sidebotham, S. E.
1986 *Roman Economic Policy in the Erythra Thalassa.* Mnesmosyne Bibliotheca Classica Batava Supplementum 91. Leiden: Brill.

Sidebotham, S. E.; Riley, J. A.; Hamroush, H. A.; and Barakat, H.
1989 Fieldwork in the Red Sea Coast: The 1987 Season. *Journal of the American Research Center in Egypt* 26: 127–66.

Sidebotham, S. E.; Zitterkopf, R. E.; and Riley, J. A.
1991 Survey of the ᵓAbu Shaᶜar-Nile Road. *American Journal of Archaeology* 95: 571–622.

Spencer, A. J.; and Bailey, D. M.
1982 *British Museum Expedition to Middle Egypt: Ashmunein (1981).* British Museum Occasional Paper 41. London: British Museum.
1985 *British Museum Expedition to Middle Egypt: Ashmunein (1984).* British Museum Occasional Paper 61. London: British Museum.

Spencer, A. J.; Bailey, D. M.; and Burnett, A.
1983 *British Museum Expedition to Middle Egypt: Ashmunein (1982).* British Museum Occasional Paper 46. London: British Museum.

Spencer, A. J.; Bailey, D. M.; and Davies, W. V.
1984 *British Museum Expedition to Middle Egypt: Ashmunein (1983).* British Museum Occasional Paper 53. London: British Museum.

Tyldesley, J. A.; and Snape, S. R.
1988 *Nazlet Tuna: An Archaeological Survey in Middle Egypt.* B.A.R. International Series 414. Oxford: British Archaeological Reports.

Vercoutter, J.
1959 The Gold of Kush. *Kush* 7: 120–53.

Weigall, A. E. P.
1909 *Travels in the Upper Egyptian Deserts.* London: Blackwood.

Whitcomb, D. S.
1982 Roman Ceramics. Pp. 51–115. In *Queseir al-Qadim 1980: Preliminary Report*, by Donald S. Whitcomb and Janet H. Johnson. Malibu: Undena.

Whitcomb, D. S.; and Johnson, J. H.
1982 *Queseir al-Qadim 1980: Preliminary Report.* Malibu: Undena.

Wilkinson, J. G.
1835 *Topography of Thebes and General View of Egypt.* London: Murray.
1843 *Modern Egypt and Thebes*, Vols. I and II. London: Murray.

Williams, B. B.
1991 *Meroitic Remains from Qustul Cemetery Q, Ballana Cemetery B, and A Ballana Settlement*, p. 1, *Text and Figures.* Oriental Institute Nubian Expedition 8. Chicago: University of Chicago.

Winlock, H. E.
1926 *The Monastery of Epiphanius at Thebes*, pt. 1: *The Archaeological Material.* New York: Metropolitan Museum of Art.

Zitterkopf, R. E.; and Sidebotham, S. E.
1989 Stations and Towers on the Quseir-Nile Road. *Journal of Egyptian Archaeology* 75: 155–89.

Madaba Plains Project: A Preliminary Report on the 1989 Season at Tell El-ᶜUmeiri and Hinterland

ØYSTEIN S. LABIANCA
Andrews University
Berrien Springs, MI 49104

LARRY G. HERR
Canadian Union College
College Heights, AB T0C 0Z0

RANDALL W. YOUNKER
Andrews University
Berrien Springs, MI 49104

LAWRENCE T. GERATY
La Sierra University
Riverside, CA 92515

DOUGLAS R. CLARK
Walla Walla College
College Place, WA 99324

GARY CHRISTOPHERSON
University of Arizona
Tucson, AZ 85716

JON A. COLE
Walla Walla College
College Place, WA 99324

P. M. MICHÉLE DAVIAU
Wilfrid Laurier University
Waterloo, ON N2L 3C5

JAMES R. FISHER
Andrews University
Berrien Springs, MI 49104

JOHN I. LAWLOR
Baptist Bible College
Clarks Summit, PA 18411

TIMOTHY P. HARRISON
University of Chicago
Chicago, IL 60637

LORITA E. HUBBARD
Andrews University
Berrien Springs, MI 49104

GLORIA A. LONDON
University of Washington
Seattle, WA

RUSSANNE LOW
University of Maryland
8900 Augsburg 1, Germany

DOUGLAS SCHNURRENBERGER
University of Maryland
8900 Augsburg 1, Germany

A third season of excavation and survey was completed in the summer of 1989 by the Madaba Plains Project, Jordan. As in previous seasons, the project has been concerned with testing the sedentarization-nomadization hypothesis. This hypothesis, which grew out of the Heshbon Expedition, has guided investigations of successive cycles of intensification and abatement in settlement and landuse in the project area, which consists of Tell el-Umeiri and the region within 5 km radius of this site, including Tell Jawa and ed-Dreijat. Highlights of the third season's findings include discovery of solid stratigraphic evidence for intensification of settlement at Tell el Umeiri during EBIII; an abatement phase during EBIV; an intensification phase again during MBIIC; followed by an abatement phase during LB. This cyclic pattern continues into the Iron Age, which reaches settlement intensification peaks during Iron I and late Iron II at both Tell el-Umeiri and Tell Jawa. During the Hellenistic period, when settlement activity at these two major tells gradually tapers off, farmsteads such as Rujm Selim and ed-Dreijat continue to thrive. The intensification of landuse which accompanied the build-up of settled life during the late Iron II and Roman periods is reflected in the discoveries of the regional surveys, which documented the existence of numerous farmsteads and intensively managed agricultural valleys dating to these periods. Finally, our research into the uses of caves and fortified residential compounds during the Ottoman period has begun to shed light on how people coped during times when settled life was precarious in the region.

INTRODUCTION

The summer of 1989 marked the 21st anniversary of archaeological explorations in the Hashemite Kingdom of Jordan by the Madaba Plains Project. As its name suggests, this project has been concerned with the Madaba Plains, in the highlands east of the northern tip of the Dead Sea. In addition to the town of Madaba, well known for its Byzantine mosaics, the region includes Mount Nebo, Tell Hesban, Umm el-ᶜAmad, el-ᶜAl, and many less well known villages and towns. In the Old Testament, the region is mentioned in connection with the Moabites, the Ammonites, and the Israelites. It also contains ruins important to our understanding of the Graeco-Roman, Byzantine, and Islamic centuries in Palestine.

The Madaba Plains Project traces its origins to the launching in 1968 of the Heshbon Expedition by S. H. Horn of the Theological Seminary at Andrews University. That expedition's original mission was to excavate Tell Hesban to see what light, if any, it could shed on biblical stories involving the Exodus (Numbers 21, Joshua 13). That the present site of Tell Hesban had once been the Heshbon mentioned in the Bible in connection with the Israelite exodus from Egypt and conquest of Canaan is a claim that most biblical scholars had taken for granted when the project began.

Instead of extensive remains from the Old Testament periods, the Tell Hesban excavations produced a prolific quantity of materials from the Graeco-Roman (ca. 200 B.C.E. to C.E. 600) and especially the Ayyubid-Mamluk (ca. C.E. 1200 to 1450) periods. It is to Horn's credit as director of the first three campaigns in 1968, 1971, 1973, as well as to the credit of R. Boraas, the expedition's chief archaeologist during all five campaigns, that these more recent layers were uncovered with the same meticulous care as the older ones. Furthermore, both men encouraged the participation of specialists on the dig. This emphasis was significantly expanded during the last two campaigns in 1974 and 1976, when L. T. Geraty, Horn's successor as professor of archaeology and the history of antiquity at Andrews, took over as director. He also expanded the regional, ethnoarchaeological, and survey aspects of the project.

The current research focus of the Madaba Plains Project, namely the concern with sedentarization and nomadization, emerged out of the final synthesis of Tell Hesban (cf. LaBianca 1990). Integral to that focus was the food system methodology. It not only supplied a solution to dealing with Tell Hesban as a multiperiod site, it also provided an integrative framework for fitting together the various multidisciplinary findings of the expedition's specialists. The final outcome of that synthesis was the formulation of the "sedentarization-nomadization" hypothesis. The hypothesis encompassed the successive cycles of intensification and abatement of the Hesban region food system as reflected in the cyclic build-up and desertion of Hesban itself and of the towns, villages, and farmsteads that surrounded it. Equally important, it changed our research design from being primarily tell oriented to being region oriented. Thus considerably more energy was devoted to regional surveys and excavations of hinterland sites.

A major reason for continuing fieldwork in the Madaba Plains region during the early 1980s was to refine and test our understanding of the sedentarization-nomadization hypothesis. Thus far, three seasons of excavation have been completed at Tell el-ᶜUmeiri, a site on the northern fringe of the Madaba Plateau, approximately 10 km northeast of Tell Hesban on the southwestern outskirts of Jordan's capital, Amman. In addition to the excavations at this site, the territory within a 5 km radius has been the focus of hinterland excavations and surveys.[1]

THE SEDENTARIZATION-NOMADIZATION HYPOTHESIS

At the risk of oversimplifying historical reality, the sedentarization-nomadization hypothesis is the idea that since the beginnings of settlement on the Madaba Plains there have been periods when the momentum of social change has been in the direction of adopting more sedentary ways; and, conversely, there have been periods when the momentum has been toward adopting more nomadic ways. Over the long term, the result has been an oscillating pattern of human occupation.

During times when people were more sedentary, permanent settlements such as farmsteads, villages, and towns sprang up and thrived. They were accompanied by gradual increases in craft specialization; production of field crops and tree crops; centralization of power, usually involving some type of state apparatus; bureaucratization of production; stratification of society; and disbursement/centralization of the food supply.

When people reverted to more nomadic ways, many formerly permanent settlements were deserted and became ruins. As that happened, some people emigrated to other settled areas, while those who remained or had arrived in the wake of the changes survived by maintaining simpler modes of livelihood. Those simpler subsistence strategies involved reliance on animals for accumulation of wealth; annual movements of households between pasture lands and cereal lands; camping in tents, caves, and ruins of farmsteads, villages, and towns; and increased reliance on tribal affiliation for access to lands and protection against hostile states and tribes.

A consequence of those dynamic processes was that a spectrum of lifestyles coexisted throughout all periods of human occupation on the Madaba Plains. To varying degrees, such a spectrum has characterized the region as a whole as well as individual tribal groups, villages, and towns. Thus within a particular tribal group, village, or town, some families' lifestyles were in the vanguard of change whereas other families clung to traditional ways. It is therefore possible that within the same village or town, some families were settled in permanent houses while others still lived in caves and tents. The same is true for the region as a whole. Parts of it may have been further along in terms of sedentarization or nomadization than others (cf. Glubb 1938).

The causes of sedentarization and nomadization are complex and synergistic. On the one hand, increased momentum in the direction of sedentarization may result from the introduction of sedentary institutions by a local strongman; imposition of such institutions by a foreign power; new opportunities for trade in the form of changes in caravan routes or new roads; and combinations of the above with other factors.

Increased momentum in the direction of nomadization, on the other hand, usually follows when sedentary institutions are weakened. That may happen as a result of either political or economic disruptions or extreme natural events such as droughts, pestilence, and earthquakes. During such times, people either emigrate to other settled areas or stay on and adopt simpler, less conspicuous lifestyles to minimize their exposure to predation and loss by capricious foreign administrators, transiting armies, bandits, or hostile tribesmen.

To avoid misunderstanding this hypothesis, four clarifications must be added. First, the hypothesis does not assume that when, for example, the momentum of social change is in the direction of sedentarization, nomadization may not be occurring

simultaneously among certain sectors of the population. It merely holds that the "prevailing" momentum is in one direction or the other.

Second, because this hypothesis offers a simplified idea of the operation of long-term changes in the Madaba Plains region, it represents at best a first approximation of what actually happened during particular centuries by examining a wide array of information sources, such as settlement patterns, flora and fauna, land use, and ceramics. The goals of the Madaba Plains Project are to address who and what the agents were that caused sedentarization and nomadization during a given century; the precise manner in which build-up or abandonment of farmsteads, villages, and towns occurred; and the character and spectrum of lifestyles that resulted from those happenings. As the details are unearthed through archaeological research, the ways in which the processes were unique or similar from one century to the next will gradually become clear.

Third, while it may appear that preoccupation with this hypothesis has upstaged the concern with biblical events that provided the spark that brought this project into existence in 1968, that is not the case. The hypothesis is a much more powerful light with which to illuminate not only the biblically relevant periods, but also those that preceded and followed them. Rather than focusing exclusively on the build up and abandonment of farmsteads, villages, and towns on the Madaba Plains during the Late Bronze and Iron Ages, this hypothesis allows us to examine those happenings in relation to similar events during earlier or later periods. In this way, much deeper insight may be gained than is possible when research is narrowly focused on one or another specific historical period.

METHODOLOGY

To the extent that research by the Madaba Plains Project has been concerned with the sedentarization-nomadization hypothesis, it has continued to be aided by the food system methodology (above). That methodology has supplied assumptions and procedures for determining the prevailing direction of social change during different periods, given the archaeological data produced by this project.

Behind the methodology lies three important assumptions. The first is that people in the past spent most of their time, in one way or another, devoted to the daily tasks of maintaining their food procurement arrangements. The second is that, of all the activities people in the region have pursued over the past five millennia, none was more instrumental in producing the archaeological record than those related to food procurement. A third assumption is that the various activities involved in those arrangements are systemically related. That is because, by definition, a food system is a dynamic and complex unity consisting of all the purposive, patterned and interdependent symbolic and instrumental activities carried out by people to procure, process, distribute, store, prepare, consume, metabolize and dispose of food (cf. LaBianca 1990: 9).

As was demonstrated in studies of Hesban's food system (Geraty and LaBianca 1985; LaBianca 1990), the extent to which sedentism or nomadism prevailed at a particular time is directly related to how intense the food system was. At Hesban, during times of "low" intensity, transhumant pastoralism prevailed; "medium" intensity indicated that village-based cereal farming prevailed; and "high" intensity meant that urban-oriented intensive farming prevailed. By comparing the intensity states of the food system over successive historical periods, the prevailing direction of change could be ascertained. Thus when intensification of the food system was occurring sedentarization was also happening, and abatement was accompanied by nomadization.

To measure the intensity of the food system during a given historical period, the environmental, settlement, landuse, operational, and dietary conditions were ascertained. Those five archaeologically traceable parameters of the food system was the most useful in the analysis of Tell Hesban data. For the current project, a variety of procedures for measuring food system intensities were implemented.

For example, on Tell el-ʿUmeiri, L. Herr and his team gave special attention to the cycles of intensification and abatement in the intensity of occupation at this site throughout the Bronze and Iron Ages.[2] At Tell Jawa and ed-Dreijat, both hinterland sites, R. Younker and his team were interested in the ways settlement conditions could cast light on our understanding of the ʿUmeiri hinterland region as a whole.[3] On the hinterland survey, Ø. LaBianca's teams focused on regional aspects of the ancient food system. For example, long-term changes over time in environmental, settlement, and landuse conditions in the region within 5 km of Tell el-ʿUmeiri were studied by the random square and the environmental surveys.[4] To under-

stand the condition of operational facilities on ancient farmsteads discovered inside the project area the farmstead documentation survey was organized. Operational facilities include those used for sheltering people and animals, for processing or storing food, for collecting and storing water, and so on.[5] The objectives of the seasonal site survey were similar, namely to learn more about the operational conditions that prevailed when people were living in tents and caves.[6] The objective of this team, whose work was mostly experimental, was to determine the feasibility of using ground-penetrating radar in locating sub-surface archaeological features. To these field operations we added those of the project's laboratories. The ceramic technology lab, headed by G. London, had the following goals: documentation of the manufacturing techniques for each archaeological period and changes or continuity from one period to another; characterization of the raw materials used for bricks and vessels of specific types, e.g., cooking pots, bowls, juglets, jugs, and jars, in each period; comparison of pottery excavated at each of the project's major sites through petrographic analysis (over 200 samples were selected); documentation of long-distance trade in pottery and its contents, as well as trade on a more localized level among the different geographic and social units; and recording of marks of manufacture and ownership to learn about those who made and used the wares.[7]

THE EXCAVATIONS AT TELL EL-ʿUMEIRI

Excavations at Tell el-ʿUmeiri took place in six Fields (figs. 1, 2) and discovered remains from Early Bronze Age III (ca. 2500 B.C.E.) to early Persian (ca. 500 B.C.E.).

Early Bronze Age at Tell el-ʿUmeiri

The earliest stratified remains found, as in previous seasons, were dated to the Early Bronze Age. Occupational remains were uncovered on both the southern and northern shelves, confirming once again that during that period Tell el-ʿUmeiri reached its greatest extent. While only fragmentary evidence was found on the northern slope, the most extensive remains came from the southern shelf, where two broad terraces and a street system organized blocks of domestic dwellings. Two long retaining walls provided support for the two ter-

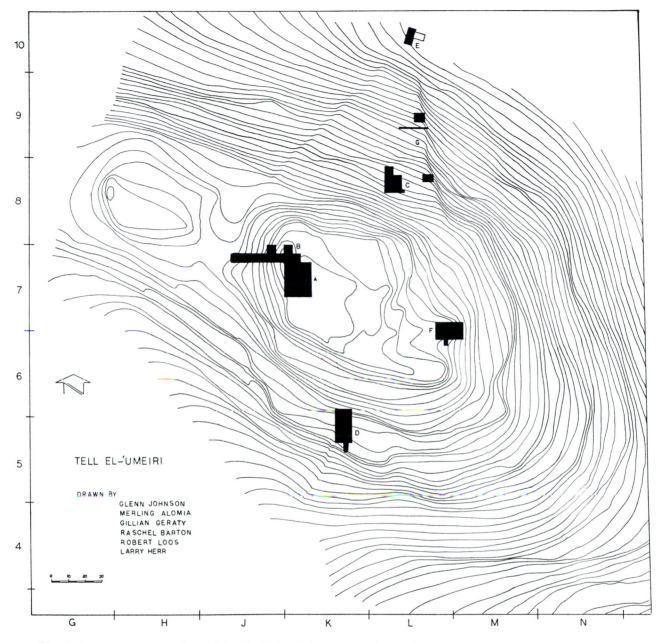

Fig. 1. Topographic map of Tell el-ᶜUmeiri with the Fields excavated through 1989.

races, which in turn held up the domestic structures. Parts of the lower, southern terrace (the
southern half of Field D in fig. 1) were first excavated in 1984 (Geraty 1985: 95), while the upper,
northern terrace (the northern half of Field D in
fig. 1) was excavated in 1987 (Geraty, Herr, and
LaBianca 1988: 241). The 1989 season marked a
return to the same grid of squares first opened in
1984 and the completion of the task of uncovering
the structures on the lower, southern terrace.

The most coherent remains of the EB III settlement have so far come from the lower terrace. A
street, approximately 1.5 m wide, ran north to
south through the excavated area, bisecting it into
two separate housing units (figs. 3, 4). A line of
stones along the eastern side of the street was possibly intended to hold fodder for a tethered beast
of burden. At its northern end, the street apparently
turned east, running along the retaining wall of the
northern terrace.

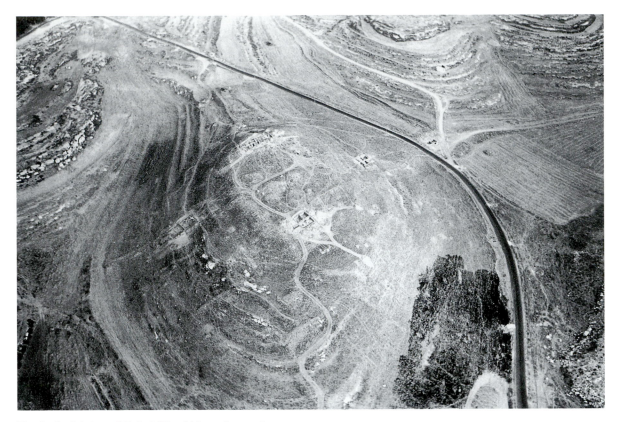

Fig. 2. Aerial view of Tell el-ᶜUmeiri from the east.

Neither of the two housing units was completely exposed. Although excavations unearthed little more than one room from the compound west of the street, the unit to the east produced three rooms with significant remains. One room, 3.5 × 3.5 m, bounded on the west and north by the street, contained two "L"-shaped bins and a cobbled surface, suggesting that it served as a courtyard, perhaps for sheltering animals. The room opened onto the northern portion of the street.

A stepped doorway to the east connected the courtyard to a large storeroom that contained the remains of some 28 storage vessels of various types, mostly jars (fig. 5). Protected by the destruction debris from the superstructure that fell on top of the vessels, and preserved by the fire that ravaged the building, many of the vessels still contained carbonized seeds. They included legumes (lentils and garbanzos), fruits (grapes and fig), and grains (wheat and barley). In addition, a small juglet was found that may have contained oil. A bench with an inset hearth was uncovered in a small room south of the courtyard. It had been constructed against the courtyard's southern wall,

and lends further evidence of the domestic nature of the compound. The pottery on the surfaces of the rooms, present at their destruction, was EB III.

Below this EB III domestic complex, the tops of several walls from yet an earlier settlement began to emerge toward the end of the season. Although the founding levels of the emerging walls were not reached, a few EB I–II sherds were found, as well as one possible Chalcolithic sherd.

On the northern slope, in Field G, two squares were excavated on the eastern line of a "V"-shaped topographic feature descending the slope toward the water source (fig. 1; see also Geraty 1985: 94). Although those topographic features strongly suggested that walls lay below, the excavations uncovered nothing but 3 m of unstratified dump above EB III tumble. No sign of a wall could be found, even when a backhoe sectioned the line. However, the presence of EB III material confirms that the town extended far down the northern slope of the tell during that period.

The Early Bronze Age in Palestine, known as the age of urbanization, witnessed the development of large, often walled, sedentary sites. The Early

Fig. 3. EB III street in Field D, Tell el-ᶜUmeiri.

Bronze settlement at Tell el-ᶜUmeiri appears to represent a modest expression of that process. The remains that have been found indicate both intensive and extensive settlement activity during EB III. While a shift toward sedentarization may have already begun as early as the Chalcolithic period, it undoubtedly did not reach its peak until EB III. Although the earlier periods still await full excavation, what has been uncovered so far does not reflect the same intensity of settlement that the EB III remains portray.

Since no trace of a city wall, or any other such defensive structure, has been discovered at Tell el-ᶜUmeiri, that feature, traditionally used to define the "urban" character of a site, cannot be used to measure the level of organization achieved at the site. Indeed, it could be argued that the lack of any fortification wall should be interpreted to mean that the settlement never became an urban center at all. However, such reasoning ignores the well-planned nature of the settlement, and the fact that the site reached its largest extent ever—approximately 16 acres—during the EB period. The arrangement and layout of EB III Tel el-ᶜUmeiri suggests an orderly and efficient use of space and indicates that a reasonably high level of social organization had already been achieved.

The Early Bronze finds from the 1989 season, along with those of the two previous seasons, have helped to further confirm the sedentarization-nomadization working hypothesis that has been adopted by the project. As has been suggested, EB III marked the culmination of a gradual process of settlement intensification. The extensive occu-

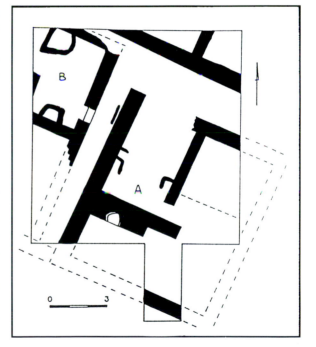

Fig. 4. Sketch plan of EB III remains in Field D, Tell el-ᶜUmeiri.

pation remains on the tell, therefore, reflect a shift toward the exploitation of sedentary subsistence strategies.

After the EB III high point, the settlement history shows signs of abatement over the succeeding two strata (probably EB IV). In the level immediately above the well-planned EB III domestic complexes in Field D, two semicircular dwellings were

Fig. 5. EB III storage vessels in Field D, Tell el-ᶜUmeiri.

Fig. 6. Astarte plaque from Field F, Tell el-ᶜUmeiri.

found, each with a single pillar holding up a roof. Those dwellings were approximately 4 m wide and are similar to early EB IV structures found at Tell Um-Hammad in the Jordan Valley (Helms 1989: #29). This settlement pattern may reflect the seasonal activity typical of a predominantly nomadic way of life.

Somewhat later, but probably still during the early EB IV, a complex of long, thin, walls of small boulders and thick mud mortar may have been used as animal pens by seminomadic pastoralists. It is therefore possible to trace a gradual shift away from the intense EB III settlement pattern typical of an "urban" or sedentary existence, toward a more nomadic settlement configuration. Following the last occupation, the site apparently was abandoned around 2200 or 2100 B.C.E. While the past three seasons have helped to confirm the general shift between sedentarization and nomadization in the Early Bronze Age, further excavation and more precise documentation of each of the stages is still needed to reach a full understanding of the cultural processes.

Middle Bronze Age

A new settlement seems to have begun toward the end of the Middle Bronze Age. No pottery that can be securely dated to MB IIA has been found; and while a few chocolate-on-white sherds were found in the earliest layers, many more were found in later Middle Bronze layers. Indeed, chocolate-on-white ware is ubiquitous, occurring together with

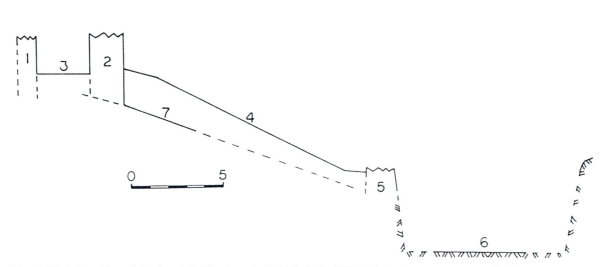

Fig. 7. Sketch section of the Iron I fortifications in Field B, Tell el-ʿUmeiri: 1—inner casemate wall; 2—outer casemate wall; 3—casemate room; 4—Iron I rampart; 5—Iron I retaining wall; 6—moat; and 7—MB II rampart.

flat-bottomed cooking pots and profiled-rim jars. The date of the resettlement should thus be within MB IIC.

The new settlers abandoned the southern shelf and did not achieve the intensity of occupation on the northern slope and eastern shelf that occurred in EB III. However, excavations in Field B on the western slope of the acropolis have probed ca. 1 m into an earthen rampart (fig. 6), suggesting that the Middle Bronze settlement was the first to be fortified at ʿUmeiri. However, a full-blown urban center did not spring up with the arrival of the new settlers. At best the first settlement started with an unfortified village or town. This is indicated by the fact that the rampart layers included earlier Middle Bronze sherds (ca. 10 percent), suggesting an earlier settlement before the rampart was built.

The top layer of the rampart (no other layers have been found yet) sloped ca. 30 degrees and was made of beaten earth with a few short, thin lenses of crushed lime. So far, nothing has been found of the city wall associated with the rampart. The presence of the rampart suggests that the walled, urban center at ʿUmeiri was not appreciably different from cities elsewhere in Syro/Palestine, although it was relatively small, covering only the acropolis (ca. 6 acres). The relatively late date of its founding, as well as the presence of strong fortifications around so small a site, suggest that the area was a frontier. Indeed, virtually no other remains have been found from the same period in the region.

How could an isolated settlement like ʿUmeiri prosper enough to intensify economically and socially? One answer is trade. Although clean Middle Bronze layers have been rare at ʿUmeiri so far (but Middle Bronze pottery is frequent in later, mixed deposits), there are significant signs of far-flung trade. An obsidian fragment found in a Middle Bronze layer in 1987 probably came from Anatolia, while a fragment of Tell el-Yahudiyeh ware suggests trade with Western Palestine or Syria.

Late Bronze Age

The isolated Middle Bronze intensification process at ʿUmeiri was a prelude to the Late Bronze settlement. Debris layers from the Late Bronze Age were uncovered behind an extraurban, Iron I terrace wall in Field F, the eastern shelf. Although no architectural remains were isolated, the layers produced a Cypriot Base-Ring sherd and a well-preserved Astarte fertility plaque common to the period (fig. 6). The pottery appears to be considerably advanced over that from the Middle Bronze settlement, probably LB IIB. It would seem that the Late Bronze settlement reused the Middle Bronze fortifications and did not grow outside the walls. The intensification process visible at the end of the Middle Bronze Age thus did not continue. In fact, the degenerate Late Bronze pottery suggests that at least a technical abatement had occurred.

Fig. 8. Iron I outer casemate wall with rampart in Field B, Tell el-ᶜUmeiri.

Fig. 9. Iron I collared-rim jars in casemate room, Tell el-ᶜUmeiri.

Iron Age I

In the 1989 season it became clear that the casemate fortification system discovered in previous seasons in Field B was indeed from Iron Age I, as suggested in earlier reports (Geraty 1985: 92; Geraty, Herr, and LaBianca 1988: 236), (figs. 6, 8). An earthen rampart, almost 2 m thick and sloping 32–35 degrees, was constructed immediately on top of the Middle Bronze rampart. That the rampart was constructed at the same time as the outer casemate wall, against which it lay, was suggested by the fact that the upper two layers within the rampart correspond to courses in the wall (see illustration in Clark 1991: 56–57). It thus appears that the rampart was constructed to provide support for the wall against the weight of debris inside. All three layers of the rampart produced significant quantities of Iron I pottery. At the bottom, a revetment wall supported the rampart where a dry moat plunged ca. 4 cm into bedrock. The rock and clay excavated from the moat appeared to have been used for the founding layer of the rampart, suggesting contemporary construction.

Inside the casemate room and further inside the town was a deep destruction layer ca. 1.8 m thick. It was composed primarily of burned mudbricks and stones but also included burned wooden roofing beams. The fire was so hot that it turned some of the wall stones to lime. Beneath the destruction debris

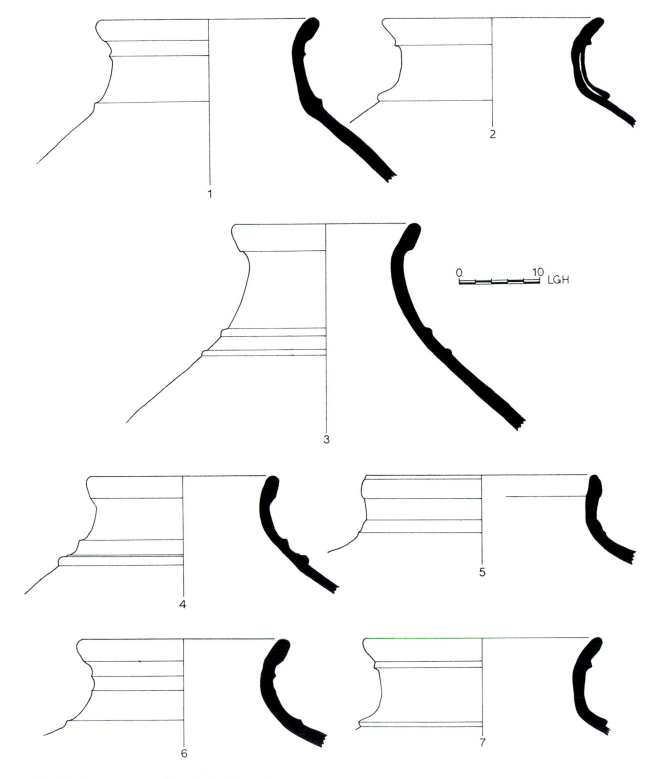

Fig. 10. Collared-rim jars from Field B, Tell el-ᶜUmeiri.

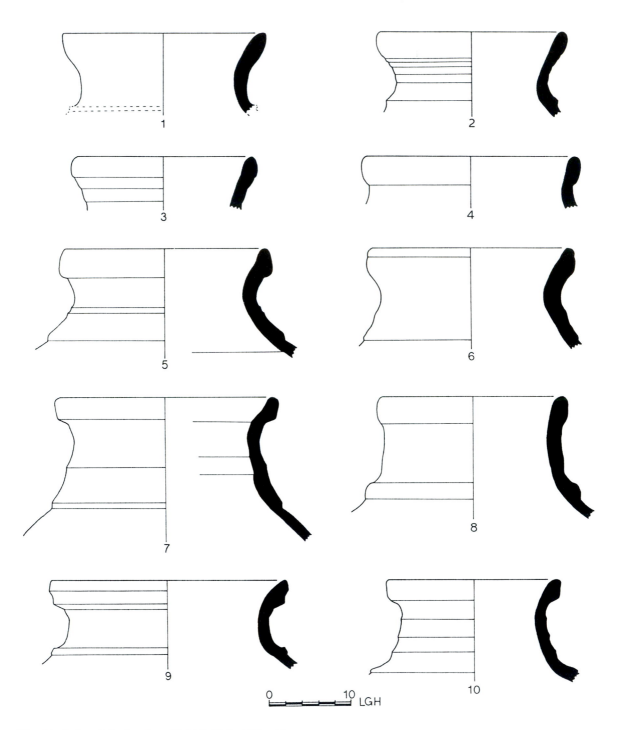

Fig. 11. Collared-rim jars from Field B, Tell el-ʿUmeiri.

in the casemate room were parts of 13 smashed storage pithoi (fig. 9), most of which had collared rims, typical of Iron I throughout Palestine (figs. 10, 11). Many species of carbonized seeds were found in those storage pithoi. Several of these large vessels contained identical potter's marks on the handles, but none had precisely the same type of collar as any of the others.

This destruction heralded the end of Iron I in Field B. In earlier seasons, we uncovered remains of an early Iron II storeroom over this destruction (Geraty 1985: 93). In Fields A and F an ash layer

Fig. 12. Late Iron II/early Persian buildings in Field A, Tell el-ᶜUmeiri.

overlay the stratigraphic boundary between Iron I and late Iron II (with no early Iron II between). It thus appears that the destruction that ended Iron I at Tell el-ᶜUmeiri was sitewide. All Iron I pottery at ᶜUmeiri was Iron IA, or 12th century B.C.E. In Field F, on the eastern shelf, a well-built terrace wall came from that period, although no occupational surfaces were found. Excavation did not proceed into the Iron I layers in Field A.

The Iron I period represents a significant intensification of occupation at ᶜUmeiri, a development that reflects a region-wide escalation of the sedentarization process. Villages and towns are more frequent, while cities gradually develop. The earliest Iron I settlement probably reused the old Middle Bronze fortifications, as the Late Bronze inhabitants had done. But as their economic and social system developed, they could afford a massive re-fortification effort. Such a development is incomprehensible without significant growth in prosperity and population.

Early Iron Age II

The prosperity of the Iron I settlement appears to have ended when the city was destroyed, probably within the 12th century. Subsequent early Iron II remains were poorly built and have been found only in Field B. Reoccupation was small and not very successful. Nearby Tell Jawa shows signs of producing more significant early Iron II remains, but the regional survey may also reflect a slightly abated settlement pattern in early Iron II.

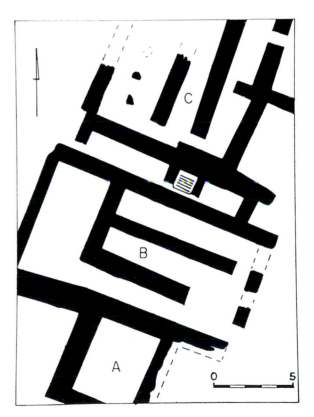

Fig. 13. Sketch plan of the late Iron II/early Persian buildings in Field A, Tell el-ᶜUmeiri.

Late Iron Age II and Early Persian Period

The west end of the acropolis in Field A continued to produce extensive remains of at least two

Fig. 14. Late Iron II/early Persian walls in Field F, Tell el-ʿUmeiri.

Fig. 15. Sketch plan of the late Iron II/early Persian walls in Field F, Tell el-ʿUmeiri.

phases, stretching from late Iron II into the beginning of the Persian period. Four new squares were opened in a north-south line immediately east of the previously excavated area. After three seasons it now seems that three large buildings have been exposed.

Only two or three rooms of a large building with very thick walls have been found in the south (Lawlor 1991), but the central building has been completely exposed. It comprised four rooms, three long rooms abutting a broad room (figs. 12, 13), a house-style typical in western Palestine and often thought to be "Israelite," but now becoming more frequent in Transjordan as Iron Age sites are excavated. The third building on the north was oriented at 90 degrees to the four-room house and included a broad room with at least five long rooms abutting it. One of the rooms was formed with a row of pillars, doorways connected all the rooms.

At least the first two buildings were apparently basement structures; that is, the walls were built into a large pit dug for the whole structure. Individual foundation trenches were not found for any of the walls, and immediately outside the buildings Iron I layers were found. Surfaces were uncovered only in the northern building, where a typical domestic repertoire of objects, such as grinding tools, was found. However, the thick walls, the basements, and the large size of the two southern buildings suggest they were used for nondomestic, administrative activities. Perhaps they should be connected with the royal seal found in the area in 1984 (Geraty, et al. 1986: 138), as well as two Persian provincial seal impressions found in the 1989 season.

Other major structures from the same period were found in Field F on the eastern shelf. Three parallels walls (figs. 14, 15) may have formed a small gate structure with a narrow passageway between the two eastern walls. Inside this possible gate was a large building constructed of the west-

Fig. 16. Figurine head from Tell el-ᶜUmeiri.

ern parallel wall; this latter wall had corners at both ends with walls extending westward out of the excavated area. Associated surfaces contained no objects.

The late Iron II phases represent another sub-period of intensification in the settlement. The large buildings seem to have covered the acropolis, whereas the early Iron II structures were smaller and fewer. However, security does not seem to have been a grave problem. The city wall apparently was still the Iron I outer casemate wall with a few patches in the rampart. The small, ephemeral "gate" in Field F fits this lack of felt security needs. Also, most of the buildings discovered were very large, suggesting administrative functions instead of domestic. Indeed, according to G. London, our ceramic technologist, the lack of a large variety of ownership marks on the pottery indicates that the population at the site was small. Elsewhere, London has called attention to indications that much of the Iron II population of Palestine lived outside the walled cities (London 1989). The large numbers of hinterland agricultural complexes in the region surrounding Tell el-ᶜUmeiri support that suggestion.

The many finds from Field A included several figurines (fig. 16). It is thus likely that the sedentarization process in late Iron II was a product of increased security in the region, perhaps due to the presence of the Assyrians. Their strong control of the territory may have resulted in a *pax assyriaca*,

which would have allowed a modest expression of prosperity.

The three buildings in Field A continued into the early Persian period with no apparent break. The typical corpus of late Iron II pottery continued with a few Persian additions, such as Attic ware. Two inscribed seal impressions with Aramaic writing of ca. 500 B.C., occurred on jar handles (figs. 17, 18). They contained the name of the Persian province, ᶜmn ("ᶜAmmon"), and the hypocoristicon of a provincial official, *šbᵓ* ("Shubaᵓ"). The impressions were made by two seals, emphasizing their official function. A third seal impression was incomplete. It was pressed into the rim of a Persian-period jar and contained the name of an individual.

Later Persian phases suggest a marked decline in quality. Poorer structures were built over the buildings of Field A described above (figs. 12, 13), seemingly ignoring the earlier walls completely. Similar building fragments have been uncovered in Field B. Unfortunately, the surfaces that went with those walls have been destroyed by agricultural activities on top of the mound in the Middle Ages, but the latest pottery associated with them in fill layers was Persian.

This new phase represents the nomadization process during the Persian period. Perhaps the administrative institutions of society had broken down, and there was no longer a need for large administrative buildings. Without central political and social control, the economic system also broke

Fig. 17. Seal impression of the Persian province of Ammon from Field A, Tell el-ᶜUmeiri.

Fig. 18. A second seal impression of the Persian province of Ammon from Field A, Tell el-ᶜUmeiri.

down; and, though inhabitants attempted to retain their lifestyle by building (inferior) houses on the acropolis, their attempt did not last long. There were no remains that would suggest a settlement at the site beyond the fifth century B.C.

Early Roman Period

In 1987 a small plastered pool or ritual bath with steps was excavated at the northern edge of Field A (Geraty, Herr, and LaBianca 1988: 234). Pottery no later than the early Persian period came from the debris inside. In the 1989 season, when we removed part of the foundation of the structure, we found two early Roman sherds. It would thus appear that the pool should be redated to the early Roman period. However, no evidence at the site suggests occupation from that period. Small amounts of pottery were found in the 1984 random surface survey, but not enough to suggest a significant occupation. Roman utilization of the site and spring instead occurred at Tell el-ᶜUmeiri East, across the modern highway.

Middle Ages

Because the plastered pool must have been subterranean, but no associated buildings or pottery of the Roman period have been found anywhere in the immediate area as might be expected, we suggest that any associated Roman buildings have disappeared and that the present surface of the mound has eroded considerably since Roman times. Agricultural activity, combined with accompanying wind erosion, has lowered the top of the tell by as much as a meter. The wind removed the soil but

left stones, pottery, and objects. As the surface of the mound eroded, farmers piled newly-exposed stones in many large mounds, scattered over the site.

Water Source

Excavations continued in one square in Field E, the water source at the bottom of the tell on the north side. Earth layers from Iron I were cut by a plaster and cobble installation built during Iron II times (fig. 19). The Iron II remains were, in turn, cut by an early Roman plastered channel. Then, during Byzantine times, all structures were cut by a deep foundation pit for a tunnel leading to the present well house. The Byzantine structure was used when the well was capped in the 1930s. None of the ancient remains except the Byzantine one were coherent enough to reconstruct the water structures.

Seal and Seal Impressions

A seal inscribed on two sides was discovered in the topsoil of Field A (Object No. 1749) (fig. 20). The name of the owner, ᵓlᵓmṣ, occurred on the top with a drawing of a bull's or ram's head. On the bottom was a bird perched atop a possible lotus flower, while the name of the owner and his patronym were inscribed around the iconography: lᵓlᵓmṣ bn tmkᵓl. We can translate and vocalize the inscription "Belonging to ᵓElᵓamats son of Tamakᵓel." Both names are found on other Ammonite seals and inscriptions. The letters suggest an early seventh century B.C.E. date, but none of the forms are strongly diagnostic. The discovery of this seal, an emblem of power and

Fig. 19. Excavations at the water source, Tell el-ᶜUmeiri.

prestige, makes sense in terms of intensification of settlement and landuse and also in terms of the bureaucratization of production that no doubt prevailed during the period.

HINTERLAND EXCAVATIONS AT TELL JAWA

During the 1987 season the survey team discovered that parts of Tell Jawa, a large, important site ca. 5 km east of ᶜUmeiri, had been recently bulldozed, apparently in preparation for a new housing development. Surface sherding indicated periods of occupation that overlapped with ᶜUmeiri, especially during the Iron II period. Obtaining an accurate understanding of ᶜUmeiri's role in the region requires taking into account its relationship with Jawa.

While the core staff had discussed the need eventually to conduct a probe of Jawa, the immediate threat to the site forced us to act more quickly than we had planned. Therefore, in the 1989 season a small team was assigned to open five squares on the south side of the tell where the bulldozer had stopped after exposing the outer face of what appeared to be an Iron Age city wall (fig. 21).

The five squares, opened in Field A—Squares 1, 2, 3, and 4 south to north, and Square 13 east of Square 3 (fig. 22)—transected three major parallel wall lines, including the outermost one, which had stopped the bulldozer. The strategy was to expose those walls, determined their construction history and function (they appeared to be city walls), and explore remains of occupation inside the walls.

Fig. 20. Seal from Field A, Tell el-ᶜUmeiri.

Early Iron Age II

The excavations revealed at least nine archaeological phases, mostly dating from the Iron II period. The earliest phase, exposed in Square 13, consisted of the intersection of two Iron Age stone walls. Both walls were covered with large (65 × 35 × 15 cm) fallen mudbricks, apparently from the collapsed superstructure. Because the bases of the walls were not reached, their date and function remain uncertain. However, the debris of the collapsed walls contained late Iron I?/early Iron II sherds, making it probable that the walls were constructed either during that period (tenth–ninth centuries B.C.E.) or later in Iron II. A fill west of the walls produced Middle Bronze, Late Bronze, and Iron I sherds. A small ash pocket south of the debris

Fig. 21. Bulldozed wall at Jawa.

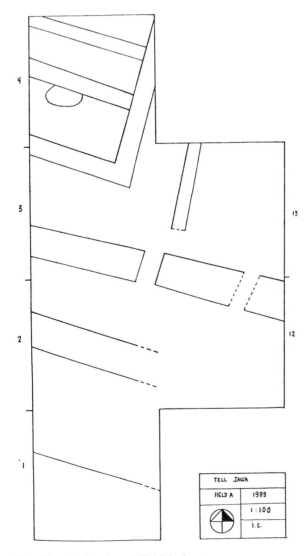

Fig. 22. Sketch plan of Field A, Jawa.

from the two Iron Age walls apparently reflects an extensive occupation in association with those walls (Phase 9B).

At least five subsequent Iron Age phases (Phases 8–4) were found in Squares 3, 4, and 13 just inside the city wall. They were particularly evident in Square 3, where two wall lines appeared to define two rectangular rooms of a large house. The lower portions of those walls were constructed of stone while the upper parts were mudbrick. On the surface associated with the lowest floor (Phase 8) was a collection of food preparation objects and ceramic vessels of a domestic nature. The objects included a saddle quern, an upper millstone (both broken, but in situ), two pounding stones, and fragments of an oven that apparently was against one of the walls. Numerous bones (55 sheep/goat, 2 cattle), ash, and flint fragments were also found on the surface. The pottery on the floor was from early Iron II (ninth–eighth centuries B.C.E.)

Middle Iron Age II

Later, probably during the middle of the Iron II period (eighth–seventh centuries B.C.E.), the floor of the room was resurfaced (Phase 7). Cooking pots, numerous animal bones (161 sheep/goat, 10 cattle), an upper millstone, and a stone pounder testify to its continued food preparation function. A broken spindle whorl might suggest spinning activity at the site. A probable contemporary phase was found in the room immediately to the east.

The latest surface in the western room (Phase 6) also had cooking pots, ash, small bowls, and animal bones (32 sheep/goat and 2 cattle). Large amounts of white plaster, possibly the result of rebuilding the inner casemate wall, had accumulated on the surface. Again, the room immediately to the east seemed to have a contemporary phase. It, too, contained remains of domestic activities, including an accumulation of charcoal, bones (57 sheep/goat, 9 cattle, 1 chicken), 2 spindle whorls, a broken stone grinder, a stone pounder, and a polished, finely serrated shark's tooth.

To the north of those two rooms was a rather large building (Phase 5) with at least two long rooms. Pottery found in the debris layers of the building suggests that it was subsequent to the rooms discussed in the proceeding paragraph (Iron II–8th–7th centuries B.C.E.).

One of the season's most interesting finds, the head of a small figurine, came from the eastern wall of this large building (fig. 23). It depicts a male wearing a headdress similar to the Egyptian *atef* crown and identical to those depicted on the well-known limestone busts displayed in the Amman Museum. S. Horn (personal communication) has suggested that the headdress was the crown of the Ammonite king. If that suggestion is accurate, this artifact would suggest that Jawa, which is near the border of Moab, was within the Ammonite sphere during the Middle Iron II period. That suggestion is further supported by the pottery, which is stylistically identical to that of nearby ᶜUmeiri where a number of distinctive Ammonite inscriptions have already been found. If Jawa is indeed an Ammonite city, Alt's (1932) identification of Jawa with biblical Mephaᶜath would have to be modified, since the latter clearly is a Moabite town (Jeremiah 48:21–24).[8]

Late Iron Age II

Excavations indicated that during the latter part of the Iron II period (ca. seventh century B.C.E.?) the city walls were rebuilt (Phase 5), although further excavation is needed to clarify their relationship to the domestic architecture found just inside.

The city walls underwent further reconstruction (Phase 4) a short time later (late seventh, early sixth centuries B.C.E.). The city walls of that phase appear to be constructed in the casemate style. A doorway leads from one of the casemate rooms into the city. An ash layer seems to represent a cooking area just inside the city wall, although there were few bones. Pottery was late Iron II (sixth century B.C.E.), although that cooking area

Fig. 23. Figurine of Ammonite King, Jawa.

could have existed subsequent to the abandonment of the town.

The Iron Age occupation at Jawa apparently was terminated during the sixth century B.C.E. Evidence for destruction or abandonment include the rock tumble that extended south down the slope from the city walls. In association with the rock tumble were the upper courses of the exterior portion of the casemate wall, which was slumped inward (uphill). Initially it was thought that the slumping should be attributed to an earthquake. However, the presence of 13 javelin points against the outside of the wall suggests that the collapse could be related to an attack on the town. The clearest sign of the destruction inside the walls was a large amount of pottery smashed against a wall and its associated floor. That pottery, all late Iron II (ca. sixth century B.C.E.), included pithoi, store jars, jugs, and one complete juglet. Amid the debris were two more javelin points, identical in style to those found outside the city wall. It is possible, although far from certain, that this destruction is related to Nebuchadnezzar's

Fig. 24. Megalithic structure, ed-Dreijat.

582/581 B.C.E. punitive campaign against the Ammonites and Moabites noted by Josephus.

After the destruction the western part of Tell Jawa was not reoccupied. The final two archaeological phases in Field A consisted of topsoils and modern field walls. Some Roman/Byzantine sherds were found, but there was no sign that this part of the tell was occupied in those periods.

HINTERLAND EXCAVATIONS AT ED-DREIJAT

A previous report of the Madaba Plains Project mentioned a large "megalithic" structure, recorded by the regional survey, which was described as a "fort" in the sense of the biblical *bîranîyôt*. Because of the extensive discussion concerning the date and precise function of similar so-called "Ammonite towers," we decided to excavate this one (fig. 24).

The site, presently known as ed-Dreijat ("the stairs"), is located on a high hill approximately 2.8 km southwest of Tell el-ᶜUmeiri. First identified by Fohrer as Site D, it was later included by the Hesban Survey as Site 135.

Prior to excavation, a site survey by the excavation team identified what appeared to be exterior walls approximately 2.5 m wide, as well as two interior walls of similar thickness. Immediately southeast of the site, a large open cave was identified. According to local villagers, a certain Umm Yusef uses the cave during the winter months as a sheep/goat pen. Farther south, on the crest of the hill, was a bell-shaped cistern, approximately 15.5 m deep, which at the time of the excavation contained 4 m to 4.5 m of water. It is still used by shepherds in the region throughout the summer.

All exterior walls were built of massive unhewn or partially hewn chert boulders (ranging from 1.1 m to 2 m in diameter) and filled with chink stones. Two major east-west interior walls were joined to the western exterior wall. The interior walls appear to have extended across and joined the north-south wall on the eastern side. It is possible that major interior walls such as these supported a second story. The complex was further subdivided into small rooms by numerous minor interior walls (fig. 25). Excavations revealed a much more complex use of the site than we had first anticipated. It appears that there were at least seven phases of occupation or activity.

Iron Age II

Although no surfaces or architectural remains could be dated definitely to Iron Age II, the presence of several Iron II surface sherds, as well as pockets of late Iron II, suggests that the site was initially occupied during that period (Phase 7). The similarity of construction with other Iron Age buildings in the region also supports the possibility that at least part of the ed-Dreijat structure (probably the main rectangular part) was built originally during that time. It appears, however, that the site was cleared to bedrock during the later Persian/ Hellenistic occupation, making a precise dating for the initial construction of the fort difficult (see below). Two cisterns or storage tanks were probably cut during this earliest phase of occupation.

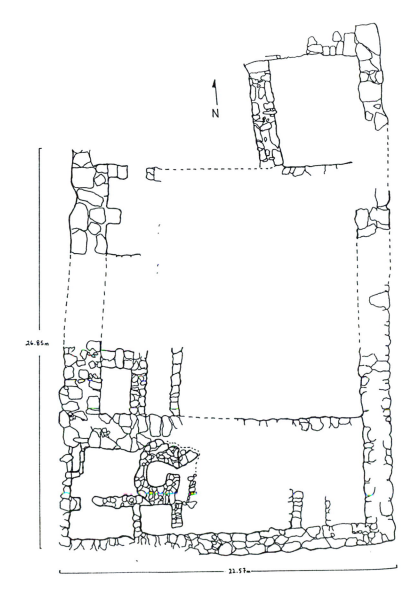

Fig. 25. Plan of ed-Dreijat.

Late Persian and Early Hellenistic Periods

The next activity phase (Phase 6) seems to have involved some remodeling during the late Persian? or early Hellenistic period. Pottery from that period was found not only in all 11 squares, but also on several bedrock surfaces, indicating that the Persian or Hellenistic occupants cleared the site down to bedrock in most areas (fig. 26). It was probably during that period that the Iron II pottery of earlier inhabitants was dumped into an abandoned cave or cistern. Several inner walls probably were constructed during the same period to create rooms along the west side of the complex (fig. 27). Several other rooms in the northeast corner of the site were also added.

Hellenistic Period

While there is no clear break between Phases 6 and 5, several Hellenistic lamps, cooking pots, and other late Hellenistic forms provide clear evidence for a later Hellenistic occupation. A circular installation, possibly used for storage, may have been constructed at that time.

Roman, Byzantine, and Ayyubid/Mamluk Periods

There is some evidence for Roman activity (Phase 4), although it does not appear that much of the structure was utilized. The circular installation may have continued in use.

A Byzantine presence is suggested by sherds, but all are small and worn. One of two coins found at the site comes from this period. It was a coin of Constans or Constantine (fourth century C.E.). The other coin has not been identified.

From the small number of sherds, 14 in all, it is possible that a temporary encampment occupied the site during the Ayyubid/Mamluk period. All the sherds are painted and may have come from the same vessel.

Modern Period

The most recent phase of activity on the site appears to be the result of modern Bedouin, according to the ceramic evidence. Portions of a modern water jar were also uncovered. Most of the modern occupation, however, appeared to be centered around the cave in the southeastern corner of the site and the blocked cave entrance to the west that was not excavated this season.

THE HINTERLAND SURVEYS

During the last three seasons, the survey's scope has shifted from extensive coverage of the entire project area to intensive scrutiny of selected sites or regions within the area. Thus the emphasis during the 1984 and 1987 seasons was on exploration and mapping of new sites and on the dominant environmental, settlement, and landuse conditions. By contrast, the 1989 season emphasized in-depth examination and documentation of aspects of the food system that, although discovered for the most part during the two prior seasons, were deemed worthy of more intensive investigation. Each of the five teams who comprised the 1989 survey had its own objectives, procedures, and staffs. These included the subsurface mapping team, the random square team, the environmental team, the farmstead documentation team, and the ethnoarchaeological team.

Subsurface Mapping

The objective of the subsurface mapping team, made up of three physicists whose work was mostly experimental, was to determine the feasibility of using ground-penetrating radar to locate subsurface archaeological features. More will be said about this in later reports.

Fig. 26. Persian/Hellenistic pottery, ed-Dreijat.

The Random Square Survey

In the 1989 season the random survey added 40 squares, each 200m² to the 60 that had been completed during the previous two seasons of fieldwork. The 100 squares are approximately 5 percent of the 1,969 such squares within a 5 km radius of Tell el-ʿUmeiri. Already this survey has heightened awareness of several important dynamics of settlement and landuse within the project area. The most significant finding, perhaps, is the discovery that pottery from the Roman and Byzantine periods and, to a lesser extent, the Iron Age is ubiquitous throughout the project area. That finding lends support to the impression, arrived at through excavations and survey at Tell Hesban, that during those three periods the food system reached peaks of intensity not equalled at any other time in history until now.

As in previous seasons, the random square survey contributed to the discovery of new archaeological sites. In the 1989 season a total of 25 new sites was recorded, including several with concentrations of agricultural features. The rapid pace at which modern construction is obliterating the archaeological record was especially obvious to the random square team, since a number of the squares selected for survey were found to be completely covered by new housing and streets. Also encountered almost daily by that team, because of its extensive coverage of the project area, were the number of new fences erected over the past two years. Typically, the fences enclose newly planted orchards or drip-irrigated vegetable fields. These are another sign of the rapid pace of sedentarization and food system intensification.

Fig. 27. Excavated rooms, ed-Dreijat.

Fig. 28. Wadi el-Bisharat.

The Environmental Survey

The environmental survey team specifically examined the landuse strategies that prevailed during the high intensity Roman and Byzantine periods. The site chosen for this in-depth examination, Wadi el-Bisharat, is approximately 2 km due west of Tell el-ᶜUmeiri (fig. 28). Adjacent to a large Roman/Byzantine town (Site 57) and a winery/church (Site 6), yet small enough to study as a complete system, it was deemed the best candidate for studying the interaction between people and environment during those high-intensity periods. Several features were mapped, photographed, and sherded by the team, including a series of various intact embankments that ran perpendicular to the fertile wadi bottom; sections of ancient terraces ascending from the wadi floor to the north and south; and diversion dams and embankments constructed along several smaller tributary wadis.

On the basis of pottery sherds found in and around those structures, a comparison could be made between present-day and Roman/Byzantine utilization of the wadi. The comparison suggests that when the ancient system was at its peak, the wadi and its surrounding slopes could have produced perhaps ten-fold its modern production in vegetable and fruit crops. The fact that terraces are again being constructed along the slopes of the wadi and repairs are beginning to be made to the embankments along its floor is confirmation that the prevailing momentum today is the direction of intensification and sedentarization.

The Farmstead Documentation Survey

The farmstead documentation team mapped, photographed, and drew features of complexes that were identified as ancient farmsteads. The sites selected for documentation represented good examples of large agricultural estates, smaller farmsteads, and agricultural camp sites (Younker 1991). While the first two types usually included clusters of buildings and agricultural installations, the third was typically represented only by a small watchtower. A total of 14 sites belonging to these categories, mostly occupied both in the Iron Age and Roman/Byzantine time, was documented. One site, Rujm Selim (excavated in 1987), was also occupied during late Hellenistic times.

The Ethnoarchaeological Survey

The primary objective of the ethnoarchaeological team was to ascertain how sedentarization and nomadization take place at the level of the tribal group and the local village. Interviews were carried out among three groups of local residents: Ajarmeh tribesmen who had occupied the region for several centuries, Christian families present since the last century, and Palestinian families, present only since the past three or four decades. In carrying out this work, the team was assisted by two artists and an interpreter. The artists helped to elicit information about how caves were utilized by the Ajarmeh earlier in the present century and before.

Perhaps the most important insights gained from the interviews have to do with advancing our understanding of why and how single households and groups of families could convert back and forth along the nomadic-sedentary continuum. Structural arrangements that have traditionally made such movement possible include: the practice of raising a mixture of crops and pasture animals; the maintenance of control over lands suitable to both pastoral or agricultural pursuits by means of tribal organization; the maintenance of a flexible tribal ideology that permits incorporation and exclusion of individuals and households as need arises; the practice of moving into tents for the warmer months of the agricultural season and into houses or caves during the cooler months; and the existence along various points on the nomad-sedentary continuum of households whose lifestyles could be followed by others.

By means of such arrangements individual households could adjust to shifting economic and political winds. For example, throughout much of the Ottoman period (ca. 1500–1900 C.E.) the majority of Ajarmeh households avoided settling in conspicuous stonehouses where they would be sitting prey for Ottoman tax authorities and hostile tribesmen. Instead they opted to live "inconspicuously" in seasonally occupied cave villages, most of them located on ancient tells. From there they could still carry on with their wheat growing in the winter months while being able to quickly disappear if the need should arise. Thus they were able to minimize their exposure to loss due to predation of various kinds while maintaining their mixed agro-pastoral food production strategy.

DISCUSSION

The evidence that has come to light from the three seasons of fieldwork at Tell el-ᶜUmeiri and vicinity has considerably advanced our understanding of the phenomena of sedentarization and nomadization on the Madaba Plains when measured against the results of the Heshbon Expedition. Although we have replicated the results of the Hesban project insofar as we have again documented the transient nature of permanent settlements in the region, by using an entirely separate set of data and improved methods of data collection, the ᶜUmeiri project has added much new insight and information:

First, we now have solid stratigraphic evidence for intensification and abatement in settlement activity throughout the Bronze Age (a period about which Tell Hesban was silent). At Tell el-ᶜUmeiri a site-wide settlement, perhaps a minor urban center, came into existence during EB III. After reaching its peak, however, settlement appears to have abated gradually. By EB IV, therefore, what was left of the town were mostly ruins. Then again, during the MB IIC, an unfortified village appears to have been established that gradually became transformed into a fortified settlement with massive ramparts. It too, however, appears to have been a transient settlement by the Late Bronze Age because all that has so far been detected is a single layer of Late Bronze Age debris.

Secondly, much more information has come to light about the Iron Age as well. Two major peaks in the intensity of settlement activity, one during Iron I and the other during late Iron II, are attested now by evidence from Tell Hesban, Tell el-ᶜUmeiri and Tell Jawa. That Tell el-ᶜUmeiri itself was some sort of administrative center during the Iron II period has already been noted. It may have been some sort of "agro-town," a settlement that was chiefly populated and serviced by farmers and agricultural laborers and included urban institutions, urban social strata, and urban functions. To this tell evidence may now be added the data yielded by the hinterland surveys which have brought to light numerous farmsteads and related agricultural installations from the Iron Age II. As was noted earlier, that evidence suggests that much of the population during the Iron II probably lived on small farmsteads throughout the hinterland (London 1989).

Thirdly, as a result of excavations in 1987 at Rujm Selim, and in 1989 at ed-Dreijat, important new information has now come to light about the Madaba Plains during the Hellenistic period. While large settlements such as ᶜUmeiri and Jawa were mostly ruins, people continued to live at Rujm Selim and ed-Dreijat. Thus, while the center of political gravity may well have been in the hands of more nomadic peoples during those centuries, the region was not without permanent settlements. It should be noted in this connection that there is evidence of people living in caves at Tell Hesban during the late Hellenistic and early Roman periods. Caves probably were widely used as shelters for people and animals during those centuries, much as they were during the Ottoman period.

Fourth, as a result of our intensive investigations in the Wadi el-Bisharat, much more information has been gained about how the large population that inhabited the ᶜUmeiri region during the Roman and Byzantine periods provided for their food needs. Their secret was intensive management of surface water to prevent soil erosion and to provide water for crops. Their strategies included building embankments at regular intervals in the main wadi, diversion dams in the larger tributary wadis, and bands of terraces on the slopes leading down to the wadis. In addition, large reservoirs and cisterns stored water for irrigation. Roads made of cobbled stones connected this and other productive wadis with surrounding cities, such as existed at ᶜUmeiri South, Site 57, Hesban (Esbus), ancient Amman (Philadelphia), and elsewhere throughout the Roman world. Thus food and other items were being imported and exported.

Fifth, while our excavations at Tell Hesban contributed significantly to our knowledge of Ayyubid-Mamluk times (ca. 1174–1516 C.E.), there were "gaps" in occupation at Tell Hesban that preceded and followed. Those gaps correspond to the Abbasid-Fatimid (ca. 750–1174 C.E.) and Ottoman (ca. 1517–1918 C.E.) periods, respectively. It is precisely because of what those gaps could teach us about how people lived in the region—when there supposedly were no or few permanent villages or towns—that the survey devoted considerable effort to finding out about them. As already noted, our efforts have focused on the residential uses of caves and fortified residential compounds (qusur) during Ottoman times. A significant discovery in this regard is ᶜUmeiri North, where a good example of an Ottoman seasonal cave village has been found.

Sixth, what we have learned through our ethnoarchaeological research about how sedentarization and nomadization actually happen on the household, tribal, and village levels also represents a significant step forward since the Hesban project. The results of this line of research have heightened considerably our confidence in our ability to test the sedentarization-nomadization hypothesis. It has also led to our becoming aware of many new questions that we would like to find ways to answer in future seasons.

FUTURE PLANS

Overall, the sedentarization-nomadization hypothesis goes a long way toward accounting for the rise and decline of permanent settlements in the Madaba Plains region. However, we still would like to address a large number of issues. Among them are the following.

• Although the excavations at Tell el-ᶜUmeiri have revealed considerable changes over time in the extent to which the site was settled, more work is needed to ascertain the precise nature of its successive settlements. Future excavations must be specifically designed to learn whether and when a site was a seasonal settlement occupied by seminomads, and when it was a village occupied year-round by subsistence farmers, a minor or major agro-town, or something completely different. The same questions need to be asked of Tell Jawa, ed-Dreijat, and Rujm Selim. Finding the answers will require in-depth analysis of the many types of artifacts and biofacts unearthed at all of those sites.

• Much more work is needed to determine what happened during such low intensity periods as the Late Bronze Age, the Early Hellenistic, Abbasid, Fatimid and Ottoman periods. An important line of research in this regard will be to excavate a number of caves to see if deposits from those periods exist. Excavation of more farmstead sites such as ed-Dreijat and Rujm Selim should also be valuable.

• One of the greatest challenges facing this project is to come to grips with the factors that generated the cyclic pattern of sedentarization and nomadization. While many of the clues to the problem are contained in the materials being excavated, a much needed additional line of inquiry involves textual sources. For example, information about influential persons, ethnic groups, and events in the Madaba Plains region can be gleaned from written sources of Egyptian, Mesopotamian, Jewish, Patristic, Arabic, and Turkish origins. While some work has already been done in this regard (cf. Geraty and Running 1989), a more concerted effort is needed.

• After two decades of archaeological involvement in the Madaba Plains, our curiosity about Tell Jalul has increased. The site is intriguing because of its size, particularly given its location. It is located about 7 km due east of Madaba, where it receives significantly less rainfall than either Hesban or ᶜUmeiri. It is also farther from major wadis or springs. Yet it is Jordan's second largest tell (after Tell Husn), covering an area of about 17 acres. Its surface has an abundance of sherds from the Bronze and Iron ages (Ibach 1988).

Excavations at Tell Jalul would not only deepen our understanding of the second and first millennia B.C.E., it would provide us with a third subregion within the Madaba Plains in which to examine the sedentarization-nomadization hypothesis. To Tell Hesban, which overlooks the western edge of the plain, and to Tell el-ᶜUmeiri, located in the hill country on the plain's northern edge, we would like to add Jalul, on the plains' eastern perimeter near the edge of the desert. These are three different ecological regions in which to test the sedentarization-nomadization hypothesis.

NOTES

[1] In 1989, the entire staff of the Madaba Plains Project numbered 130 persons, of whom about 80 worked on Tell el-ᶜUmeiri, about 40 worked in the hinterland, and the rest stayed behind at the project's headquarters in Amman, housed at the Amman Baptist School.

[2] In pursuing this interest Herr has been assisted by field supervisors J. Lawlor (Baptist Bible College), Field A; D. Clark (Walla Walla College), Field B; T. Harrison (University of Chicago), Field D; R. Low (University of Maryland), Field F and J. Fisher (Andrews University), Field G.

[3] Assisting Younker were field supervisors M. Daviau (Wilfrid Laurier University), Tell Jawa and L. Hubbard (Andrews University), ed-Dreijat.

[4] These teams were headed by G. Christopherson (University of Arizona) and D. Schnurrenberger (University of Maryland) respectively.

[5] This survey was headed by J. Battenfield (Grace Theological Seminary).

[6] D. Irvin (Durham, North Carolina) and Ø. LaBianca (Andrews University) headed this survey. J. Cole (Walla Walla College) led the subsurface mapping team, assisted by G. Sandness and B. Matson.

[7] In the object registration lab, E. Platt recorded all objects, including those related to the quest for food and long-distance trade networks and social stratification represented at Tell el-ᶜUmeiri, Tell Jawa, and ed-Dreijat. Also important are the contributions of the ecology lab, in which lithic samples, soil samples, plant and animal remains produced by the excavations were processed. Through preliminary analysis of these remains in the field, information directly relevant to ascertaining environmental, landuse, and dietary conditions in the past has been made available.

[8] See subsequent discussion on the identity of Tell Jawa in R. W. Younker and P. M. Daviau, "Is Mefaᵓat to be Found at Tell Jawa (South)?" in IEJ 43/1, pp. 23–28, 1993; Z. Kallai, "A Note on 'Is Mefaᵓat to be Found at Tell Jawa (South)?" by R. W. Younker and P. M. Daviau, IEJ 43/2, pp. 249–251, 1993. While Kallai raises some questions concerning the dating of the reference to Moab's occupation of Mephaath in Jeremiah 48, most biblical references seem to locate Mephaath on the *Meshor*, or the plain. However, Tell Jawa is clearly on the highlands south of Amman and not on the plain. This still raises in our minds the question whether Jawa can be Mephaath.

BIBLIOGRAPHY

Alt, A.
1932 *Palästina Jahrbuch des Deutschen Evange-lischen Instituts für Altertumswissenschaft des Heiligen Landes zu Jerusalem*, Vol. 29, p. 26.

Clark, D. R.
1991 Field B: The Western Defense System. Pp. 53–73 in *Madaba Plains Project 2: The 1987 Season at Tell el-ᶜUmeiri and Vicinity and Subsequent Studies*, eds. L. G. Herr, L. T. Geraty, Ø. S. LaBianca, R. W. Younker. Berrien Springs, MI: Andrews University/Institute of Archaeology.

Geraty, L. T.
1985 The Andrews University Madaba Plains Project: A Preliminary Report on the First Season at Tell el-ᶜUmeiri (June 18 to August 8, 1984). *Andrews University Seminary Studies* 23: 85–110.

Geraty, L. T.; Herr, L. G.; and LaBianca, Ø. S.
1987 The Madaba Plains Project: A Preliminary Report on the First Season at Tell el-ᶜUmeiri and Vicinity. *Annual of the Department of Antiquities of Jordan* 31: 187–99.

1988 The Joint Madaba Plains Project: A Preliminary Report on the Second Season at Tell el-ᶜUmeiri and Vicinity (June 18 to August 6, 1987). *Andrews University Seminary Studies* 26: 217–52.

Geraty, L. T.; et al.
1986 Madaba Plains Project: A Preliminary Report of the 1984 Season at Tell el-ᶜUmeiri and Vicinity. *Bulletin of the American Schools of Oriental Research Supplement* 24: 117–44.

1990 Madaba Plains Project: A Preliminary Report of the 1987 Season at Tell el-ᶜUmeiri and Vicinity. *Bulletin of the American Schools of Oriental Research Supplement* 26: 59–88.

Geraty, L. T., and LaBianca, Ø. S.
1985 The Local Environment and Human Food-Procuring Strategies in Jordan: The Case of

Tell Hesban and its Surrounding Region. Pp. 323–30 in *Studies in the History and Archaeology of Jordan II*, ed. Adnan Hadidi. Avon: Bath.

Geraty, L. T., and Running, L. G.
1989 *Historical Foundations. Hesban 3*. Berrien Springs, MI: Andrews University Press/Institute of Archaeology.

Glubb, J. B.
1938 The Economic Situation of the Trans-Jordan Tribes. *Journal of the Royal Central Asian Society* 25: 448–59.

Helms, S.
1989 An EB IV Pottery Repertoire at Amman, Jordan. *Bulletin of the American Schools of Oriental Research* 273: 17–36.

Ibach, R. D., Jr.
1988 *Archaeological Survey of the Hesban Region. Hesban 5*. Berrien Springs, MI: Andrews University/Institute of Archaeology.

LaBianca, Ø. S.
1990 *Sedentarization and Nomadization: Food Systems at Hesban and Vicinity in Transjordan. Hesban 1*. Berrien Springs, MI: Andrews University Press/Institute of Archaeology.

London, G.
1989 A Comparison of Two Contemporaneous Lifestyles of the Late Second Millennium B.C. *Bulletin of the American Schools of Oriental Research* 273: 37–55.

Younker, R. W.
1991 Architectural Remains from the Hinterland Survey. Pp. 335–42 in *Madaba Plains Project 2: The 1987 Season at Tell el-ᶜUmeiri and Vicinity and Subsequent Studies*, eds. L. G. Herr, L. T. Geraty, Ø. S. LaBianca, R. W. Younker. Berrien Springs, MI: Andrews University/Institute of Archaeology.

The Combined Caesarea Expeditions: The Excavation of Caesarea's Byzantine City Wall, 1989

Clayton Miles Lehmann
Department of History
University of South Dakota
Vermillion, SD 57069

This article summarizes previous research on the Byzantine city wall of Caesarea Maritima (Israel), and reports on the excavation of the wall by the Combined Caesarea Expeditions in 1989. The wall, ca. 2 m wide, consists of two faces of large ashlars bonded by a rubble and concrete core, founded on a bedding of field stones in the sand. The inner face carried a decorative plaster finish. Archaeological and historical evidence indicate a date in the fifth century for the founding of the wall. The wall presumably went out of use after the Muslim conquest of ca. 640. Several burials within the wall belong to the Byzantine or early medieval period.

The Combined Caesarea Expeditions (CCE) renewed exploration of the Byzantine city wall at Caesarea Maritima in 1989. A team of nine volunteers supported CCE's professional staff in the excavation of Area V/4 from 28 May to 23 June. Because we plan no further excavation of the area, this article constitutes the final report.

STATE OF THE PROBLEM

Caesarea's Byzantine city wall runs in a broad semicircle enclosing some 110–120 hectares. A. Frova, of the Missione Archeologica Italiana, excavated several segments of the wall in its northeastern arc (our Area V) in 1959.[1] The wall had long been known, but it was considered Roman (either Herodian or third century) until Frova established its Byzantine date (Levine 1975: 9). Additional work since 1959 has contributed further information about the wall, but many questions remain regarding its chronology, construction, and purpose. Recent agricultural activity, moreover, has destroyed or buried much that was visible on land and by aerial photography at mid-century. It therefore seems advisable to review the state of the problem in addition to describing the work of CCE on the wall in 1989.

The Italian excavators cleared a square tower 7.5 m wide and projecting 2.5 m from the wall (map reference 140800/212525; figs. 1–3). CCE cleaned the area around the tower to reexamine the structures. The builders of the tower made it integral with the wall and of the same type of construction (described below). An opening on the inner face of the wall gives access to the inside of the tower, and the interior walls retain traces of plaster. Inside the city wall Frova found a second wall abutting but not bonded to the main wall, with an opening to permit access to the tower. The secondary wall, ca. 1.6 m wide, consists of mortared ashlars founded on sand at a level much higher than the curtain wall and tower. Excavation weakened part of the secondary wall, which has now toppled away from the tower. Frova identified the secondary wall as a reinforcing wall and found that it continued in other trenches to the northeast (Frova 1959: 18). It does not continue southeast into Area V/4.

A circular installation of poor construction occupies the northern angle between the tower and the curtain wall. A single wythe of small, irregularly dressed stones, laid in earth with some brick, survives up to three courses high; remarkably, the builders actually carved out part of the angle of the wall and tower to secure a circular plan (fig. 4). An

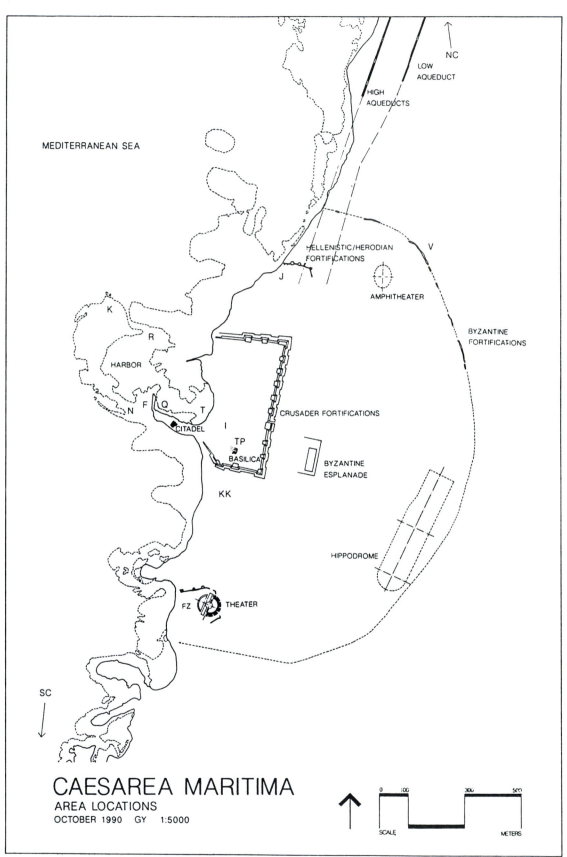

Fig. 1. Map of Combined Caesarea Expeditions' excavation areas, 1989–90. CCE drawing; repr. with permission from Holum, et al. 1992: fig. 1.

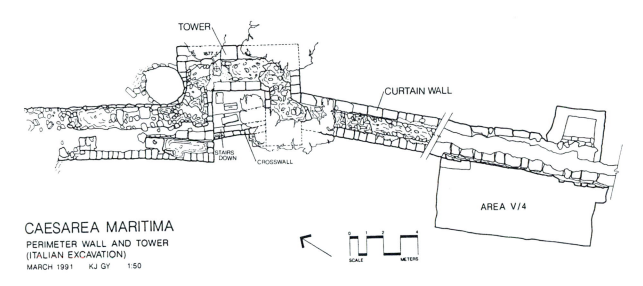

CAESAREA MARITIMA
PERIMETER WALL AND TOWER
(ITALIAN EXCAVATION)
MARCH 1991   KJ GY   1:50

Fig. 2. Plan of tower and city wall at Area V/4. This plan does not plot a fragmentary and unstable extension of the secondary wall adjacent to the curtain wall just south of the tower (but visible in fig. 3). CCE drawing.

opening ca. 0.3 m wide furnished access to the inside. Variously identified as a granary or a round tower (Frova 1959: 18; Ringel 1975: 75), the structure probably functioned as a lime kiln. About 2 m in front of the tower lies a pavement of large stones; its full extent remains unknown. Frova found no evidence for an earlier city wall.

Inside the wall just south of the tower, Frova uncovered a sarcophagus within a stone-lined pit and inexplicable clusters of Byzantine amphorae with their tops sawed off, some placed upright and others upended. The sarcophagus held some of the bones of two persons, and just to the south lay two human skulls.

The Italian expedition recovered pottery, a lamp, and a corroded coin, all Byzantine, from near the wall and the tower. Merely on the basis of levels and without stratigraphic evidence, Frova dated the retaining wall to the end of the Byzantine period, long after the construction of the main wall earlier in the Byzantine period and after the placement of the sarcophagus and amphorae.

The Survey of Western Palestine plotted a circuit wall complete except at the southwestern end near the theater (Conder and Kitchener 1882). Fifty years later, dune sand had obliterated any trace of the wall south of the hippodrome. Beginning in the middle of the 20th century, Reifenberg (1950–51: 20–32, pl. 16), Levine (1975: Map B), and Ringel (1975: 41, fig. 3; 75) studied the city wall of Caesarea with the aid of aerial photographs and identified a second square tower some 150 or 200 m to the northwest

and a third ca. 450–500 m to the southeast. They also located a monumental gateway at the eastern extremity of the city, where the modern road intersects the conjectured line of the wall.[2] I can detect no evidence for those features in aerial photographs that I have seen, and none appears on the surface today. Only the segment from Area V/4 northwest to the coast appears on the surface, along with a short section that the sea has exposed where the wall reaches the coast on the south.

The Caesarea Ancient Harbor Exploration Project tried to locate Caesarea's eastern gate in 1988; three trenches exposed only large demolished segments of the wall pushed to the edges of modern fields.[3] Those vermiform rows of rubble probably account for much of the supposed line of the wall that appears in plans of the city.

In the winter of 1985–1986 Peleg and Reich conducted a rescue excavation on behalf of the Israel Antiquities Authority below a tile factory inside Kibbutz Sdot Yam on Caesarea's southern side, ca. 300 m east of the shore (map reference 14015/21125; Peleg and Reich 1992). They discovered a segment ca. 22 m long of the city wall, pierced by two of the openings of a presumed triple gate (Stratum II) built over a massive Herodian or early Roman building (Stratum I). The gate went through several phases. The excavators dated the wall's original construction to after the mid fourth century because they found a coin of Constantius II (324–361) sealed below a floor from the time of the construction of the gate (Peleg and Reich 1992: 141,

Fig. 3. View northwest over city wall, with tower (to right) and secondary or reinforcing wall (to left). Photograph by Mark Little.

Fig. 4. Kiln built into city wall, view from the west. Photograph by Mark Little.

142, 165). The ceramic material from this phase points to a date in the fifth century for the wall's construction (Peleg and Reich 1992: 148–53; the ceramic evidence includes fifth century but no clearly sixth century types like those attested in the following phases of Stratum II). No earlier than the sixth century the gate received a "balcony" (Peleg and Reich 1992: 165). Numismatic evidence indicates that no later than the early seventh century, and probably as an emergency defense against the Persian threat in 614 or the Muslim attack about 640, the people of Caesarea blocked the gates.[4] Finally, Humphrey, leading a team for the Joint Expedition to Caesarea Maritima in 1974, explored a short segment of the inner face of the city wall behind the hippodrome (Humphrey 1975: 9–15, figs. 7–9; Riley 1975: 25). A thick coat of plaster carried incisions that indicate the joints of the stones beneath and hatch marks that mimic rusticated masonry. Humphrey found a large quantity of broken pottery

dumped against the inside of the city wall in two distinct layers. The lower layer dated predominantly to the fourth century, the upper layer to the sixth. Humphrey suggested that the lower layer of pottery stabilized the city wall and tentatively dated its construction to the fourth to early fifth century. He also thought that the upper layer of pottery put the wall out of use at the end of the Byzantine period or early in the Muslim period. But a few fragments of Islamic fine ware no earlier than the eighth or ninth century, found in the lower layer, make the entire dump post-Byzantine, of no value as evidence for the date of the wall's construction (Humphrey 1975: 6, 9, 15; for the pottery of the lower layer [Levels H1B and H2B], including three fragments of Islamic fine wear, see Riley 1975: 25–26, 40–43).

An inscription found near the conjectured site of the eastern gate furnishes the only possible documentary evidence for the date of the Byzantine wall. The text commemorates the construction of a βοῦρ-

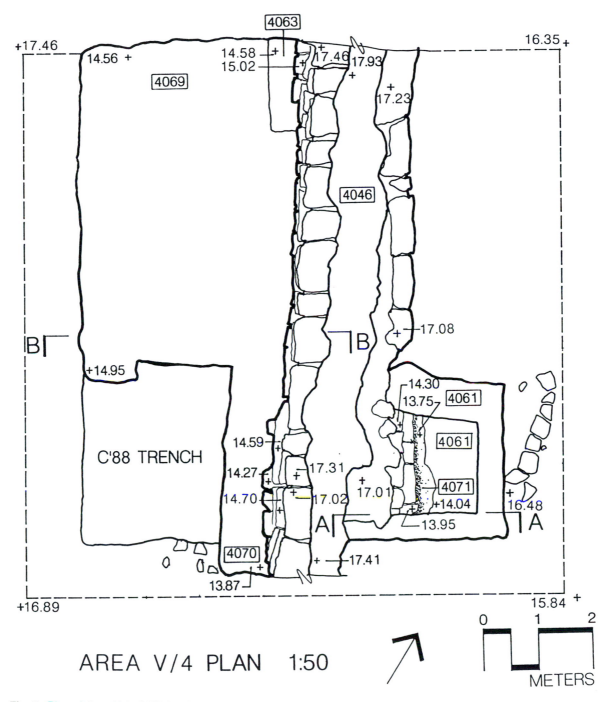

Fig. 5. Plan of Area V/4. CCE drawing.

γος (< πύργος, "tower") in the time of the otherwise unknown consular governor Flavius Procopius Constantius Severus Alexander (Lifshitz 1961; no. 16; first published by Schwabe 1950). That luminary held office sometime between the end of the fourth century and 536, because before and after that period governors of the province held proconsular rank (Mayerson 1988). Alexander's tower might have graced his capital's city wall, either in its original construction or in a remodeling.

Fig. 6. View looking north over Area V/4, soon after the start of excavation. The trench dug in 1988 lies in the foreground. Photograph by Mark Little.

Fig. 7. Western face of wall in Area V/4. Photograph by Mark Little.

THE EXCAVATIONS OF 1989

In the 1989 season, CCE volunteers excavated Area V/4, laid athwart the city wall ca. 25–30 m southeast of the tower that the Italian Mission had cleared (figs. 2, 5, 6). We hoped that the excavation, which continued an effort begun the previous summer, would secure additional information on the structure and chronology of the wall.

The trench exposed nearly 10 m of the inner face and nearly 2 m of the outer face of the wall to its entire extant height. A core of concrete and rubble bonds together two faces of large ashlars of the local calcareous sandstone, called *kurkar*, finished

with the drove, and now badly eroded and discolored where exposed or in contact with topsoil.

On its western face the wall survives eight courses above the footings, to a height of ca. 2.8 m (fig. 7). The footings consist of large fieldstones and some small ashlars in one or two courses, with chinks and earth but no mortar, on a bedding of sand and cobblestones. Following the inclination of the terrain, the footings slope and step from 15.02 m above mean sea level at the northern side of the trench down to 14.50 m at the southern side. The footings support two courses of ashlars of irregular size with no evidence of mortar. Above them lie courses of much larger blocks of varying

Fig. 8. Eastern face of wall in Area V/4. Photograph by Mark Little.

dimensions, usually greater in length than in height except in the fourth and fifth courses toward the southern part of the square. The masons laid the upper courses dry, with chinks, then pointed them with a fine, white plaster that has a porous and chalky composition, with very fine sand. Below the fourth course they pointed some joints with a gray, soft mortar with many charcoal inclusions. Finally, the masons pargeted the face of the wall with the fine plaster and cut rectilinear incisions over the joints of the ashlars beneath. Portions of the parget survive near the southern end of the trench. It recalls the decorative treatment of the walls of the Byzantine intramural fortress around Caesarea's theater and the wall in Humphrey's trench behind the hippodrome, but in Area V/4 the plaster lacks the rusticating hatch marks (Humphrey 1975: fig. 8).

The eastern face of the wall survives to a lower elevation than the western, e.g., 17.20 m as opposed to 17.45 m (fig. 8). The eastern face eroded more than the other because wind-blown sand, which drifted high against the western face and protected it from the weather, accumulated more slowly and to a lesser depth against the eastern face. Furthermore, the acidic topsoil that constitutes much of the fill on the eastern side exacerbated the outleeching of minerals from the limestone and its subsequent erosion. A probe against this face of the wall exposed its footings at 13.75 m (fig. 9). Stepped in two courses, the footings rest on a bedding of cobblestones and sand. Six to seven courses of ashlars survive above the footings, mortared together and not merely pointed with the fine white plaster described above. The ashlars approximate those on the west in size. No traces of plaster survive on this badly

Fig. 9. Probe at southern end of eastern face of wall in Area V/4, with southern balk. Photograph by Mark Little.

eroded face, but the soil next to it contains chunks of plaster that might once have adhered to the face of the wall.

A core of fieldstones, gravel, pottery sherds, and concrete binds together the two faces of the wall. The concrete has a light gray color and contains

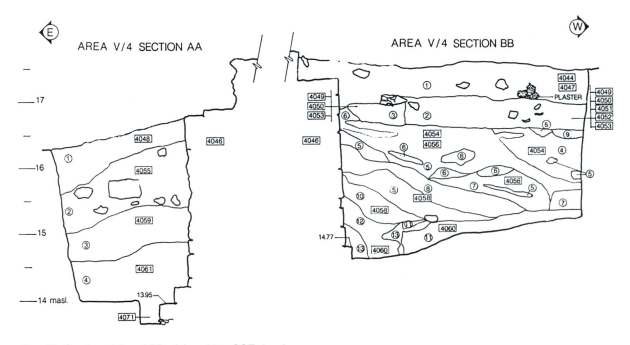

Fig. 10. Sections AA and BB of Area V/4. CCE drawing.

pebbles, sand, and pieces of charcoal. The core measures ca. 0.70 m wide, the wall a little over 2 m, and the footings nearly 2.5 m.

Grade at the time of founding probably lay just over 15 m above mean sea level, sloping down to the east. The hill on which the tower and this segment of the wall stand rises higher than any other point in the city except for its extreme eastern edge. The designers placed the wall for optimum strategic value near the top and on the outer or eastern side of the crest. Excavation on the western side of the wall showed that its foundation lies in a trench cut in sand. Section BB (fig. 10) gives a possible profile of the trench, although later burials along the inside of the wall disrupted the stratification; the burials (described below) and movement of the dunes (evident from the layers blown up against the wall[5]) introduced material of the Early Roman to Crusader periods. A probe along the northern balk proved that the footings of the wall rest on nothing but sand (Magness, this issue, pp. 133–45, presents a ceramic analysis of the pottery from this and the other loci mentioned here). Just outside the excavated area to the east a line of stones, perhaps the exposed part of a retaining wall, runs parallel to the wall. Between the wall and the line of stones we found a layer of trash (Locus 4061)—mostly broken pottery and glass—over 1.25 m thick (figs. 9,

10), dating from the sixth to the first half of the seventh century. Locus 4071, next to the footings, contained much less pottery and a more silty, almost claylike, darker soil. Unfortunately, the pottery from Locus 4071, which should have provided the most secure date for the wall's construction, includes no diagnostic sherds; nor does the pottery from the last four or five baskets of Locus 4061, just above Locus 4071. Because the evidence from Peleg and Reich's excavation of the southern gate indicates a date in the fifth century, and because for historical reasons discussed below the seventh century seems far too late for the wall's construction, we prefer to understand Locus 4061 as a post-construction dump rather than backfill from the time of construction (see Magness, this issue, pp. 133–45). The dump, within the possible retaining wall on the eastern edge of Area V/4, might have buttressed the wall just above the level of the footings and strengthened the city's fortifications on the eve of the Persian or Muslim siege. According with this conjecture, we may understand that the secondary wall inside the tower and the blockage of the southern gate fulfill the same role.

Palestine's Byzantine emperors tried repeatedly to enhance the province's urban amenities and defenses. According to Procopius of Gaza, for example, the emperor Anastasius's efforts to restore the prosperity of Palestine after a Samaritan uprising in 484 included the improvement of Caesarea's harbor (Procop. Gaz. *Pan.* 19 [Chauvot 1986]). Procopius of Caesarea reports that Justinian embellished many cities and monasteries in Palestine by building or restoring churches, walls, wells or cisterns, and charitable institutions, and that he responded to Samaritan violence by restoring Christian holy places and building a wall around the Christian church on the Samaritans' Mt. Garizim (Proc. *Aed.* 5.6–29; cf. Holum 1982). Caesarea's wall seems far less formidable than the walls of other imperial cities that faced threats from large, organized, and well-equipped armies—as, for example, Antioch on the highway to Persia did—or from the huge plundering expeditions of Germans and Huns—for example, Thessalonica and Constantinople itself. Nor does Caesarea's wall measure up to the standards set in the anonymous *De Strategica* of the sixth century, which recommends a thickness of some 3 m for a city's fortifications. But Caesarea's wall does compare favorably to border forts on the Arabian frontier, like the late fourth century fort at ᵓEn Boqeq in southern Palestine on the western shore of the Dead Sea, which has walls 1.75–2.0 m thick. Such fortifications, like Caesarea's, defended settled communities from bandits and raiders and did not require the thick walls and deep foundations necessary to resist artillery, ramming, and mining.[6] Caesarea received its circuit wall in the context of Samaritan violence and banditry, imperial generosity, and the remarkable growth of the city in the Byzantine period (Holum, et al., 1988: 155–200). The pottery from the southern gate suggests a date in the fifth century, and if the *bourgos* inscription mentioned above does indeed record an addition to the new or existing wall, it furnishes a terminus ante quem of 536 for the foundation of the Byzantine city wall.

The 1989 season uncovered no evidence for abandonment of the wall. The complex layering created by wind and sand cannot determine chronology (Rim 1950–51: 44). Presumably the wall went out of use after the Muslim conquest about 640, when large tracts of intramural Caesarea reverted to fields, cemeteries, and sand dunes as the population plummeted (Holum, et al. 1988: 203–5).

We found no evidence of occupation in Area V/4 previous to the construction of the wall. After the Byzantine period the area became a cemetery. We recovered an unrestorable fragment of a Byzantine tombstone (V4073.I1) and five or six burials, poor graves with no associated artifacts, interred at indeterminate dates after the wall's founding. Pottery intrusive from the soft sand around the bodies dated early Roman to Byzantine. Two or three burials lay right up against the footings of the wall, the others within two or three meters of the wall and at a slightly higher elevation, in irregular orientation and body position. Our physical anthropologists identified burial no. 1 (Locus 4066) possibly as an adolescent female; no. 2 (Locus 4065) as an adult female; no. 3 (Locus 4064) as an adult male; no. 5 (Locus 4068) as an adult; and no. 6 (Locus 4070) as an adult male (no. 4 [Locus 4067], very disturbed, may belong with no. 6).[7] Numerous Byzantine tombstones come from outside the wall in this region of the city, and the sarcophagus that the Italian excavators found just inside the tower north of Area V/4 dated to the Byzantine period. We lack sufficient evidence to identify the burials in Area V/4 as either Byzantine or Muslim.

From the dunes we extracted one unreadable coin and numerous fragments of such materials as glass, animal bones, shells, and tesserae of too little interest to describe here.

ACKNOWLEDGMENTS

I thank K. G. Holum and A. Raban, directors of CCE, for permission to publish the results of the excavation of Area V/4 in 1989. A brief report appears in Holum, et al. (1992: 95–97). I am grateful for financial support from CCE and the University of South Dakota General Research Fund, and for assistance in preparing this report from J. Magness and K. G. Holum. Finally, I thank the volunteers who excavated Area V/4 under my direction: K. Sheeler (Assistant Supervisor), R. Avigad, B. Dickinson, B. Grier, M. Horton, B. Hurley, M. Spiegel, D. Wessel, and A. Yellin.

NOTES

[1]Frova published a short preliminary report of this work (Frova 1959: 14–21). A promised further report has not appeared. Except for brief notices, only one other report describes the Italian excavation of the Byzantine city wall (Frova 1961–1962: 649–50). The area enclosed by the wall depends on the hypothetically restored course of the southern and southeastern part of the circuit; thus planimetric measurement of Conder and Kitchener (1988: 14) yields ca. 109 ha (ca. 269 acres), Holum, et al. (1992: fig. 1) ca. 123 ha (ca. 304 acres).

[2]All three scholars publish maps showing these features without any explanation. The map of the Survey of Western Palestine shows only one feature in the wall, a rectilinear deviation much too large for a tower (Conder and Kitchener 1882: 14).

[3]Raban, et al. 1990: 252–54. The plan published in this report (fig. 5, p. 253) does not accurately give the relation between the tower and Area V/4.

[4]Peleg and Reich (1992) associated the blockage of the gate with the Muslim attack only, but there seems no reason to exclude the period of Persian threat as well, even though in the event the Persians took the city without resistance. Holum 1992: 73–75 reviews the literary evidence for these conquests.

[5]The layers visible in the balk, particularly on the windward or western side, graduate subtly in color and texture according to the action of wind and sand. Unless we found the distinction between given layers remarkable we did not differentiate them by locus during excavation.

[6]Lawrence 1983: 175–76 (Arabian frontier); 188–200, esp. pp. 189–90 (De Strategica). See De Strategica 12 for the recommended thickness of a wall (Dennis 1985). For banditry in Palestine see Isaac 1990: 69–97. Foss and Winfield restrict their survey almost exclusively to Thrace and western Asia Minor, but Caesarea's Byzantine wall can accommodate their most general conclusions about Late Antique walls (Foss and Winfield 1986: 129–31, 161–62).

[7]P. Smith and her students from The Hebrew University Hadassah Medical School supervised the excavation of human remains and have undertaken their analysis, which will appear in a separate general study of burials excavated by CCE.

REFERENCES

Chauvot, A., ed.
1986   *Procope de Gaza, Priscien de Césarée: Panégyriques de l'Empereur Anastase Ier.* Antiquitas 35. Bonn: Habelt.

Conder, C. R., and Kitchener, H. H.
1882   *The Survey of Western Palestine.* Vol. 2: *Samaria.* London: Palestine Exploration Fund.

Dennis, G. T., ed.
1985   *Three Byzantine Military Treatises.* Corpus Fontium Historiae Byzantinae 25. Washington: Dumbarton Oaks.

Foss, C., and Winfield, D.
1986   *Byzantine Fortifications: An Introduction.* Pretoria: University of South Africa.

Frova, A.
1959   *Caesarea Maritima (Israele): Rapporto preliminare della prima campagna di scavo della Missione Archeologica Italiana.* Milan: Istituto Lombardo, Accademia di Scienze e Lettere.
1961–   Gli scavi della Missione Archeologica Itali-
1962   ana a Cesarea (Israele). *Annuario della Scuola Archeologica di Atene* 39–40, n.s. 23–24: 649–57.

Holum, K. G.
1982   Caesarea and the Samaritans. Pp. 65–73 in *City, Town, and Countryside in the Early Byzantine Era*, ed. R. L. Hohlfelder. East Eu-

ropean Monographs 120, Byzantine Series 1. Boulder, CO: East European Monographs.
1992   Archaeological Evidence for the Fall of Byzantine Caesarea. *Bulletin of the American Schools of Oriental Research* 286: 73–85.

Holum, K. G., Hohlfelder, R. L., Bull, R. J., and Raban, A.
1988   *King Herod's Dream: Caesarea on the Sea.* New York: W. W. Norton.

Holum, K. G., Raban, A., Lehmann, C. M., le Berrurier, Diane, Ziek, R., and Sachs, S. F.
1992   Preliminary Report on the 1989–1990 Seasons. Pp. 79–111 in *Caesarea Papers: Straton's Tower, Herod's Harbour, and Roman and Byzantine Caesarea*, ed. R. L. Vann. *Journal of Roman Archaeology*, Suppl. Ser. 5. Ann Arbor: Journal of Roman Archaeology.

Humphrey, J. H.
1975   A Summary of the 1974 Excavations in the Caesarea Hippodrome. *Bulletin of the American Schools of Oriental Research* 218: 1–24.

Isaac, B.
1992   *The Limits of Empire: The Roman Army in the East.* Rev. ed. Oxford: Clarendon.

Lawrence, A. W.
1983   A Skeletal History of Byzantine Fortification. *Annual of the British School at Athens* 78: 171–227.

Levine, L. I.
1975   *Roman Caesarea: An Archaeological-Topo-graphical Study*. Qedem: Monographs of The Institute of Archaeology, The Hebrew University of Jerusalem 2. Jerusalem: Hebrew University.

Lifshitz, B.
1961   Inscriptions grecques de Césarée en Palestine. *Revue Biblique* 68: 115–26.

Magness, J.
1994   The Byzantine Pottery from Area V/4 at Caesarea Maritima. *Annual of the American Schools of Oriental Research* 52: 133–45.

Mayerson, P.
1988   Justinian's Novel 103 and the Reorganization of Palestine. *Bulletin of the American Schools of Oriental Research* 269: 65–71.

Peleg, M., and Reich, R.
1992   Excavation of a Segment of the Byzantine City Wall of Caesarea. *ʾAtiqot* 21: 137–70.

Raban, A., Hohlfelder, R. L., Holum, K. G., Stieglitz, R. R., and Vann, R. L.
1990   Caesarea and Its Harbours: A Preliminary Report on the 1988 Season. *Israel Exploration Journal* 40: 241–56.

Reifenberg, A.
1950–   Caesarea: A Study in the Decline of a Town.
1951   *Israel Exploration Journal* 1: 20–32.

Riley, J. A.
1975   The Pottery from the First Session of Excavation in the Caesarea Hippodrome. *Bulletin of the American Schools of Oriental Research* 218: 25–63.

Rim, M.
1950–   Sand and Soil in the Coastal Plain of Israel,
1951   *Israel Exploration Journal* 1: 33–48.

Ringel, J.
1975   *Césarée de Palestine: Étude historique et archéologique*. Association des Publications près les Universités de Strasbourg. Paris: Editions Ophrys.

Schwabe, M.
1950   The Bourgos Inscription from Caesarea Palaestina. *The J. N. Epstein Jubilee Volume. Tarbiz* 20: 273–83. (Hebrew)

The Pottery from Area V/4 at Caesarea

JODI MAGNESS

Departments of Classics and Art History
Tufts University
Medford, MA 02155

In 1989, the Combined Caesarea Expeditions (CCE) excavated a sounding (Area V/4) along a section of the Byzantine city wall. Next to the foundations of the wall, a thick layer of pottery was discovered which represents a homogeneous dump of sixth to mid-seventh century date.[1] It appears to have been deposited to strengthen the line of fortifications on the eve of the Muslim siege. The evidence from Area V/4 and from other excavations around Caesarea suggests that the Byzantine city wall was constructed in the fifth century. Modifications and changes were carried out during the sixth century, and efforts to strengthen it were made in preparation for the Muslim siege. Following the fall of the city to the Muslims, the wall went out of use and some formerly settled areas within it were abandoned.

INTRODUCTION

The corpus of pottery presented here derives from a single locus (4061) in Area V/4 at Caesarea. Area V/4 represents a sounding along a section of the Byzantine city wall on the northeastern side of the site (Lehmann, this issue, pp. 121–31). The excavation in this area was carried out in the hope that it would shed light on the date and constructional history of the wall. Unfortunately, the stratification on the inner (western) face of the wall had been disturbed by later burials and by the movement of the sand dunes. Therefore no ceramic material recovered from inside the line of the wall could be associated with its foundation. Furthermore, no diagnostic sherds were recovered from locus 4071, which represents the foundation trench on the outer (eastern) side of the wall. However, a 1.25 to 1.50 meter thick layer of pottery and debris (locus 4061) was discovered above Locus 4071, between the outer face of the wall and a line of stones further east. Its position just above the foundation level suggests that it was intended to stabilize and buttress the wall against the sand dunes. The presence of many large fragments, none of which could be restored as whole vessels, indicates that the dump represents material brought in from elsewhere and deposited at this spot. That impression is reinforced by the freshness of the breaks and the generally unworn appearance of the

sherds. The ceramic types represented in this dump constitute a remarkably homogeneous assemblage. Although no coins were recovered, most, if not all, of the ceramic types can be dated from the sixth to the first half of the seventh century. These include pieces that do not antedate the beginning of the seventh century (see fig. 1:3).

Another pottery dump was discovered by Humphrey in his excavations against the upper part of the inner face of the Byzantine city wall by the hippodrome (Humphrey 1975; Riley 1975). He distinguished two layers, an upper one (H2A and H1A) and a lower one (H1B and H2B). Almost all of the pottery from the upper layer consisted of fifth to sixth century ceramic types, while the lower layer contained mostly third to fourth century material. On the basis of the ceramic evidence, Humphrey dated the dump to the end of the Byzantine period or beginning of the Islamic period, suggesting that it rendered the wall ineffective as a line of defense (Humphrey 1975: 15). However, three later sherds found deep in the lower layer, including two Islamic pieces that do not appear to antedate the eighth to ninth centuries, suggest that the dump was deposited long after the end of the Byzantine period.[2] Humphrey's dump therefore differs from the one in Area V/4, which contained no Islamic material and was located next to the base of the wall.

During the 1989 season at Caesarea Maritima, I worked alone as the staff's ceramic specialist.[3] I attempted to develop a system for counting and weighing all the ceramic material recovered, to provide a basis for quantifying types and wares. In light of my experiences that summer, and with the addition of other ceramic specialists to the staff, the system was later refined. For example, due to my inexperience, and the overwhelming amount of material recovered from the field, I did not quantify amphoras according to type during the 1989 season. Despite its relatively general nature, however, the information recorded is worth presenting. First, it is necessary to describe the system used for processing the material. Individual "bucket" numbers were assigned in the field to each physical bucket of pottery. A locus could include one or more such buckets, depending on the amount of pottery recovered. The sherds from each bucket were washed and laid out in boxes to dry. Each bucket of sherds was weighed as a whole, then sorted on a table into groups according to wares. These groups consisted of various fine wares ("black-glazed," "terra sigillata," "Late Roman Red Wares," "glazed"), cooking wares, amphoras and storage jars, other coarse wares, miscellaneous wares (such as oil lamps and terracottas), and roof tiles. Because in most cases even body sherds could be assigned without difficulty to one of those categories, they were included in the count. After the sorting was completed, the sherds were counted and weighed according to the ware group. A rough estimate of the chronological range of the bucket was recorded, and diagnostic sherds were selected to be saved.

The data recovered from that process provide a clear indication of the proportions of the various wares represented in Locus 4061. They confirm the impression that storage jars and amphoras predominate in the Byzantine corpus at Caesarea (Riley 1975; Adan-Bayewitz 1986; Blakely 1987). Of the 137.9 kg of pottery recovered from Locus 4061, 130 kg (94%) consisted of storage jar and amphora fragments. In terms of numbers, this represents 1246 (90%) of the 1381 sherds recovered from the locus. The remainder consisted of cooking wares (103 sherds [7.4%] that weighed 5.05 kg [3.6%]); Late Roman Red Wares (13 sherds [0.94%] that weighed 0.25 kg [0.18%]); other coarse wares and miscellaneous wares (10 sherds [0.72%]), including two oil lamp fragments, which weighed 0.2 kg [0.14%]; and roof tiles (9 fragments [0.65%] that weighed 2.4 kg [1.7%]). The only non-Byzantine sherd from the locus, a fragment of terra sigillata, is not included in this count. Its presence high-lights the remarkable homogeneity of this assemblage in terms of date.

THE POTTERY

A sample of the ceramic types found in Locus 4061 is illustrated in figs. 1–3. A description of each piece and a list of parallels appears in the catalogue below. The types are arranged and discussed in the following order: bowls, casseroles, cooking pots, amphoras, storage jars, lids, jugs, flasks, and juglets. Bowls and cooking wares are illustrated in fig. 1. A sample of the imported Late Roman Red Wares present in the assemblage appears in fig. 1:1–3. In the absence of numismatic evidence, these pieces provide the basic chronological framework. They include examples of African Red Slip Ware (fig. 1:1) and Late Roman "C" or Phocean Red Slip Ware (fig. 1:2, 3), all dated from the late sixth to the mid-seventh century. The rim of a bowl of African Red Slip Ware Form 94, Type A, dated from the late fifth to the early sixth century, is not illustrated here (but see Hayes 1972: 146–48, 158–66, 343–46). The cooking wares include various types of casseroles (fig. 1:4–9) and cooking pots (fig. 1:10–17). It is difficult to establish an internal typology for casseroles, which are common during the late Roman and Byzantine periods in Palestine. However, the casserole with wishbone handle (fig. 1:9) is a characteristic Judaean type of the sixth and seventh centuries. The type is rare at Caesarea, which seems to mark the northernmost point of its distribution (Magness 1992a: 133 and fig. 65.9; 1993: Casseroles Form 2). The parallels for the casserole in fig. 1:8, which is made of a coarse, gritty, dark red-brown ware, also point to a Judaean origin (see Birger 1981: pl. 12:12; Aharoni 1962: fig. 17:14). The one in fig. 1:4 is distinguished by its unusual folded rim and relatively smooth, hard-fired, orange-brown ware. Although no parallels were found, I suspect that it represents a western Galilean or Egyptian type.

The cooking pots include types found throughout the country during the late Roman and Byzantine periods. The parallels for those in fig. 1:10–11, which have a straight, vertical neck and thickened rim, point to a Judaean origin. On the other hand, the cooking pots in fig. 1:12–14, with their short, everted rims, are clearly a characteristic northern Palestinian type. Most of the parallels for both types are dated to the sixth and seventh centuries. No parallels were found for the cooking pot in fig. 1:15, which is made of a thin, smooth, hard-fired, orange-brown ware covered with a dark grey slip. The swollen rims and angular, flattened strap handles of the cooking pots in fig. 1:16–17 identify them as a Cypriot type and highlight the cosmopolitan character of Caesarea's corpus (Magness 1992a: 133). That the pieces from Area V/4 represent imports rather than local imitations is suggested by the quality of their ware, which matches that of the Cypriot products.[4] The presence of imported cooking pots at Caesarea provides striking evidence for the site's commercial contacts with other parts of the eastern Mediterranean during the Byzantine period.

Imported amphoras are illustrated in fig. 2:1–7. Figure 2:1–2 presents two variants of the most common type of amphora found at Yassi Ada, both of which have published parallels from Caesarea (Magness 1992a: 150; Adan-Bayewitz 1986: fig. 2:4 [Amphora Type 5] and fig. 2:6 [Amphora Type 6]). Peacock and Williams (1986: 187) have suggested an early fifth to mid-seventh century range for amphoras of this type, which may come from Cyprus or Asia Minor. No close parallels were found for the amphoras in fig. 2:3, 5, but the one in fig. 2:4 represents a type attested at Jalame, for which a Palestinian origin and fourth century date are suggested (Johnson 1988: fig. 7–49:721 [Amphora Form 1]). The amphora base in fig. 2:6 has possible North African parallels dating to the fifth and sixth centuries (Keay 1984: fig. 130:3 [Type LVII]). The base in fig. 2:7 might also represent a type of amphora of Tunisian origin and fourth to mid-fifth century date (Keay 1984: 209 no. 8 [Type XXV Variant 1]). It was recut for apparent use as a stopper, a phenomenon attested elsewhere at Caesarea (Adan-Bayewitz 1986: fig. 3:18; Siegelmann 1974: fig. 2:6; Peleg and Reich 1992: fig. 13:2).

Storage jars or amphoras of Palestinian origin are illustrated in figs. 2:8–15 and 3:1–8. Three types are represented: southern Palestinian "bag-shaped" storage jars (fig. 2:8–15), "Gaza" storage jars or amphoras (fig. 3:1–6), and northern Palestinian white-painted storage jars (fig. 3:7–8). Although those jars were not counted and weighed according to type, this sample does reflect the relative proportions in which they were represented. Our evidence accords with Riley's findings that the southern Palestinian bag-shaped storage jars predominate at Caesarea, while Gaza storage jars are the second most common type, and the northern Palestinian white-painted storage jars are a distant third (Riley 1975; for a more recent discussion of these storage jar types and references see Magness 1992a: 130–32). The southern Palestinian bag-shaped jar rims from Locus 4061 (fig. 2:8–13) appear to represent Riley's Type 1B, which has a lower, simpler rim than his Type 1A. The pieces in fig. 2:9, 11, 13, though belonging to the southern Palestinian type in form and ware, have concretions adhering to the outside of the rim, neck, and shoulder like those found on Gaza storage jars (Magness 1992a: 131). The bodies of the southern Palestinian bag-shaped storage jars are sometimes painted with white or yellow designs, like the fragments in fig. 2:14–15. The Gaza storage jars (fig. 3:1–6) have relatively simple rims and pointed bases, features that may indicate a sixth to seventh century date. Both the rim and the body sherd in fig. 3:7–8 have the metallic, dark-surfaced ware and white-painted decoration characteristic of the northern Palestinian storage jars. The prominent ridge marking the transition from the shoulder to the body on the piece in fig. 3:8 is another characteristic feature of the type.

Lid handles are illustrated in fig. 3:9–12. The lid with a loop handle (fig. 3:9) is made of a thin, smooth, hard-fired, pink-red ware. The parallels suggest that this is a northern Palestinian or Egyptian type, as examples are also found at Kellia in Egypt (Magness 1992a: figs. 61:12; 66:13, with references). On the other hand, the pierced knob handle of thin, brittle, gritty, dark red cooking ware in fig. 3:10 represents a Judaean type that seems to be most common in contexts of the sixth to seventh century. The only parallels found for the rather unusual knob handle of a lid or stopper in fig. 3:11 come from Caesarea and Kellia (Adan-Bayewitz 1986: fig. 3:14; Egloff 1977: pl. 55:7 [Type 350]). It is made of a thick, dark orange cooking ware covered on the interior with a purple-red slip. A number of parallels from sites around Palestine were found for the pierced knob handle in fig. 3:12, which is made of a thick, gritty, dark orange-brown ware covered with an orange-brown slip. Its identification as the handle of a lid rather than as the base of a jug is indicated by the hole pierced through its center before firing. It probably belongs to a type of bell-shaped lid common at Jalame, where it is dated to the third and fourth centuries (Johnson 1988: figs. 7–55; 7–56).

The jug base illustrated in fig. 3:13 is distinguished by the pare-burnishing (or knife-paring) that covers its exterior, even on the base. Parallels for this piece come from beneath the pavement of Justinian's "Nea" Church in Jerusalem and from the foundations of the octagonal church on top of Caesarea's "temple platform," which appears to be of the same date (Magness 1992a: 132; fig. 59:17). These pieces seem related to "Fine Byzantine Ware," which appeared around the middle of the sixth century. The knob base of a jar or jug is illustrated in fig. 3:14, while spouts belonging to jugs made of cooking ware appear in fig. 3:15–16. The molded fragment in fig. 3:17, made of thick, pink-brown ware, is part of a ceramic mirror plaque (Baly 1962: pl. 26:10–11; Rahmani 1964; Israeli 1974; Avni and Dahari 1990: 310; fig. 7). It is flat and circular, and is decorated in relief with concentric circles surrounding a circular ridge.

Two flasks with asymmetrical bodies are illustrated in fig. 3:18–19. They differ in form and ware from contemporary flasks published from Khirbet Karak, Kursi, and Pella (Delougaz and Haines 1960: pl. 57:5–6; Tzaferis 1983: fig. 8:20; Walmsley 1982: CN2028; Smith and Day 1989: pl. 54:12). The form and ware of the rims in fig. 3:20–21, and the parallels found, suggest that they belong to Fine Byzantine Ware juglets, which are often decorated with incised gashes on the shoulder (Magness 1993: "Fine Byzantine Ware Jars, Jugs, and Juglets"; Magness 1992b: 160; fig. 9:10). The same might be true of the stump-based juglet in fig. 3:22, which represents a common type of the late Roman and Byzantine periods in Palestine (Magness 1992b: 153).

CONCLUSION

The ceramic material from Locus 4061 is rich in terms of the diversity of types represented, and homogeneous in terms of its date. Most if not all of the types can be assigned to the sixth to mid-seventh century, while none has to be later than that. What is the relation of this dump to the Byzantine city wall? Prior to the final analysis of the pottery, we believed the dump to be contemporary with the construction of the wall. However, since that would mean dating the establishment of the wall to the first half of the seventh century or later, we prefer to understand it as a post-constructional dump. Its position just above the foundation level suggests that it was intended to stabilize and buttress the wall against the sand dunes. The pottery may have been deposited to strengthen the line of fortifications on the eve of the Muslim siege.

Recently published evidence from a rescue excavation at Caesarea helps to refine the chronology of the Byzantine wall. The excavation was carried out in 1985–1986 on behalf of the Israel Antiquities Authority, under the direction of M. Peleg and R. Reich (1992). The excavation site was located along the southern segment of the Byzantine city wall, approximately 300 m east of the shoreline. Two main building phases, Strata I and II, and four subphases of Stratum II, were distinguished. The earlier Stratum I contains the remains of a massive substructure belonging to a Herodian or early Roman building. In Stratum II, the building was incorporated into the line of the Byzantine city wall. The excavators have suggested that the remains of two gateways found in this line of wall originally formed part of a triple gate. A coin of Constantius II sealed beneath the earliest surface associated with the wall and gates provides a mid-fourth century *terminus post quem* (Peleg and Reich 1992: 165). However, the ceramic material from that subphase (Stratum II/1) points to a fifth century date for the wall's construction. That date is indicated by the presence of a Yassi Ada amphora and by the absence of clearly sixth century types such as those attested in the following subphases.[5] After their establishment in the fifth century, the wall and gateway underwent a series of modifications, which are clearly visible in the architectural and stratigraphic record. In the last subphase of Stratum II (II/4), architectural elements such as pieces of columns and statuary were brought in to reinforce the wall and block the gates (Peleg and Reich 1992: 144–45). The latest types associated with that subphase parallel those from Locus 4061 in Area V/4,[6] suggesting that this activity was carried out at the time of the Muslim siege. This chronology is supported by the numismatic evidence, since the latest coins recovered by Peleg and Reich do not postdate the late sixth to early seventh century (Peleg and Reich 1992: 163–64).

The Byzantine city wall seems to have fallen out of use after the Muslim conquest, when large intramural areas reverted to fields, cemeteries, and sand dunes. This is evident in many of the excavated areas around Caesarea. In Area V/4, five or six poor post-Byzantine burials were discovered adjacent to the wall (see Lehmann, this issue, p. 121–31). In Humphrey's excavation, the pottery dump seems to have rendered the fortifications ineffective (Humphrey 1975: 9–15). Peleg and Reich have noted that after the Muslim conquest their area was abandoned and covered with sand dunes (Peleg and Reich 1992: 145). That also appears to be true in the area just south of the Crusader city (the Combined Caesarea Expedition's Area KK), where rich Byzantine levels are covered with relatively sterile sand dunes with no evidence of post-Byzantine occupation (see Holum et al. 1992: 100).

All available evidence points to a date in the fifth century for the construction of Caesarea's Byzantine city wall. Modifications and changes were carried out during the sixth century, and efforts to strengthen it were made on the eve of the Muslim siege. Following the fall of the city to the Muslims, the Byzantine city wall went out of use and some formerly settled areas within it were abandoned.

NOTES

[1] All dates in this article refer to the Common Era.

[2] See Humphrey 1975: 15; Riley 1975: 25, 37. Unfortunately, the pieces are not illustrated; the descriptions seem to refer to "Mefjer" or buff ware and glazed pottery.

[3] In subsequent seasons, A. M. Berlin and A. Boaz joined the staff as the Hellenistic to Early Roman and Islamic to Crusader ceramic specialists, respectively.

[4] The ware of the Cypriot pots is described in Williams 1989: 68, as follows:

The clay is basically orange red (5YR6/8) to a dirty red (somewhat like 10R5/8) but tends to be fired grey or dark reddish grey on the exterior (10R4/1 or 4/2). It is very hard fired and often will emit an almost metallic ping when flicked with a fingernail. It is also very gritty to the touch and is full of white lime particles (often up to 0.001 in diameter). There are occasional dark grits and sometimes silver mica appears.

[5] For the Yassi Ada amphora from Stratum II/1 see Peleg and Reich 1992: fig. 15:15; for the dating of this type see Peacock and Williams 1986: 187. The bowl in Peleg and Reich 1992: fig. 14:1, which comes from a Stratum II/3 context, represents a relatively late variant of Late Roman "C" or Phocean Red Slip Ware Form 3 (Hayes 1972: 329–34).

[6] See, for example, Peleg and Reich 1992: fig. 13:7 (Late Roman "C" or Phocean Red Slip Ware Form 10) and fig. 13:9 (a Cypriot cooking pot).

BIBLIOGRAPHY

Adan-Bayewitz, D.
1986   The Pottery from the Late Byzantine Building (Stratum 4) and its Implications. Pp. 90–129 in *Excavations at Caesarea Maritima 1975, 1976, 1979—Final Report. Qedem* 21, eds. L. I. Levine and E. Netzer. Jerusalem: Hebrew University.

Aharoni, Y.
1962   *Excavations at Ramat Rahel*. Rome: Centro di Studi Semitici.

Avni, G., and Dahari, U.
1990   Christian Burial Caves from the Byzantine Period at Luzit. Pp. 301–14 in *Christian Archaeology in the Holy Land, New Discoveries*, eds. L. Di Segni and E. Alliata. Jerusalem: Studium Biblicum Franciscanum.

Baly, T. J. C.
1962   Pottery. Pp. 270–303 in *Excavations at Nessana I*, ed. H. D. Colt. London: British School of Archaeology in Jerusalem.

Bar-Natan, R., and Adato, M.
1986   Pottery. Pp. 160–75 in *Excavations at Caesarea Maritima 1975, 1976, 1979—Final Report. Qedem* 21, eds. L. I. Levine and E. Netzer. Jerusalem: Hebrew University.

Bass, G. F.
1982   The Pottery. Pp. 155–88 in *Yassi Ada*, vol. 1, eds. F. G. Bass and F. H. van Doorninck, Jr. College Station, TX: Texas A & M.

Ben-Tor, A.
1963   Excavations at Horvat ᶜUsa. ᶜAtiqot 3, Hebrew series: 1–24.

Birger, R.
1981   Pottery and Miscellaneous Finds of the Byzantine Period. Pp. 75–77 in *Greater Herodium. Qedem* 21, ed. E. Netzer. Jerusalem: Hebrew University.

Blakely, J. A.
1987   *Caesarea Maritima, The Pottery and Dating of Vault 1: Horreum, Mithraeum, and Later Uses*. New York: Mellen.

Catling, H. W.
1972   An Early Byzantine Pottery Factory at Dhiorios in Cyprus. *Levant* 4: 1–82.

Catling, H. W., and Dikigoropoulos, A. I.
1970   The Kornos Cave: An Early Byzantine Site in Cyprus. *Levant* 2: 37–62.

Crowfoot, J. W., and Fitzgerald, G. M.
1929   *Excavations in the Tyropoeon Valley, Jerusalem, 1927. Annual of the Palestine Exploration Fund* 5. London: Palestine Exploration Fund.

Delougaz, P., and Haines, R.
1960   *A Byzantine Church at Khirbet al-Karak.* Chicago: University of Chicago.

Dothan, M., and Freedman, D. N.
1967   *Ashdod I (1962).* ᶜAtiqot 7, English series. Jerusalem: Israel Department of Antiquities and Museums.

Egloff, M.
1977   *Kellia, La poterie copte.* Geneva: Libraire de l'université.

Feig, N.
1985   Pottery, Glass, and Coins from Magen. *Bulletin of the American Schools of Oriental Research* 258: 33–40.

Fitzgerald, G. M.
1931   *Beth-shan Excavations 1921–1923: The Arab and Byzantine Levels.* Philadelphia: University of Pennsylvania.

Fritz, V.
1983   Das nestorianische Kloster (Area D); Die Keramik. Pp. 153–58 in *Ergebnisse der Ausgrabungen auf der Ḫirbet el-Mšāš (Tēl Māśōś), 1972–1975,* eds. V. Fritz and A. Kempinski. Wiesbaden: Harrassowitz.

Hamilton, R. W.
1944   Excavations Against the North Wall of Jerusalem, 1937–8. *Quarterly of the Department of Antiquities in Palestine* 10: 1–54.

Hayes, J. W.
1972   *Late Roman Pottery.* London: British School at Rome.

Holum, K. G.; Raban, A.; Lehmann, C. M.; le Berrurier, D.; Ziek, R.; and Sachs, S. F.
1992   Preliminary Report on the 1989–1990 Seasons. Pp. 79–111 in *Caesarea Papers, Strato's Tower, Herod's Harbour, and Roman and Byzantine Caesarea. Journal of Roman Archaeology supplementary series* no. 5, ed. R. L. Vann. Ann Arbor, MI: University of Michigan.

Humphrey, J. H.
1975   A Summary of the 1974 Excavations in the Caesarea Hippodrome. *Bulletin of the American Schools of Oriental Research* 218: 1–24.

Israeli, Y.
1974   A Mirror Plaque from the Clark Collection, Jerusalem. *Israel Exploration Journal* 24: 228–31.

Johnson, B. L.
1988   The Pottery. Pp. 137–226 in *Excavations at Jalame, Site of a Glass Factory in Late Roman Palestine,* ed. G. D. Weinberg. Columbia, MO: University of Missouri.

Keay, S. J.
1984   *Late Roman Amphorae in the Western Mediterranean, A Typology and Economic Study: The Catalan Evidence.* BAR International Series, 196. Oxford: British Archaeological Reports.

Kelso, J. L., and Baramki, D. C.
1949–   Excavations at New Testament Jericho and
1951   Khirbet en-Nitla. *Annual of the American Schools of Oriental Research* 29–30. New Haven, CT: American Schools of Oriental Research.

Landgraf, J.
1980   La céramique Byzantine. Pp. 51–99 in *Tell Keisan (1971–1976), une cité phénicienne en Galilée,* eds. J. Briend and J.-B. Humbert. Paris: Gabalda.

Lehmann, C. M.
1994   The Combined Caesarea Expeditions: The Excavation of Caesarea's Byzantine City Wall, 1989. Pp. 121–31 in *Annual of the American Schools of Oriental Research* 52. Baltimore, MD: Scholars Press.

Loffreda, S.
1974   *Cafarnao II, La ceramica.* Jerusalem: Studium Biblicum Franciscanum.

Magness, J.
1987   The Pottery from the 1980 Excavations at Maᶜon (Nirim). Pp. 216–24 in *Eretz-Israel* 19. Jerusalem: Israel Exploration Society.

1992a   Late Roman and Byzantine Pottery, Preliminary Report, 1990. Pp. 129–53 in *Caesarea Papers, Strato's Tower, Herod's Harbour, and Roman and Byzantine Caesarea. Journal of Roman Archaeology supplementary series* no. 5, ed. R. L. Vann. Ann Arbor, MI: University of Michigan.

1992b   The Late Roman and Byzantine Pottery from Areas H and K. Pp. 149–85 in *Excavations at the City of David 1978–1985 Directed by Yigal Shiloh, Vol. 3 Qedem* 33, eds. A. DeGroot and D. T. Ariel. Jerusalem: Hebrew University.

1993   *Jerusalem Ceramic Chronology, circa 200–800 C.E.* Sheffield: Academic.

Meyers, E. M.; Kraabel, A. T.; and Strange, J. F.
1976   Ancient Synagogue Excavations at Khirbet Shemaᶜ, Upper Galilee, Israel 1970–72. *Annual of the American Schools of Oriental Research* 42. Durham, NC: American Schools of Oriental Research.

Meyers, E. M.; Strange, J. F.; and Meyers, C. L.
1981   *Excavations at Ancient Meiron, Upper Galilee, Israel 1971–72, 1974–75, 1977.* Cambridge, MA: American Schools of Oriental Research.

Nevo, Y. D.
1985   *Sde Boker and the Central Negev, 7th–8th Century A.D.* Paper presented to the Third International Colloquium: From Jahiliyya to Islam, The Hebrew University of Jerusalem, June 30 to July 6, 1985. Jerusalem: Israel Publication Services.

Peacock, D. P. S., and Williams, D. F.
1986 *Amphorae and the Roman Economy, An Introductory Guide*. New York: Longman.

Peleg, M., and Reich, R.
1992 Excavations of a Segment of the Byzantine City Wall of Caesarea Maritima. ʿAtiqot 21: 137–70.

Prausnitz, M. W.
1967 *Excavations at Shavei Zion*. Rome: Centro per le Antichita e la Storia dell'Arte del Vicino Oriente.

Rahmani, L. Y.
1964 Mirror-Plaques from a Fifth-Century A.D. Tomb. *Israel Exploration Journal* 14: 50–60.

Riley, J. A.
1975 The Pottery from the First Session of Excavation in the Caesarea Hippodrome. *Bulletin of the American Schools of Oriental Research* 218: 25–63.
1981 Coarse Pottery. Pp. 91–449 in *Excavations at Sidi Khrebish Benghazi (Berenice)*, Vol. 2, ed. J. A. Lloyd. Tripoli: Department of Antiquities.

Robinson, H. S.
1959 *The Athenian Agora*. Vol. 5, *Pottery of the Roman Period*. Princeton, NJ: American School of Classical Studies at Athens.

Rosenthal-Heginbottom, R.
1988 The Pottery. Pp. 78–96 in *Excavations at Rehovot-in-the-Negev*. Vol. 1, *The North Church*. Qedem 25, ed. Y. Tsafrir. Jerusalem: Hebrew University.

Saller, S. J.
1957 *Excavations at Bethany*. Jerusalem: Studium Biblicum Franciscanum.

Sauer, J. A.
1973 *Heshbon Pottery 1971*. Berrien Springs, MI: Andrews University.

Sellers, O. R., and Baramki, D. C.
1953 A Roman-Byzantine Burial Cave in Northern Palestine. *Bulletin of the American Schools of Oriental Research Supplementary Studies* 15–16. New Haven, CT: American Schools of Oriental Research.

Schaefer, J.
1979 *The Ecology of Empires: An Archaeological Approach to the Byzantine Communities of the Negev Desert*. Unpublished Doctoral dissertation, University of Arizona.

Siegelmann, A.
1974 A Mosaic Floor at Caesarea Maritima. *Israel Exploration Journal* 24: 216–21.

Smith, R. H.
1973 *Pella of the Decapolis*. London: Clowes.

Smith, R. H., and Day, L. P.
1989 *Pella of the Decapolis*, Vol. 2. Wooster: College of Wooster.

Tubb, J. N.
1986 The Pottery from a Byzantine Well Near Tell Fara. *Palestine Exploration Quarterly*: 51–65.

Tushingham, A. D.
1972 The Excavations at Dibon (Dhiban) in Moab, The Third Campaign, 1952–53. *Annual of the American Schools of Oriental Research* 40. Cambridge, MA: American Schools of Oriental Research.
1985 *Excavations in Jerusalem 1961–1967, Vol. 1*. Toronto: Royal Ontario Museum.

Tzaferis, V.
1983 *The Excavations of Kursi-Gergesa*. ʿAtiqot 16, English series. Jerusalem: Israel Department of Antiquities and Museums.

Walmsley, A.
1982 The Umayyad Pottery and its Antecedents. Pp. 143–57 in *Pella in Jordan 1: An Interim Report on the Joint University of Sydney and the College of Wooster Excavations at Pella 1979–1981*, eds. A. McNicoll, R. H. Smith, and B. Hennessy. Canberra: Australian National Gallery.

Wightman, G. J.
1989 *The Damascus Gate, Jerusalem: Excavations by C.-M. Bennett and J. B. Hennessy at the Damascus Gate, Jerusalem, 1964–66*. BAR International Series, 519. Oxford: British Archaeological Reports.

Williams, C.
1989 *Anemurium, The Roman and Early Byzantine Pottery*. Canada: Pontifical Institute of Mediaeval Studies.

Zemer, A.
1978 *Storage Jars in Ancient Sea Trade*. Haifa: National Maritime Museum Foundation.

CATALOGUE OF POTTERY

All vessels are wheel-made unless otherwise indicated. Where it is known, the basket number is indicated in parentheses after the designation of the type of vessel; some pieces were returned from restoration without their basket number.

FIGURE 1

Fig. 1:1 Bowl

Rim fragment; est. dia. 32 cm. Thick, dark orange-red ware (2.5YR5/8), with orange-red slip and burnish (10R5/8) on interior and exterior. Many tiny to small white and dark grits.

See Hayes 1972: African Red Slip Ware Form 104, Type B, dated ca. 570–600, with late variants to 625+.

Fig. 1:2 Bowl

Rim and wall fragment; est. dia. 21 cm. Orange-red ware (10R5/8), with orange-red slip and burnish (10R6/8) on interior and exterior, fired purple-red (7.5R5/4) on rim. Some tiny to medium white grits.

See Hayes 1972: Late Roman "C" (Phocean Red Slip) Ware Form 10, Type A, dated late sixth to early seventh century.

Fig. 1:3 Bowl (B0078.06)

Rim fragment; est. dia. 24 cm. Hard-fired, dark orange-brown ware (2.5YR5/8), with dark red slip (10R4/6) over interior, dripped over exterior; fired brown (5YR5/3) on rim. Many tiny to small white grits.

See Hayes 1972: Late Roman "C" (Phocean Red Slip) Ware Form 10, Type C, dated early to mid-seventh century.

Fig. 1:4 Casserole (B0084.04+0086.01)

Rim and upper wall fragment; est. dia. 16 cm. Relatively smooth, hard-fired, orange-brown ware (2.5YR5/6). Some tiny to large white grits. Much of the surface is blackened.

Fig. 1:5 Casserole

Rim and horizontal handle; est. dia. 25 cm. Thin, gritty, dark red-brown ware (2.5YR4/8). Signs of burning on handle. Many tiny to small white grits.

Fig 1:6 Casserole (B0104.018)

Rim and horizontal handle; est. dia. 28 cm. Gritty, red-brown ware (10R5/6). Many tiny dark and some tiny to large white grits. Light ribbing on exterior; blackened on exterior.

Fig. 1:7 Casserole (B0104.07)

Rim and horizontal handle; est. dia. 30 cm. Thick, gritty, dark orange-brown ware (2.5YR5/6). Many tiny dark and some tiny to large white grits.

Fig. 1:8 Casserole (B0104.014)

Almost whole profile from rim to base with horizontal handle; est. dia. 25 cm. Gritty, coarse, dark red-brown ware (2.5YR5/6). Many tiny to very large white grits. Blackened on bottom of exterior.

Parallels from Aharoni 1962: fig. 17:14, dated fifth to seventh century; Birger 1981: pl. 12:12, dated first to sixth century.

Fig. 1:9 Casserole (B0084.05)

Complete wishbone handle with attached rim; est. dia. 26 cm. Gritty, hard-fired, thin, brittle, red-brown ware (2.5YR4/8). Many tiny to small white and dark grits; micaceous. Light, narrow ribbing on exterior.

Parallels from Hamilton 1944: fig. 7:7, dated sixth to seventh century; Adan-Bayewitz 1986: fig. 3:22, dated ca. 630–660; Bar-Natan and Adato 1986: fig. 1:19, dated fifth to seventh century.

Fig. 1:10 Cooking pot

Rim and shoulder fragment with handle; est. dia. 10 cm. Gritty, red-brown ware (2.5YR5/6). Many tiny and some medium to large white grits.

Parallels from Kelso and Baramki 1949–1951: Type 11A (N33), dated Byzantine; Riley 1975: 36 no. 33, dated Byzantine; Birger 1981: pl. 12:10, dated ca. fifth to sixth century; Feig 1985: fig. 2:14, dated Byzantine; Tushingham 1985: fig. 32:1, dated late sixth to early seventh century.

Fig. 1:11 Cooking pot (B0100.02)

Rim and neck fragment; est. dia. 11 cm. Thin, hard-fired, relatively smooth, red-brown ware (2.5YR5/6), with a purple-red slip (10R5/6) on exterior, fired dark purple (2.5YR4/2) on rim. Many tiny to medium white and dark grits.

Parallels from Saller 1957: fig. 46:3933, dated late Roman to early Arab: Baly 1962: Shape 134:11, dated Hellenistic to Byzantine, if not later.

Fig. 1:12 Cooking pot (B0100.03)

Rim fragment with handle; est. dia. 11 cm. Gritty, hard-fired, orange-brown ware (5YR5/8). Many tiny to small white and dark grits.

Parallels from Fitzgerald 1931: pl. 31:10, dated fifth to early seventh century; Johnson 1988: fig. 7–39:593, dated fourth century; Smith and Day 1989: pl. 51:8, dated sixth to early seventh century.

Fig. 1:13 Cooking pot (B0079.07)

Rim fragment with upper part of handle; est. dia. 11 cm. Gritty, hard-fired, pink-orange ware (2.5YR6/6), with a purple slip (10R4/3) on exterior. Many tiny to large white, dark, and red grits; micaceous.

Parallels from Sellers and Baramki 1953: fig. 32:3, dated Roman to Byzantine; Delougaz and Haines 1960: pl. 53:39, dated Byzantine; Ben-Tor 1963: fig. 11:6, dated Byzantine; Meyers, Kraabel, and Strange 1976: pl. 7.18:29, dated fourth to fifth century; Meyers, Strange, and Meyers 1981: pl. 8.14:14, dated late fourth century; Walmsley 1982: CN1083, dated late sixth to early seventh century; similar to Smith and Day 1989: pl. 51:13, dated sixth to early seventh century.

Fig. 1:14 Cooking pot (B0076.06)

Rim fragment: est. dia. 14 cm. Gritty, brown ware (5YR5/6). Many tiny and a few small to medium white grits. Signs of burning on exterior and on rim.

Parallels from Tushingham 1972: fig. 9:18, dated probably third quarter of sixth century; Smith 1973: pl. 43:1252, dated Byzantine; Riley 1975: 36 no. 31b, dated Byzantine; Walmsley 1982: CN512, dated late sixth to early seventh century; Tushingham 1985: fig. 30:15, dated late sixth to early seventh century; Johnson 1988: fig. 7-35:534, dated fourth century; Smith and Day 1989: pl. 53:7, dated sixth to early seventh century.

Fig.1:15 Cooking pot (B0104.011)

Rim fragment; est. dia. 17 cm. Thin, hard-fired, relatively smooth, orange-brown ware (2.5YR5/8), with a dark grey slip (10YR5/1) on exterior. Some tiny white grits.

Fig. 1:16 Cooking pot (B0097.07)

Rim and shoulder fragment with one handle; est. dia. 12 cm. Thin, hard-fired, relatively smooth, red-brown ware (2.5YR5/8), with a dark grey slip (10YR4/1) on exterior. Many tiny to large white and red grits; slightly micaceous.

Parallels from Catling and Dikigoropoulos 1970: fig. 7:7, dated ca. 650–725; Catling 1972: fig. 7:P96, dated seventh to eighth century; Egloff 1977: pl. 52:3 (Type 140), dated seventh century; Bass 1982: fig. 8-15:P53, dated first half of seventh century; Adan-Bayewitz 1986: fig. 4:3, 4, dated ca. 630–660; Williams 1989: fig. 37:406–8, dated sixth to seventh century.

Fig. 1:17 Cooking pot (B0104.010)

Rim fragment; est. dia. 16 cm. Thin, hard-fired, relatively smooth, dark orange-brown ware (2.5YR5/6), with a dark grey slip (5YR4/1) on exterior. Some tiny to large white grits.

For parallels see fig. 1:16

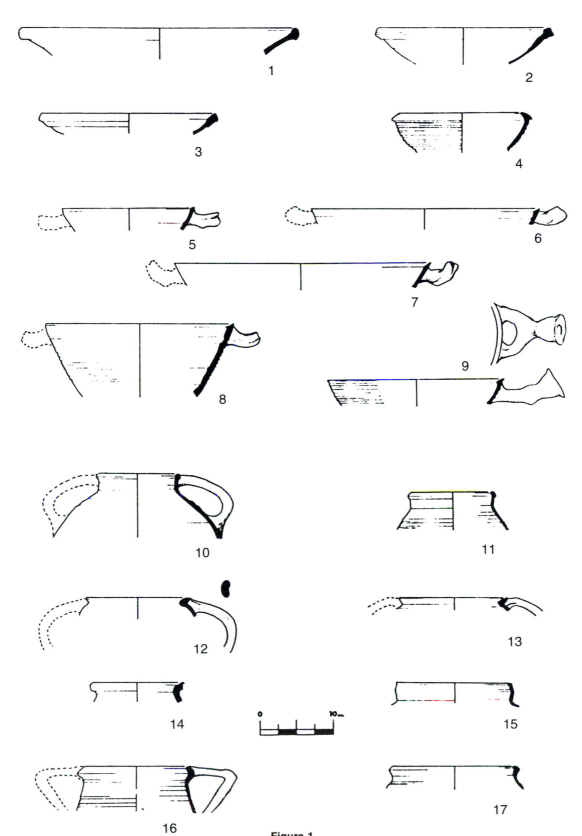

Figure 1.

FIGURE 2

Fig. 2:1 Amphora (B0094.020)

Rim and neck fragment; est. dia. 8 cm. Orange-brown ware (2.5YR6/6). Some tiny to small dark and some tiny to very large white grits; micaceous.

Parallels from Robinson 1959: pl. 32:M333, dated early sixth century; Prausnitz 1967: fig. 11:6, 7, 11, dated third to fourth century; Keay 1984: fig. 117:10 (Type LIIIA), dated late fifth to seventh century; Bass 1982: 155–57 (Type 1), dated first half of seventh century; Fritz 1983: pl. 169:10, dated seventh to early eighth century; Adan-Bayewitz 1986: fig. 2:4 (Amphora Type 5), dated ca. 630–660; Rosenthal-Heginbottom 1988: pl. 3:127, dated sixth to seventh century.

Fig. 2:2 Amphora

Rim and neck fragment with handle attachment; est. dia. 7 cm. Light brown ware (7.5YR6/4). Many tiny to large white and some dark grits; slightly micaceous.

Parallels from Riley 1981: fig. 91:346, 347 (Late Roman Amphora 1a), dated late fourth to seventh century; Bass 1982: 155–57 (Type 1), dated first half of seventh century; Keay 1984: Type LIII, dated late fifth to early seventh century; Adan-Bayewitz 1986: fig. 2:6 (Amphora Type 6), dated ca. 630–660; Tubb 1986: fig. 2:4 (Amphora Type 2), dated sixth to seventh century.

Fig. 2:3 Amphora

Rim and neck fragment; est. dia. 9 cm. Thick, hard-fired, light yellow-brown ware (10YR8/6). Many tiny to small dark grits.

Fig. 2:4 Amphora

Rim and neck fragment; est. dia. 6.5 cm. Light orange-brown ware (7.5YR7/6). Many tiny dark and some medium to large white and dark grits.

Parallel from Johnson 1988: fig. 7-49:721 (Amphora Form 1), dated fourth century.

Fig. 2:5 Amphora (B0094.015)

Rim and neck fragment with upper part of handle; est. dia. 11 cm. Orange-brown ware (5YR6/6). Many tiny to very large white and dark grits; micaceous.

Fig. 2:6 Amphora (B0088.07)

Solid toe. Orange-brown ware (5YR6/6). Many tiny to medium white and dark grits.

Parallel from Keay 1984: fig. 130:3 (Type LVII), dated mid-to-late fifth century to some time in sixth century.

Fig. 2:7 Amphora (B0088.11)

Solid toe recut for use as a stopper. Coarse, gritty, dark orange-brown ware (2.5YR5/8). Many tiny to very large white grits and some tiny to small dark grits; micaceous.

Parallel possibly from Keay 1984: 209 no. 8 (Type XXV Variant 1), dated fourth to mid-fifth century. For amphora toes recut as stoppers, see Siegelmann 1974: fig. 2:6; Adan-Bayewitz 1986: fig. 3:18.

Fig. 2:8 Storage jar (B0100.08)

Rim and shoulder fragment with one handle; est. dia. 9 cm. Gritty/sandy orange ware (2.5YR5/6), with light orange slip (5YR7/4) on exterior. Many tiny to very large white grits; slightly micaceous. Deep band of combining covering entire shoulder.

Fig. 2:9 Storage jar (B0100.013)

Rim and upper shoulder fragment; est. dia. 9 cm. Gritty/sandy orange ware (2.5YR6/6), with pink-orange slip (2.5YR6/6) on exterior. Many tiny dark and tiny to very large white grits, and some large red grits. Ribbing and clay concretions on shoulder.

Parallel from Blakely 1987: fig. 39:150 (Amphora Class 63), dated fourth to seventh century.

Fig. 2:10 Storage jar (B0104.01)

Rim and shoulder fragment with handle attachment; est. dia. 8 cm. Gritty/sandy orange ware (2.5YR6/6), with light orange slip (5YR7/4) on exterior. Many tiny dark and tiny to very large white grits. Faint white-painted lines possibly visible on exterior.

Fig. 2:11 Storage jar

Rim and shoulder fragment; est. dia. 9 cm. Orange-brown ware (2.5YR5/6). Many tiny to large white grits. Clay concretions on neck.

Parallels from Dothan and Freedman 1967: fig. 13:11, dated sixth to seventh century; Loffreda 1974: fig. 9:7, dated Byzantine; Feig 1985: fig. 2:2, dated Byzantine; Nevo 1985: pl. 5:2, dated seventh to eighth century; Tushingham 1985: fig. 28:25, dated third quarter of sixth century or slightly later; Adan-Bayewitz 1986: fig. 1:4, dated ca. 630–660.

Fig. 2:12 Storage jar (B0093.08)

Rim and upper shoulder fragment; est. dia. 13 cm. Thick, dark orange-brown ware (2.5YR5/8), with a light brown slip (10YR8/4) on exterior. Deep combing on shoulder; ridge at base of neck.

Fig. 2:13 Storage jar (B0082.07)

Rim and upper shoulder fragment; est. dia. 9 cm. Gritty/sandy, dark orange-brown ware (2.5YR6/6). Many tiny dark and tiny to large white grits. Clay concretions on rim; ridge at base of neck, and beginning of combing on shoulder.

Parallel from Tushingham 1985: fig. 30:29, dated late sixth to early seventh century.

Fig. 2:14 Storage jar

Body sherd. Sandy/gritty, orange ware (5YR6/6). Many tiny to very large white and a few tiny to very large dark grits. White-painted lines on exterior.

Fig. 2:15 Storage jar

Body sherd. Sandy/gritty, orange ware (5YR6/6). Many tiny to very large white and a few tiny to very large dark grits. White-painted lines on exterior.

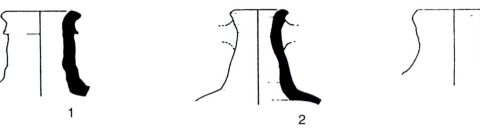

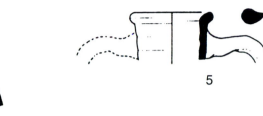

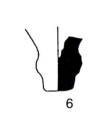

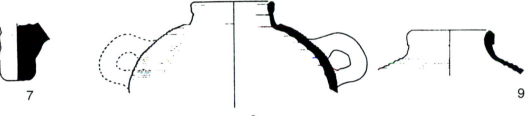

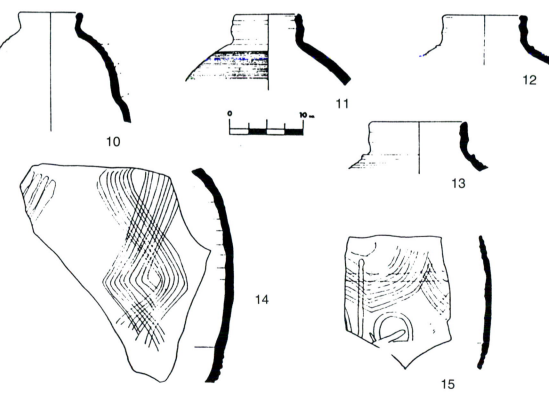

Figure 2.

FIGURE 3

Fig. 3:1 Storage jar/amphora (B0093.010)
Rim and shoulder fragment with one handle; est. dia. 8 cm. Red-brown ware (5YR5/6). Many tiny and some small to large white and dark grits; slightly micaceous. Clay concretions adhering to rim.

Fig. 3:2 Storage jar/amphora (B0094.010)
Rim and shoulder fragment; est. dia. 9 cm. Brown ware (2.5YR5/6). Many tiny to very large white grits. Roughly finished rim and upper shoulder.

Fig. 3:3 Storage jar/amphora (B0094.09)
Rim and shoulder fragment with one handle; est. dia. 8 cm. Red-brown ware (2.5YR5/6). Many tiny and some medium to very large dark and white grits. Some clay concretions adhering to shoulder; roughly finished rim; sharp band of combing on shoulder.
Parallels from Smith 1973: pl. 45:324, dated Byzantine; Schaefer 1979: fig. B-4:28, dated Byzantine; Adan-Bayewitz 1986: fig. 1:9 (Amphora Type 2), dated ca. 630–660.

Fig. 3:4 Storage jar/amphora
Rim and shoulder fragment with handle attachment; est. dia. 11. Brown ware (5YR4/8). Many tiny-very large white and a few tiny-large dark grits. Clay concretions adhering to rim; roughly finished rim; band of deep combing on shoulder.

Fig. 3:5 Storage jar/amphora
Rim and shoulder fragment with one handle; est. dia. 9 cm. Thick grey core, fired dark red-brown (2.5YR5/6) at surfaces, with a light red-brown slip (5YR7/4) on exterior. Many tiny to large white grits. Clay concretions adhering to rim.
Parallels from Smith 1973: pl. 29:1190, dated Byzantine; Tushingham 1985: fig. 31:1, dated late sixth to early seventh century.

Fig. 3:6 Storage jar/amphora
Toe. Brown ware (5YR5/6). Many tiny to large dark and some tiny to medium white grits. Band of deep combing above base.
Parallels from Egloff 1977: pl. 61:1, dated second quarter of seventh century; Zemer 1978: pl. 18:49, dated third/fourth century to fifth/sixth century; Magness 1987: fig. 1:9 (=2:9 in text), dated mainly sixth to early seventh century.

Fig. 3:7 Storage jar (B0104.05)
Rim and shoulder fragment; est. dia. 9 cm. Hard-fired, dark grey ware (10YR4/1), with a brown core (5YR6/6); traces of white-painted lines on shoulder. Many tiny to large white grits. Ribbing on shoulder.
Parallels from Landgraf 1980: pl. 21:16, dated Byzantine; Walmsley 1982: CN287, dated late sixth to early seventh century; Adan-Bayewitz 1986: fig. 2:1 (Amphora Type 3), dated ca. 630–660.

Fig. 3:8 Storage jar (B0083.12)
Body sherd (shoulder and upper wall). Hard-fired, brown ware (5YR6/6), with a thick, dark grey core (10YR4/1). Purple-grey slip (5YR5/2) on exterior, with white-painted lines on exterior wall. Many tiny to medium white and dark and some very large white grits. Light ribbing on shoulder and upper wall.

Fig. 3:9 Lid
Loop handle. Thin, hard-fired, pink-red cooking ware (2.5YR6/6). Some tiny to small white and dark grits. Light, narrow ribbing on body.
Parallels from Prausnitz 1967: fig. 15:4, dated Byzantine; Egloff 1977: pl. 55:7 (Type 350), dated before 450; Walmsley 1982: pl. 55:1, dated first quarter of eighth century.

Fig. 3:10 Lid (B0104.016)
Pierced knob handle. Thin, brittle, gritty, dark red cooking ware (10R4/6). Many tiny to small white and dark grits.
Parallels from Crowfoot and Fitzgerald 1929: pl. 15:22, dated late sixth to early seventh century; Aharoni 1962: fig. 3:16, dated fifth to seventh century; Fritz 1983: pl. 167:10, dated seventh to early eighth century; Adan-Bayewitz 1986: fig. 4:9, dated ca. 630–660.

Fig. 3:11 Lid/stopper (B0083.11)
Knob handle. Thick, dark orange cooking ware (2.5YR4/8), with a purple-red slip (10R5/4) on interior and exterior. Some tiny to medium white grits; micaceous.
Similar to Egloff 1977: pl. 55:11 (Type 352), dated seventh century; Adan-Bayewitz 1986: fig. 3:14, dated ca. 630–660.

Fig. 3:12 Lid
Knob handle. Thick, sandy/gritty, dark orange-brown ware (5YR5/6), with an orange-brown slip (5YR7/6) on exterior. Many tiny and some small to medium white grits.
Parallels from Fitzgerald 1931: pl. 31:12, dated fifth to early seventh century; Prausnitz 1967: fig. 11:9, dated fourth century; Sauer 1973: fig. 2:91, dated fifth century; Riley 1975: 36 no. 34 ("base"), dated Byzantine; Tushingham 1985: fig. 28:36, dated third quarter of sixth century or slightly later; fig. 32:16, dated late sixth to early seventh century; Johnson 1988: fig. 7-56:847, dated third to fourth century; Wightman 1989: pl. 11:13, dated mid-sixth century; Smith and Day 1989: pl. 52:6, dated sixth to early seventh century ("jug base").

Fig. 3:13 Jug
Low ring base. Hard-fired, orange-brown ware (2.5YR6/6), covered with lines of pare-burnishing on exterior (even on bottom). Some tiny to medium white grits.
Parallels from Magness 1993: Jugs and Juglets: Bases, Form 6B.

Fig. 3:14 Jar/jug (B0086.02)
Knob base. Thick, orange-brown ware (2.5YR5/6). Many tiny to very large pieces of quartz and some tiny dark grits.

Fig. 3:15 Jug
Spout. Thin, hard-fired, dark brown cooking ware (2.5YR4/6), with a dark purple-red slip (10R4/6) on exterior. Some tiny white and dark grits. Light, narrow ribbing on body.

Fig. 3:16 Jug
Spout. Thin, hard-fired, dark orange-brown cooking ware (2.5YR5/8). Many tiny to small white and dark grits.

Fig. 3:17 Mirror plaque (B0076.02)
Mold-made; fragment of edge decorated in relief with concentric circles around a circular ring. Pink-brown ware (5YR6/6), with a light, grey-brown core (7.5YR6/2). Some tiny to small white and dark grits.
Parallel from Avni and Dahari 1990: 310, fig. 7, dated Byzantine.

Fig. 3:18 Flask (B0104.22)
Rim and neck fragment; est. dia. 5 cm. Thick, coarse, dark red-brown ware (2.5YR5/6). Many tiny to very large white grits.

Fig. 3:19 Flask
Rim and neck fragment; est. dia. 6.5 cm. Gritty/sandy orange-brown ware (5YR6/6). Many tiny to very large white grits.

Fig. 3:20 Juglet
Rim and neck fragment with upper part of handle; est. dia. 1.5 cm. Purple-brown ware (5YR6/3), fired orange (2.5YR6/8) on and next to handle. Many tiny to small white grits.
Parallel from Fitzgerald 1931: pl. 31:6, dated fifth to early seventh century.

Fig. 3:21 Juglet (B0081.05)
Rim and neck fragment with upper part of handle; est. dia. 2.5 cm. Light yellow-brown ware (10YR7/3). Many tiny to small dark grits.
Parallels from Saller 1957: fig. 58:202, dated Byzantine to early Arabic; Delougaz and Haines 1960: pl. 56:8, dated Byzantine; Baly 1962: Shape 96:1, dated Byzantine; Fritz 1983: pl. 168:5, dated seventh to early eighth century.

Fig. 3:22 Juglet (B0076.08)
Stump base. Thin, hard-fired, orange ware (2.5YR6/8), with a light orange-brown slip on exterior. Some tiny to large white grits. String-cut base.
Parallels from Kelso and Baramki 1949–51: N16 (Type 8), dated Byzantine; Delougaz and Haines 1960: pl. 56:8–12, dated Byzantine; Aharoni 1962: fig. 17:17, dated fifth to seventh century; Smith 1973: pl. 29:1203, dated Byzantine.

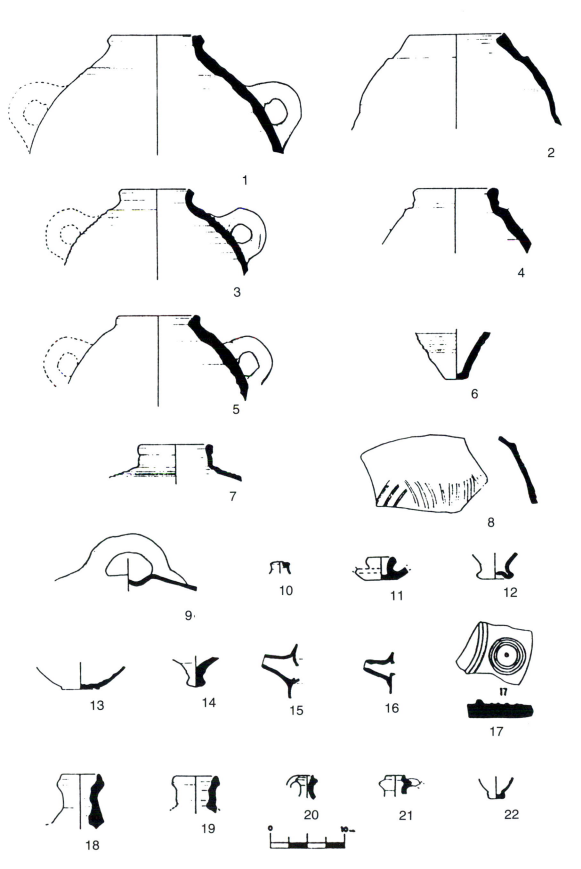

Figure 3.

Tell Dothan: The Western Cemetery, with Comments on Joseph Free's Excavations, 1953 to 1964

ROBERT E. COOLEY and GARY D. PRATICO

Gordon-Conwell Theological Seminary
South Hamilton, MA 01982

Tell Dothan is an impressive archaeological mound in the northern Samaria hills, some 22 km north of Shechem. The site was excavated by Joseph Free in nine seasons between 1953 and 1964. Notable among the discoveries was the western cemetery, three tombs on the western edge of the tell that date between the LB IIA and the early Iron Age. Tomb 1 was the largest and best preserved of the three burial contexts and was unusual in that it was stratified in five distinct levels. Each level produced a wealth of pottery and other artifacts, together with some 250–300 burials. As part of the publication phase of the Dothan Archaeological Project, this article will introduce the largely unpublished tombs of the western cemetery, focusing on Tomb I.

THE TELL

Location and Description

Tell Dothan is in the northern Samaria Hills on the eastern side of the Dothan Valley, some 22 km north of Shechem and 10 km south of Jenin (fig. 1). Rising approximately 60 m above the surrounding valley, Tell Dothan is a prominent mound composed of nearly 15 m of stratified remains on top of a natural hill of some 45 m high. The site has a fairly flat top with steeply sloping sides. The summit comprises approximately 10 acres and the occupied area of the slopes includes another 15 acres. Its area of occupation, therefore, consists of approximately 25 acres. The eastern and southern slopes are terraced today with olive groves that are watered from a spring on the south side of the tell. That water source likely served the site in antiquity.

The rock formations exposed in the immediate environs of Tell Dothan are Eocene beds of limestone, chalky limestone, and soft chalk. The settlement was founded on a gently sloping ridge that consists of a thin cap of chalky limestone over the chalky subsurface. Though the upper unit is basically a chalky limestone, a few exposures approach the classification of micritic limestone. Fresh exposures of the chalk are white, turning to gray with exposure to natural elements. Most of the chalk is homogeneous; iron stains are common, likely from pyrite inclusions. The site offered the ancients a suitable location for digging cisterns and tombs. The building material that was utilized in the settlement's architecture was quarried nearby.

Identification

Tell Dothan has been identified with the biblical city of the same name, mentioned in Genesis 37 as the place where Joseph found his brothers during their wanderings with their father's flocks. According to the narrative, Joseph was sent by his father Jacob from the Valley of Hebron to find his brothers in the region of Shechem but learned that they were tending the flocks in the area of Dothan. Thereafter, the narrative describes the intrigue that led to Joseph's being taken to Egypt by a caravan of Ishmaelites (or Midianites) who were traveling to Egypt via Dothan from Gilead.

Fig. 1. Aerial view of Tell Dothan and its immediate environs. The mound is clearly visible in the upper left of the photograph. Ruins are discernible across he summit, especially on the southern side of the tell. The Dothan Valley stretches to the west of the site, through which the Jerusalem–Nablus–Jenin road runs. The compass orientation of this road is basically north–south.[3]

During the Monarchy, Dothan is described as a well-fortified city to which the Aramean king sent emissaries in search of the prophet Elisha (2 Kgs 6:13–14). It was in that context that Elisha's servant was encouraged by a vision of heavenly forces arrayed on a hill east of town. Other literary references include three notations in the Book of Judith (3:9; 4:6, 7:3) and one in the Onomasticon of Eusebius (76:13).

Strategic Importance of the Site

Dothan is surrounded on the north, east, and south by hills that enclose the fertile Dothan Valley (figs. 1, 2). The site dominates this plain, which has always been of strategic importance as the easternmost of the three main passes between the Sharon Plain and the Jezreel Valley through the mountainous ridge created by the northern Ephraimite hill country and the Carmel range. The main pass followed the Wadi ᶜAra (Naḥal ᶜIron) and had the advantage of being the shortest route between the coast and the Jezreel Valley, despite the strategic disadvantages of the narrow defiles. The other passes

were somewhat easier but longer. The southernmost of these alternative routes negotiated the mountainous spine via the Dothan Valley, reaching the Jezreel Valley south of Taᶜanach. The Ishmaelite/ Midianite caravan of Gen 37:25 probably traveled this route on its way from Gilead to Egypt.

Excavation History and Publications

Dothan was excavated by Joseph Free in nine seasons between 1953 and 1964 (fig. 3).[1] The expedition was not in the field in the years of 1957, 1961, or 1963. According to the excavator, the site yielded a nearly continuous occupational sequence in 21 levels, dating from the end of the Chalcolithic through the Byzantine period, with later occupation as late as the 14th century C.E. Free's excavations have never been published in technical detail, and even the preliminary reports provide few details on the site's rich architectural traditions and artifact assemblages (Free 1953; 1954; 1955; 1956a; 1956b; 1958a; 1959; 1960a; 1962 [see Supplemental Readings list for Free's popular writings]; Ussishkin 1975).[2] Preliminary reports were

Fig. 2. View of the Tell Dothan excavations taken during the 1960 season. Beyond the edge of the mound, the Dothan Valley stretches to the distant horizon.

prepared for the eighth (1962) and ninth (1964) seasons, but they were never published.

The 1953–1964 excavations represented the first of two phases in the Dothan Archaeological Project. The second phase of the project is a long-range undertaking that seeks to publish a multivolume final report on the nine-year campaign. The first volume will publish the western cemetery (Tombs 1, 2, and 3), excavated during the sixth to the ninth seasons. Subsequent publications will focus on the tell excavations, with emphasis on selected studies such as the city's various fortification systems, the Iron Age city, and the ruins of the acropolis area. The current article will introduce the largely unpublished tombs of the western cemetery, focusing on Tomb 1, with brief comment on the tell excavations.[4]

Location of the Western Cemetery in the Context of the Tell Excavations

Dothan was investigated in six major areas of excavation (T, B, A, D, L, and K, moving from east to west). The western cemetery, which is the primary focus of this article, is located in Area K on the western end of the tell.

Area T is located on the eastern extremity of the tell's summit. It encompassed the highest part of the mound and that designated by Free as the "acropolis" area (Free 1956a: 16–17; 1959: 26). Published data for Area B, just west of Area T and north of Area A, are exceptionally meager and consist of only a few observations related to remains of the Roman and Hellenistic periods. The

Fig. 3. Joseph Free, director of the Tell Dothan excavations.

and Late Bronze Age defenses (Free 1958: 10–12). Further east in Area L, large sections of an Iron Age administrative building were uncovered (Free 1959: 22–24, 1960: 7–9).

THE WESTERN CEMETERY:
TOMBS 1, 2, AND 3

Discovery and Excavation

Toward the end of the 1959 season, the excavators uncovered a circular, stone-lined pit in Area K (on the western side of the tell) that diminished in size until it funneled into a square-cut shaft in the bedrock. About 1 m down the shaft, a stone slab was uncovered, leaning against a vertical rock-cut doorway. Thus began the excavation of one of Dothan's most significant discoveries, the so-called western cemetery (fig. 4).

The largest tomb of this cemetery (Tomb 1) was discovered four days before the conclusion of the 1959 season (figs. 5, 6). During those four days, the team worked around the clock in eight-hour shifts in the hope of clearing the burial chamber. Approximately 1 m of the tomb chamber was exposed; 52 objects were removed, including chalices, lamps, bowls, pyxides, and numerous other objects. Many vessels were complete, though fragmented, and some were intact. The pottery dated to the early Iron Age. The excavators could not finish clearing the burial chamber before the end of the season, and sealed the tomb with reinforced concrete until the following season. No one could have imagined that 2756 more vessels, 234 bronze objects, and several hundred burials awaited discovery. Archaeologists had uncovered the largest single-chambered tomb with the largest number of burial deposits to have been excavated in Palestine at that time.

As noted above, the western cemetery was excavated over four seasons (1959, 1960, 1962, and 1964). Although Free was director of the Dothan Archaeological Project during those years, the tomb excavations were conducted under the direction of R. E. Cooley, who is in charge of the publication phase of the Dothan Archaeological Project, assisted by Gary Pratico.

Very little of this stratified tomb has been published to date. Apart from dictionary and encyclopedia articles, the most substantive studies are to be found in preliminary reports (Free 1959: 26–28; 1960: 10–15) and in works largely concerned with

excavation records and Free's unpublished ninth season report provide a few more details regarding occupation during the Roman, Byzantine, and Medieval Arab periods. The central section of the top of the mound (Area A) was occupied by a Hellenistic settlement, dating to the third and second centuries B.C.E., beneath which was a substantial Iron Age settlement (Free 1954: 15–16; 1955: 3–7; 1956a: 11, 14–15, fig. 2). The excavator's unpublished ninth season report provides some details regarding a Middle Bronze Age "citadel" that was partially excavated during the eighth and ninth seasons. Area D, on the south side of the summit of the tell yielded remains that dated between the beginning of the Early Bronze Age and the beginning of the Iron II period (Free 1953: 16–18; 1956b: 45–46). Subsequent work extended the later range to include the Hellenistic and Roman periods.

The largest area of excavation was Area L, on the western summit of the mound, contiguous with the eastern side of Area K and the western cemetery. The slope section of that area yielded substantial fortifications of the Early Bronze Age; and, although few published details are available, the area also produced sections of the city's Middle

Fig. 4. The area of Tell Dothan's western cemetery, on the western edge of the mound (Area K), looking west. The opening that resulted from the collapse of the Tomb 1 ceiling is seen in the lower half of the photograph. The vertical shaft is clearly visible on the other side of the modern doorway. Note also the portion of the stepped entryway that is within the tomb chamber, together with Crypts B (right) and A (left) on the northern and southern sides of the tomb chamber, respectively. Tombs 2 and 3 are just west of Tomb 1 (upper center).

matters of interpretation (Cooley 1968; 1983). The western cemetery in general and its largest tomb in particular will be the primary focus of the remainder of this article.

Tomb Architecture (figs. 4–12)

During the Late Bronze Age, a pit (approximately 6 to 7 m deep) was cut into Early Bronze Age debris and lined with stones (fig. 7). The pit gradually diminished in circumference until it reached bedrock, at which point it became a shaft that opened to a stomion with seven steps that led into a very large burial chamber.

Tomb 1 therefore consists of three architectural components: a vertical shaft, a stepped entryway, and the main tomb chamber in which were located eight crypts or loculi (figs. 4 and 5). Access to the

stepped entryway and the main chamber was provided through a well-cut vertical shaft on the western side of the tomb (figs. 8, 9). The chamber has a west–east orientation. The shaft measures 1.75 m × 1.00 m wide and is 1.51 m deep. Of the seven steps that lead into the tomb chamber, three were located within the shaft. The shaft depth to the first step is 1.00 m, 1.32 m to the second step, and 1.51 m to the third step. The remaining four steps were within the tomb chamber; the seventh step is 3.30 m below the uppermost level of the shaft. The doorway to the tomb chamber was blocked by a stone slab that measured 1.10 m high × 1.00 m wide × 0.12 m thick.

The tomb chamber is irregularly shaped, although basically rectangular with rounded corners. At its largest extremities, the chamber measures 10.65 m west to east (Crypt H to the western wall

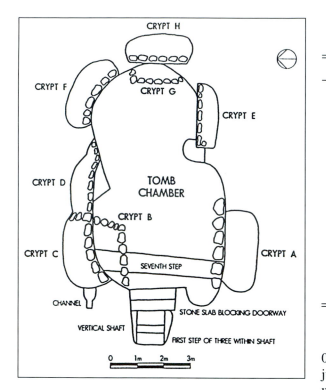

Fig. 5. Plan of Tomb 1 of Tell Dothan's western cemetery, Area K. Drawing by I. S. Chow, after the plan by R. E. Cooley.

TABLE 1. Section Measurements for the Levels and Fills of Tomb 1

Level, fill	Thickness, m
Collapsed limestone ceiling	1.50
Level 1	0.10
Limestone fill	0.15
Level 2	0.10
Limestone fill	0.05
Level 3	0.15
Limestone and earthen fill	0.40
Level 4	0.25
Limestone and earthen fill	0.40
Level 5	0.15
Limestone and earthen fill between lowest level and the tomb floor	0.40

of the shaft) and 6.90 m north to south (Crypt A to Crypt C). Excluding the crypts, the chamber walls measure 8.30 m west to east and 5.00 m north to south. The chamber contained eight crypts of which six were cut into the rock (A, C, D, E, F, and H) and two were constructed at a later time (B in the northwestern corner of the tomb and G at the extreme eastern end; figs. 6, 10–12, 14–16). The two later crypts were created by constructing stone walls below Crypts C and H respectively. Crypt dimensions are as follows: Crypt A (1.20 m × 2.80 m), Crypt B (1.10 m × 2.30 m), Crypt C (1.13 m × 2.60 m), Crypt D (0.81 m × 2.25 m), Crypt E (0.79 m × 2.25 m), Crypt F (0.88 m × 2.30 m), Crypt G (0.80 m × 2.20 m), and Crypt H (1.20 m × 2.20 m). The depth of the tomb chamber, from the bedrock surface at the center to the collapsed ceiling, is 5.50 m.

A small channel was discovered on the northwestern side of the tomb, directly above Crypt C. This channel created an opening from the outside of the tomb to the interior of one of the chamber niches. The opening was roughly square on the interior, measuring 0.60 m × 0.60 m, narrowing to roughly circular on the exterior with a diameter of

0.20 m. Two large storage jars, each with a dipper juglet, were associated with this channel. Both were discovered on the outside of the tomb chamber, just below the channel entrance. This opening, together with the associated pottery, obviously served a ritual function, perhaps for libation offerings for "feeding the tomb." Similar installations were discovered in the great tombs of Ugarit, dating to the 14th and 13th centuries B.C.E. (Schaeffer 1939: 50–51).

Tomb Stratification

Although atypical for multiple burial tombs, Tomb 1 was clearly stratified. The uppermost level (Level 1) was completely sealed by the debris from the collapsed ceiling. Each of the five burial levels was clearly and completely separated from the next by a layer of limestone and/or earthen fill. The earliest level of burials (Level 5) was separated from the bedrock floor of the tomb by a layer of limestone and earthen fill. Table 1 presents the section measurements for the five levels of the tomb and the intervening fills.

Pottery and Chronology of Tomb 1 (figs. 13:1–13; 14–16, 19–35)

Pottery vessels constitute the largest class of burial deposits, numbering approximately 2800 pieces categorized as lamps, bowls, jugs, dipper jugs, juglets, dipper juglets, pyxides, flasks, kraters,

Fig. 6. Detail of the view through the collapsed ceiling of Tomb 1, looking west. Crypt A is on the southern side of the tomb chamber. Crypts B and C are on the right, the northern side of the chamber.

pots, strainer pots, jars, jar stands, storage jars, funnels, vases, stirrup cups, zoormorphic vessels, *kernoi* rings, chalices, cooking pots, pitchers, and bowl stands (fig. 13:a–c). It should be noted that these categories represent the vessel nomenclature of the Dothan field records. Vessel designations will be refined in the final report, most importantly in the categories of jug, dipper jug, pot, jar, jar stand, vase, pitcher, and bowl stand. For an assemblage of selected pottery types from each of the five levels of Tomb 1, see figs. 19–35.

Table 2 provides numerical details, level by level, for vessel types attested by more than ten examples. The vessel nomenclature represents that utilized in the field records and pottery register. The tabulations are based on the numerical summaries recorded in the field reports. Vessel categories represented by less than ten examples throughout the five levels of the tomb include: jar, funnel, vase, milkbowl, strainer, bilbil, cooking pot, incense burner, kernos ring, special lamp forms, and anthropomorphic vessels.

The pottery plates (figs. 19–35) present a representative assemblage of selected vessel types for the five levels of Tomb 1 (pyxides, biconical jars, chalices, krater-mugs, and lamps), together with examples of unique and unusual forms such as multihandled kraters and stirrup jars. The plates do not represent the range of vessel types present in this tomb or the many variations of form attested

TABLE 2. Level Distribution of Selected Vessel Types in Tomb 1

Pottery	Tomb Levels					Total pieces
	1	*2*	*3*	*4*	*5*	
Bowl	109	197	123	114	64	607
Lamp	115	163	108	116	76	578
Pyxis	173	196	129	52	17	567
Jug/juglet	95	145	118	64	50	472
Pot	37	53	45	50	13	198
Chalice	25	33	31	24	6	119
Flask	15	12	14	11	5	57
Storage jar	5	14	13	11	7	50
Krater	32	11	1	0	0	44
Stirrup jar	1	3	8	9	0	21
Spouted jug	4	2	2	3	0	11

within the vessel categories that are depicted and discussed below. Discussion will focus on the typological distinctions of the various vessel types as they evolve through the five distinct levels of the tomb, together with some reference to comparative examples. These observations should be regarded as preliminary and tentative. The final report on the western cemetery will present the full range of pottery from Tombs 1 to 3, together with comparative and typological studies and complete technical descriptions.

Fig. 7. The relationship between Tomb 1 and its Early Bronze Age context in Area K. The chamber of this cave burial was constructed beneath a level of Early Bronze Age remains. Cooley is kneeling on the bedrock surface just right of the collapsed ceiling of Tomb 1. A study of the balk to the left of the group reveals the following stratigraphic details: A 1-m-thick ash layer, dating to the Early Bronze Age, extends horizontally between the workman standing on the far left and the second vertical fissure, a distance of approximately 2 m. A 10 to 15 cm slippage in this ash layer (clearly seen in the first vertical fissure) was created when the tomb ceiling collapsed. Note the 1-m-wide section of the tomb ceiling that dropped the same distance, visible below and to the left of the bedrock surface upon which the group is standing. Further left, both the ash layer and the tomb ceiling collapsed nearly 2 m (to the left of

the second vertical fissure), dropping well into the tomb chamber. The balk clearly documents, therefore, the construction of the tomb chamber beneath a level of Early Bronze Age remains. This ash layer obviously was penetrated with the construction of the vertical shaft that gave access to the tomb chamber beneath the earlier remains.

Fig. 8. Detail of the entrance to Tomb 1, photographed from within the tomb chamber and and looking west. The meter stick is resting on the sixth step, the second step above the floor of the tomb chamber. Six of the seven entryway steps are within the tomb chamber; three are within the shaft. A portion of the vertical shaft is visible above the uppermost step.

Pyxides. The five levels of Tomb 1 produced more bowls than any other vessel type (607), followed by lamps (578) and pyxides (567). The pyxides of this tomb are a particularly rich and interesting assemblage with discernible evolution of form through the five levels of this burial context. The numbers are significantly greater in Levels 1 to 3 (173, 196, and 129 respectively), with 52 pyxides from Level 4 and only 17 from the earliest level. A selection of Level 1 pyxides is presented in fig. 19:1–12. Level 2 forms are depicted in fig. 24:1–9; Level 3, in figs. 28:1–12; Level 4, in fig. 32:1–7; the smaller numbers of Level 5 are represented by the vessels of fig. 35:1–4, 6. These figures present a representative selection of the main pyxides types for each level of Tomb 1, although variations abound in each level.

As one studies the level-by-level arrangement of pyxides at Saint George's College in Jerusalem—the largest collection of this vessel type—the most obvious observation with respect to the evolution of this form is that the disk base predominates in the later levels of the tomb (Levels 1 and 2: figs. 19:2–12; 24:4–9,11) and a rounded bottom characterizes the majority of vessels in the earlier levels (Levels 4 and 5: fig. 32:1–4,6,7; 35:1–4). Level 3 pyxides are fairly evenly divided between these two categories (fig. 28:1–4,6,7 with disk base; fig. 28:5, 8–12 with rounded bottom). A few rounded bottoms are attested in Levels 1

Fig. 9. Detail of the entrance to Tomb 1 as seen through the vertical shaft, looking east. The stepped entryway is clearly visible with the meter stick resting on the sixth step. The floor of tomb chamber is visible beyond the seventh step with a few stones of Crypt B on the left or northern side of the tomb.

Fig. 10. Detail of the western half of Tomb 1. The chamber floor occupies the lower third of the photograph. The modern doorway rests on the fourth step. Rock-hewn Crypts A and C are seen on the extreme southern (left) and northern (right) sides of the tomb chamber. Crypt B, a later construction, was located just below Crypt C.

(19:1) and 2 (24:10,12). Note the flat base of fig. 32:5 (Level 4). The rounded bottom of pyxides in Levels 3 to 5 should be characterized as slightly rounded, though some forms have bottoms that are sharply rounded (figs. 28:9,11; 32:2; 35:6).

There are few significant variations in the body profile of Level 1 pyxides. The most common profile is illustrated by the vessels depicted in fig. 19:1–12 (cf. Guy 1938: pl. 62:19 with vertical loop handles; Loud 1948: pls. 77:7; 84:9; [fig. 24:12 here]; Guy 1938: pl. 69:2 [fig. 19:2 here];

pls. 14:5; 35:26 [fig. 19:4 here]; pl. 30:12 [fig. 19:9 here, lower body profile only]; McGovern 1986: fig. 53:48 [fig. 19:1 here]). As a general impression, the body shape of the pyxides in subsequent levels tends increasingly to become bottom heavy; that is, the lowest of the two body carinations drops with respect to the base (figs. 24:1,2,4,8–10,12; 28:5,7,10–12; 32:1,3,4,6; 35:1–4; cf. Guy 1938: pls. 62:19; 69:2 with flat base; Tufnell 1958: pl. 82: 927, 928 [fig. 24:1,2, 12 here]; Guy 1938: pls. 14:5; 62:18 [fig. 24:4 here]; Tufnell 1958:

Fig. 11. A view of the stepped entryway from the south with Crypts B (lower) and C (upper) on the northern side of the tomb. The meter stick is resting on the sixth step. Note that the stone wall that creates the southern side of Crypt B is constructed over the sixth and seventh steps. Tomb 1 had six rock-hewn and two constructed crypts. Crypt C is rock-hewn; Crypt B is a later construction.

Fig. 12. Detail of rock-hewn Crypt H, constructed on the eastern end of the tomb chamber. The deposits associated with this burial included seven pottery vessels and a clam shell. The oversized flask and dipper juglet are at the head of the skeleton. No personal adornments, implements, weapons, or ritual objects were included in the burial assemblage.

pl. 82: 922 [figs. 24:10 here]; 82:923 [fig. 28:9,10–12 here]; Pritchard 1963: figs. 8:23; 12:66 [fig. 24:2 here, with unusual decoration; cf. 24:11 with ring base]). As is clear in these examples, the vessel takes on a squat appearance compared to the more upright body profile of Level 1 forms. The lower body profile of fig. 24:9,12 is common in Levels 2 and 3 (cf. fig. 28:1 from Level 3), with parallels in imitation Mycenaean pyxis forms from

Tell es-Saᶜidiyeh (Pritchard 1980: fig. 37:2) and Megiddo (Guy 1938: pls. 30:12; 62:18).

Another common body profile in Levels 2 and 3 is that represented by figs. 24:11 (Guy 1938: pl. 20:5; Loud 1948: pl. 64:6) and 28:3 (Pritchard 1980: fig. 43:1, though with different rim profile). Beginning in Level 3, the body profile becomes slightly more angular between the two body carinations, as in fig. 28:2, 3, 7 (cf. Guy 1938: pl. 35:26).

The pyxis presented in fig. 32:2 from Level 4 represents the earliest example of the bag-shaped body profile attested in all later levels of the tomb. The form is paralleled by other imitation Mycenaean pyxides, dating from Late Bronze II into Iron I (Pritchard 1980: figs. 8:2; 23:5; Tufnell 1958: pl. 82:925, 926; de Vaux 1952: 563, fig. 6:8; Loud 1948: pls. 68:9; 73:12; 77:7, 9; Yadin 1961: pl. 201:28). The vessel wall of earlier level pyxides at Tell Dothan is more angular between the two body carinations (figs. 28:2,3,5,7–9; 32:6,7; 35:2; cf. Pritchard 1980: fig. 31:1 [fig. 28:7 here] with vertical loop handles).

A simple or straight rim (vertical to slightly everted) is one of the most common rim profiles in all levels of the tomb (figs. 19:1,2,4,12; 24:1,3–7,11,12; 28:3–6,8,11; 32:1,2,4; 35:1–3,6), though the vessels of Levels 4 and 5 tend to have shorter and more sharply everted necks (fig. 24:10). Although it has many subtle variations, a small triangular rim is also common in the three latest levels (figs. 19:5,8–10; 24:2,8; 28:2,12), with a few examples in Levels 4 (fig. 32:3) and 5 (fig. 35:4). Note the grooved rim of fig. 19:7, which may also be characterized as triangular. Unusual and unique rim profiles are depicted in figs. 19:9,11; 24:9 and 32:5–7.

Levels 1–3 produced both small and large pyxides, with the majority of forms classified in the small-to-medium range. Levels 4 and 5 produced very few large pyxides. Figures 32:1–4 and 35:1–4 are illustrative of the typical vessel size of these earlier levels.

Decoration is attested in all levels of the tomb, though more common in Levels 1 to 3. The pottery plates are not representative at this point, depicting mostly painted forms for these levels and few plain vessels. The latter are attested in significant numbers. While the most common pattern in all levels consists of two clearly defined registers around the body of the pyxis with diagonal or vertical lines within the registers, there are discernible differences between the earlier and later patterns. The pyxides of Level 1 are quite consistent in the painted patterns as described above. In most examples, the two registers are of roughly equal size, though a few exceptions are attested. In figure 19:1, 6 and 7, the lower register is larger than the upper register. The same patterning prevails in the pyxides of Levels 2 and 3, though there is greater variation in the size of the registers. In some pyxides of both levels, the upper register is smaller (figs. 24:1, 3,4,7,8; 28:12); whereas in other examples it is

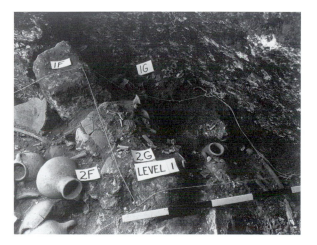

Fig. 13. The concentration of vessels throughout the five levels of the tomb is illustrated by this sequence of photographs from Level 1 of Squares 2E, 2F, and 2G.

Fig. 14. This is the first in a sequence of three photographs (figs. 14–16) that document the progress of excavations in the eastern end of the Tomb 1 chamber. These three photographs also serve to illustrate the wealth and condition of the burial deposits. This first image depicts the concentration of pottery and skeletal remains in Level 1, the latest of the tomb's strata, looking east. Crypt F, a rock-hewn loculus on the northeastern side of the chamber, is visible in the upper left, just above and slightly left of the two multihandled kraters. Though barely visible through the debris, the uppermost portions of rock-hewn Crypt E are discernible in the upper center portion of the photograph.

larger (fig. 28:1,3,4,8,9). A smaller upper register is more frequent in Levels 4 and 5 (figs. 32:1,3,4; 35:6), though the larger upper register is attested as well (fig. 32:2). Less frequent or unique decorations include those depicted in figs. 19:10,11 (cf. Guy 1938: pl. 62:17); 24:2; 28:6,10, and 35:1. Painted (rounded) bottoms (figs. 24:2,4; 28:10,12; 32:3,4) and handle decoration (figs. 19:1,3,4,6; 24:2; 28:1,3,6,8,9; 32:3,4; 35:1,6) are attested, but not with any discernible frequency or distribution.

Biconical Jars. Biconical jars are evenly distributed through Levels 1 to 4 with few examples attested in Level 5 (figs. 20:1–7; 25:1–6; 29:1–6; 32:8,9; 33:1,2). The biconical jars in Level 1 evidence great variety in rim profiles, unlike the bicon-

icals in earlier levels of the tomb (fig. 20:1–5,7; cf. Yadin 1960: pl. 134:5 [20:3 here]). There are two dominant rim profiles in Level 2 vessels: rectangular rim with a groove and near vertical stance (fig. 25:5,6); and triangular rim with groove and near vertical or slightly everted stance (fig. 25:1–4; cf. Pritchard 1980: fig. 11:2 [25:3 here]; Yadin 1960: pls. 120:15; 134:4). The triangular grooved rim of Level 2 continues into Level 3 (fig. 29:6), though sometimes without a groove (fig. 29:4). The rectangular grooved rim is also attested (fig. 29:3,5). A new and dominant rim profile is represented by the biconicals of fig. 29:1,2 (Guy 1938: pl. 17:12; Yadin 1960: pls. 134:5; 152:5; fig. 9:15 for rim profile and body carination only). Note the similar rim profile and stance of the Level 1 biconical jar in

Fig. 15. This second photograph in the sequence depicts the progress of excavations down to Level 4, looking east. Although filled with stones, the full extent of rock-hewn Crypt F is now visible in the upper left. Crypt H, the rock-hewn loculus in the extreme eastern end of the chamber, is discernible in the upper right, though blocked with stones. Just below Crypt H, the stone wall of Crypt G is clearly visible. Rock-hewn Crypt E, on the southern side of the eastern end of the tomb, is visible in the upper right.

fig. 20:3, though the body carination is higher and slightly less sharp. Level 4 rim profiles vary (fig. 32:8,9; 33:1), though few examples of the rectangular and triangular grooved rims were found in that level (Loud 1948: pls. 58:3 [32:8 here]; 63:7 [33:1 here]; Yadin 1960: pl. 134:11 [32:8 here]). Flat and shallow-to-moderate disk bases are attested in all levels. As a general impression, the body carination that characterizes this vessel type tends to be more pronounced in Levels 3 to 5 (cf. figs. 20:1,2,7; 25:2–6 [Levels 1 and 2] with figs. 29:1–6; 32:8,9; 33:1,2 [Levels 3 and 4]). There is consistency through all levels of the tomb in terms of point of handle attachment. Biconicals with one or two handles are documented in all levels. The biconical spouted vessel with basket handle shows little change through the tomb levels (figs. 20:6, 33:2).

Lamps. Tomb 1 produced nearly 600 lamps, with significant numbers in each level of the tomb. The distribution is fairly uniform in Levels 1, 3, and 4, but with significantly higher numbers in Level 2 and slightly lower numbers in Level 5. The characteristic MB II–LB I lamp with slightly pinched mouth is not attested. The lamps of Level 5 are closer to the typical LB II form: sharply pinched mouth; and shallow to moderately deep bowl and definite rim, though many lamps are without a rim. The lamps of Levels 2 to 4 are quite uniform in these basic typological features. Figure 26:7 depicts the most common Level 2 form; the lamp of fig. 31:6 is typical of Level 3; and fig. 34:1 preserves the characteristic features of the Level 4 horizon. Although not depicted in the plates, minor variations are attested. Figure 26:9 is unusual in

Fig. 16. Level 5, the earliest stratum in the tomb, looking east. Crypts F, G, H, and E are clearly visible.

the repertoire of Levels 2 to 4. By way of comparison with the lamps of Levels 1 and 5, the forms of Levels 2 to 4 have deeper bowls and more sharply pinched mouths. Many examples are attested in which the pinch almost closes the folded-over flaps, and most lamps have a definite rim. The typical lamp of Levels 2 to 4 preserves the basic typological features of the form in LB II. Lamp typology for these levels of Tomb 1 appears to be uniform, with no typological distinctions discernible. Level 1 lamps appear to fall into two categories: a smaller lamp with definite rim, moderately deep bowl, and a slightly less pronounced pinch in the mouth; and a form that preserves the features described above for the form in Levels 2 to 4. In many examples in both categories, the rim tends to be slightly wider than in previous levels. Level 1 lamps have rounded bases. The flat base of Iron I is not attested.

Chalices. Chalices are well-attested in all levels of Tomb 1 except Level 5 (figs. 21:1,2; 26:1–5; 30:1–6; 33:3–5; 35:7); and subtle typological distinctives are observable between the levels, especially between Levels 1 and 4. The rims of Level 1 chalices are triangular and inverted, frequently with a pronounced or slight ridge (fig. 21:1,2; cf. Loud 1948: pl. 72:11–13). The triangular rim is occasionally elongated, as in fig. 21:2. The flared foot is common in early Iron I (Guy 1938: pls. 8:3; 16:9,10; 19:17; 71:17). The ridge continues into Level 2 forms (fig. 26:2,3; Loud 1948: pl. 67:5 for the former), with as many rims evidencing a slight to pronounced groove (fig. 26:4–6). The triangular rims of this level are both inverted (fig. 26:6) and everted (fig. 26:5). Figure 26:1 represents a slight variation in the profile of the ridged rim (cf. Yadin 1960: pl. 118:24), though the stepped foot is attested in chalices of early Iron I (Guy 1938:

pl. 8:14). The inverted, triangular grooved rim is the most common profile in Level 3, and the groove is usually pronounced (fig. 30:4,5; Guy 1938: pls. 16:9; 19:17; Yadin 1960: pl. 141:20). Everted rims with groove are also attested in this level (fig. 30:3,6), as are triangular ridged rims (30:1). The chalices of Level 4 perpetuate the rim profiles of the previous level (fig. 33:3–5), though more pronounced. Level 5 produced only six chalices, one with the unusual profile of fig. 35:7.

The chalice base in Levels 1 to 3 evidences several forms; straight (figs. 21:1; 26:2; 30:5), and slightly to moderately stepped or flared (figs. 21:2; 26:3,4,6; 30:2,3). The chalices of Level 4 have a more pronounced flare (fig. 33:3–5; cf. fig. 35:7). Unusual base profiles are represented by the forms of fig. 26:1,5. Each level yielded forms with shallow and deep bowls, as well as low and high bases.

Krater-mugs. The so-called krater-mug (figs. 21:3; 31:1–3, 33:6–7) is attested in small numbers in Levels 3 and 4 of Tomb 1 (less than 15 examples in each level), with one to three examples each in Levels 1, 2, and 5. In Levels 3 and 4, the form is quite uniform in appearance (cf. the Level 3 forms of fig. 31:1–3 with the Level 4 examples of 33:6,7). The only variations in evidence for the krater-mugs of these two levels are the sharpness of the body carination and the type of base, though flat and disk bases are attested in both levels. With the exception of the rim in fig. 21:6, this Level 1 example is very close to the krater-mugs of earlier levels. Precise parallels are unknown, though certain features (such as the pronounced body carination and the high vertical rim) are reminiscent of similar features on other vessel types from the MB II, Late Bronze, and early Iron Ages, as well as local imitations of Late Bronze Cypriot imports (Guy 1938: pls. 31:4; 32:22,23; 34:8,10; 59:8; 60:35; 64:34,35; 68:3; 70:12–17; 71:1; 73:3; Yadin 1960: pl. 116:11).

Multihandled Kraters, Stirrup Jars, and Flasks. Tomb 1 produced a remarkable assemblage of multihandled kraters, of which only a small selection has been presented in the pottery plates. It must be emphasized that the forms depicted in the plates are not predominant types, nor are they representative for the levels in which they are attested. The majority of the multihandled kraters and some of the most interesting forms were uncovered in the later levels of the tomb. The kraters of figs. 21:6; 22:1–3; and 23:1,2 are from Level 1; those depicted in 27:1–3 are from Level 2. The vessel pictured in fig. 34:5 is from Level 4. Level 1 kraters have numerous parallels in Iron I (Guy 1938: pls. 8:9 [22:1 here]; 68:16 [22:2 here]; 70:13; 73:3 [22:3 here, with fenestrated pedestal]; 70:15 [23:1 here]; Loud 1948: pl. 69:14. For Level 2, multihandled kraters, see Guy 1938: pl. 68:3 [27:1 here]; 68:16 [27:3 here]); McGovern 1986: fig. 51:24,25,27,28. The final report will provide a detailed study of this important and unique vessel type.

Tomb 1 yielded fewer than ten stirrup jars, the majority from Levels 3 and 4 (figs. 30:7, 34:4, respectively). The closest parallels come from Late Bronze II contexts, and included several from Late Bronze IIB, the period of Mycenaean IIIB (for parallels to the Level 3 stirrup jars, see Pritchard 1980: fig. 10:3; 53:10; Guy 1938: pls. 14:7; 34:22; Yadin 1960: pl. 137:11,12; Baramki 1959: 133:5,8,10,11; p. 135:14,15,21 [though the Sarepta imports are more angular in body profile]; for Level 4, see Pritchard 1980: figs. 13:6,7; 21:10; Loud 1948: pl. 62:9; Hankey 1974: 139, fig. 7:81–83).

The ring flask of fig. 30:8 (and several other closed-form flasks of Level 3) find many close parallels in Late Bronze IIB contexts: Lachish (Tufnell 1958: pl. 84:955); Megiddo (Guy 1938: pl. 14:6; 34:13); Tell es-Saᶜidiyeh (Pritchard 1980: figs. 12:2; 13:9; 18:2); Tell el-Farᶜah (de Vaux 1951: 570, fig. 3:6); Hazor (Yadin 1960: pl. 130:8–13); Gibeon (Pritchard 1963: fig. 8:25); Beth Shean (Oren 1973: pls. 50:3; 48b:32; 44b:31); Sarepta (Baramki 1959: 137:27–29,31).

Figures 19–35 and the accompanying preliminary observations only begin to explore the incredible wealth of this tomb's pottery traditions. The combination of a clearly stratified burial context in five levels and nearly three thousand vessels holds great promise for the study of pottery typology for the period in which the western cemetery was in use at Dothan. Based on the pottery and other material remains, the following chronology is suggested for the five levels of Tomb 1:

Level 5 Late Bronze IIA (1400–1300 B.C.E.). The tomb consisted of the central chamber with the shaft measuring 0.90 × 1.45 m. Remains of this earliest level were restricted to an area in the back of the tomb chamber.

Level 4 Late Bronze IIA (1400–1300 B.C.E.). The chronology of this and the earliest level are established on the basis of both domestic and imported pottery (Cypriot and Mycenean wares). Burials occupied the entire chamber in Level 4.

Level 3 Late Bronze IIB (1300–1200 B.C.E.), though some LB IIA forms are still attested in this level. The tomb was enlarged by the addition of crypts.

Level 2 This level evidences a mixture of Late Bronze IIB and Early Iron I domestic pottery.

Level 1 Early Iron I (1200–1100 B.C.E.). As noted above, diagnostic Iron I pottery was discovered in this latest level. No Iron II pottery was present. The shaft was widened from 0.90 × 1.45 m to 1.25 by 1.45 m with a depth of 1.00 m. The blocking stone fit into the reworked shaft and rested on large stones that were placed on the shaft steps below.

Although some chronological refinement for the individual levels is possible in the final publication of the western cemetery, Tomb 1 dates between the 14th and 12th centuries B.C.E.

Other Tomb 1 Deposits. Several unique deposits are worthy of note: three seven-spouted lamps (Free 1960: 14); a simply decorated *kernos* ring with free communication between the ring and the seven spouts; five zoomorphic vessels, each fashioned in the shape of a bull with sexual attributes clearly represented; a bronze lamp manufactured in identical form to its ceramic counterparts; and a collection of 25 scarabs. Imported Mycenaean and Cypriot wares are represented among the burial vessels. The tomb also yielded bronze weaponry (daggers, spearheads, and various projectiles), a collection of 39 bronze bowls, and a complete faience bowl with painted lines on the bottom of the vessel. Other deposits included an alabaster chalice, basalt vessels, limestone platters, grinding stones, spindles, whorls, and jewelry (bracelets, necklaces, finger rings, toggle pins, beads, and pins). Two ivory pendants, fashioned in the shape of a mallet or hammer, were discovered on the chest area of two skeletons. Very few remnants of the food offerings survived. Olive pits, sheep bones, shellfish remains, and a fish vertebra were among the few discoveries.

As would be expected in a multiple burial tomb, the level of disturbance made it very difficult to associate deposits with individual burials, except

TABLE 3. Personal Ornaments found in Tomb 1

| | Tomb Levels | | | | | |
	1	2	3	4	5	Total
Bracelet	1	0	0	1	0	2
Ring	6	6	2	30	10	54
Earring	0	9	0	9	0	18
Gold earring	0	0	0	0	1	1
Toggle pin	0	0	0	3	1	4
Button	0	0	0	1	0	1
Ivory pendant	1	1	0	0	0	2
Pin	3	0	0	9	0	12
Total Personal Ornaments						94

TABLE 4. Weapons found in Tomb 1

| | Tomb Levels | | | | | |
	1	2	3	4	5	Total
Dagger	9	18	18	10	16	71
Projectile points	2	10	1	1	0	4
Spear point	2	7	5	3	2	19
Total weapons						94

TABLE 5. Amulets and Ritual Objects Found in Tomb 1

| | Tomb Levels | | | | | |
	1	2	3	4	5	Total
Scarab	4	7	4	10	0	25
Kernos ring	0	0	1	0	0	1
Zoomorphic	2	2	1	0	0	5
Total amulets and ritual objects						31

for the interment in Crypt H (fig. 12). The deposits associated with this burial included seven pottery vessels and one clam shell. A dipper juglet and an oversize flask were placed at the head of the skeleton, presumably to quench the thirst of the deceased. A medium-sized bowl, rounded-bottom juglet, jug, pot, and a Cypriot bowl were placed at the feet. The clam shell was associated with this latter group. No personal adornments, implements, weapons, or ritual objects were included in the burial assemblage.

Tables 3 to 8 present the numbers of selected artifacts, according to distribution throughout the tomb's five levels.

TABLE 6. Flora and Fauna Found in Tomb 1

| | Tomb Levels | | | | | |
	1	2	3	4	5	Total
Olive pit	0	2	6	0	2	10
Fish bone	0	0	1	0	0	1
Sheep bone	1	1	0	0	0	2
Shell	0	0	0	1	4	5
Total flora and fauna						18

TABLE 7. Implements Found in Tomb 1

| | Tomb Levels | | | | | |
	1	2	3	4	5	Total
Needle	0	1	0	0	0	1
Knife	0	2	1	1	0	4
Hook	0	0	0	2	0	2
Whorl	3	3	6	0	3	15
Spindle	3	2	1	0	0	6
Total implements						28

TABLE 8. Miscellaneous Deposits
Found in Tomb 1

| | Tomb Levels | | | | | |
	1	2	3	4	5	Total
Bronze bowl	3	12	14	8	2	39
Bronze lamp	1	0	0	0	0	1
Ivory cup	0	0	0	1	0	1
Limestone bowl	0	0	0	0	1	1
Basalt bowl	1	0	0	3	0	4
Basalt platter	0	0	0	0	2	2
Basalt chalice	0	0	1	0	0	1
Total miscellaneous deposits						49

Tomb 1 is one of the largest and richest multiple burial tombs discovered to date in the Levant. As will be detailed below, only Megiddo, Shechem, Lachish, and Tell el-ʿAjjûl have yielded burial contexts comparable in size, tomb construction, or wealth of finds.

Figurine Lamp (figs. 17a–c, 18a–d). Numbered among the rich artifact finds of Tomb 1 was an anthropomorphic lamp of unique design and significance (Reg. No. T1-2010-P1344; see figures 17a–c and 18a–d).

The lamp is likely wheelmade, though only radiographic imaging will provide a definite determination. The interior surface shows traces of wheel finishing by smoothing of the surface with a rotary movement. The clay is composed of several types of aplastic inclusions (including small fragments of calcite or gypsum with medium to coarse limestone and sandstone inclusions well distributed) and an organic material that has burned out. The hardness of the clay (MOHS 4) suggests a firing temperature above 700° C. The lack of evidence of extreme vitrification in the body indicates a firing temperature below 1000° C and probably below 900° C. No refiring tests, microstructure evaluations, or radiographic imaging were conducted. These conclusions are based on visual and low-power optical microscopy.

The vessel has a sharply pinched spout. The fold of the spout is so pronounced that it encompasses half of the lamp form. The reservoir of the lamp has an exterior depth of nearly 6 cm (bottom exterior to the tip of the figure's head) with an interior depth of 3.7 cm. The form has a definite rim with the appearance of a slight base, though the body features of the applied figure may simply create the impression of a base. No traces of burning are evident. As is typical of many Tomb 1 vessels, this buff-colored lamp is of relatively poor manufacturing quality.

The molded and applied human figure makes this lamp unique to the Dothan pottery assemblage. The applied human form extends from a point beyond the tip of the spout to the start of the slightly flaring rim. The figure's overall length is approximately 16 cm. The head extends 2 cm beyond the tip of the spout and is 3 cm wide × 4 cm high. Five clay globulets, applied high on the forehead and extending ear to ear, create the impression of a coiffure or some type of head adornment. The skull terminates in a pointed ridge, 1 cm higher than the uppermost globulet. The ears are created by elongated globulets of clay. The right ear is 1.4 cm long; the left is 1.2 cm.

The nose is prominent (1.5 cm in length), flaring slightly from the sloping forehead. The eyes were created by pushing excess clay upward, forming a rounded depression. The lips consist of two thin coils of applied clay 1.3 cm in width by 0.7 cm thick). The arms (each 7.5 cm long) were created by applying a small coil of clay along the bottom fold of the pinched spout. The ends of the arms are splayed, with no hands or fingers distinguishable. The legs are rather short in relation to the body (5.5 cm to 6.0 cm long). Similar to the

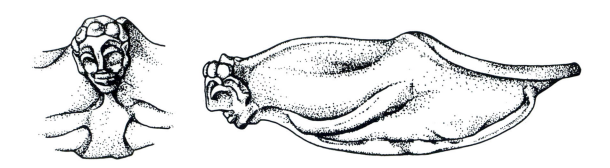

a

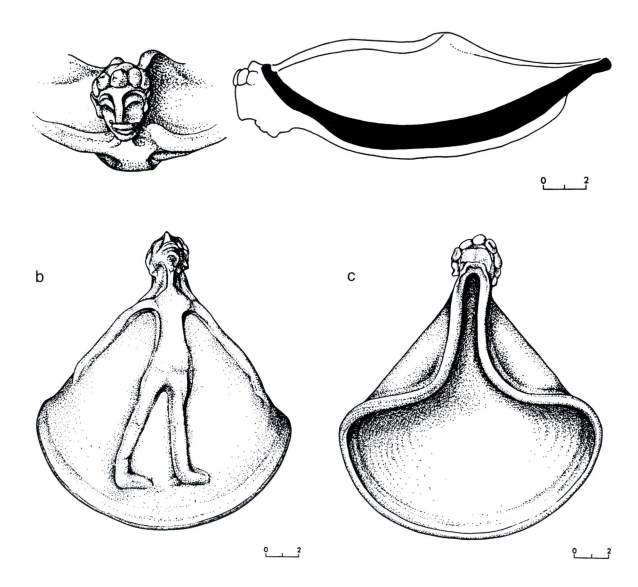

b   c

Fig. 17. Drawings of the figurine lamp (Reg. No. T1-2010-P1344). **a.** First in a sequence of three drawings that detail the figurine lamp (#T1-2010-P1344); side and section drawings with details of the figure's head and upper body; **b.** bottom of the figurine lamp; **c.** drawing of the figurine lamp from above.

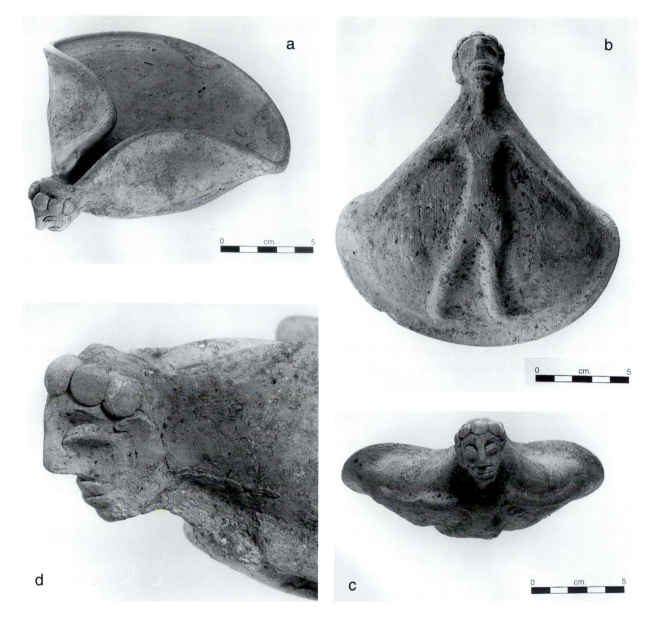

Fig. 18. Photographs of the figurine lamp. **a**. First in a sequence of four photographs that detail the figurine lamp (#T1-2010-P1344); **b**. bottom of the figurine lamp; **c**. frontal view of the figurine lamp; **d**. detail of the head of the figurine lamp.

arms, the legs were created by the application of clay coils that were smoothed onto the bottom of the lamp. The feet are also splayed with no toe features discernible. The figure exhibits a two-directional stance. The feet are molded in a left to right stance, whereas the body and head are applied in a frontal stance. No gender characteristics are evident. The absence of breasts suggests that the figure is a male. Several imprints of the sculptor's fingers indicate that the clay was quite wet

during the application of the figure to the bottom of the vessel.

Skeletal Remains. Although skulls were better preserved in Levels 3 to 5, the skeletal remains in all levels of this tomb were very fragmentary and in a state of complete disorder, often fused in limestone. The poorer state of preservation of the skeletal remains, especially the skulls in Levels 1 and 2, may be explained by the damage incurred when the tomb ceiling collapsed. The five levels yielded a total of 204 skulls: 47 fragmentary skulls in Level 1; 57 fragmentary and 9 complete skulls in Level 2 (one infant skeleton was discovered); 22 fragmentary and 26 complete skulls in Level 3; 3 fragmentary and 30 complete skulls in Level 4; and, in Level 5, 3 fragmentary and 7 complete skulls. Based on these and other skeletal remains, it has been estimated that Tomb 1 contained between 250 and 300 skeletons.

OBSERVATIONS ON TOMB 1
MORTUARY PRACTICE

The following observations are advanced regarding the reconstruction of Tomb 1 burial ritual. Upon the death of a family member, the body was taken to the ancestral tomb in the limestone escarpment on the western side of the settlement. The bones of earlier burials were unceremoniously swept to the sides of the chamber, thereby providing space for the new interment. The body was then placed on the floor of the chamber or on the debris of earlier burials, either in an extended or full-length position without regard to a fixed orientation. No evidence for contracted positioning was discerned. Numerous burials were documented in which the skeletal remains were covered with the body sherds of large storage jars. Vessels, furnishings, and personal possessions were either placed around the circumference of the tomb or carefully arranged around the body. The deposits appear to represent a full complement of everyday articles that presumably would provide the deceased with the necessary material needs in the afterlife. Food and drink were included in the deposits, and the presence of clay lamps in large numbers suggests the importance of light. Following interment, the doorway to the chamber was closed with the blocking stone. The shaft was then filled with debris.

When a second death in the family occurred and the tomb was to be used again, the debris in the shaft and then the blocking stone were removed, and the corpse and its deposits were placed in the chamber. As before, the previous burials and deposits were brushed aside to make room for the new interment with its adornments.

As noted above, the practice of multiple successive burials resulted in significant destruction to the skeletal remains. In many instances, the skeletal remains were fused into a solid mass, making it difficult to study the components of the individual interment. The few burials that had not suffered destruction indicate that full-length or extended positioning was preferred. Tibia and fibula bones were in an excellent state of preservation. Some were stacked like cordwood; though most were scattered throughout the burial debris.

Several inferences may be drawn from the study of Tomb 1 mortuary practices relating to such issues as the treatment of the body, the nature of the tomb as a temporary residence, and the significance of the burial deposits. The evidence suggests that there existed a contrast in attitude regarding the corpse between the time of interment and its later treatment after the decomposition of the flesh. At the time of burial, scrupulous care was exercised in the placement of the corpse and in the arrangement of the burial deposits. Once the body was transformed into a pile of bones, it was treated with little respect. It was normal practice to sweep aside the bones and deposits into a heap, often destroying both in the process to make room for subsequent burials. Apparently it was believed that the deceased was conscious of feeling and in need of sustenance as long as the flesh had not completely decomposed. With the decomposition of the flesh, however, the descendants could with impunity destroy or perhaps even remove certain of the burial deposits. The tomb was not considered the permanent residence of the dead, but only a temporary station on the way to the netherworld. There is no evidence that burials deposits were renewed periodically, nor were additional supplies placed in the tombs in the years that followed interment (see Cooley 1968: 80–188; 1983 for further study of Tomb 1 mortuary practices).

SUMMARY OBSERVATIONS ON TOMB 1
IN THE CONTEXT OF EASTERN
MEDITERRANEAN BURIAL PRACTICES

Based on clearly prescribed burial characteristics, a recent study by Gonen discerns two distinct groups of burials of the Late Bronze Age in Canaan: pit burials for individual interment and cave burials for multiple interment (Gonen 1992: 9–31). Both burial types are regarded as indigenous to Canaan, having been practiced since the beginning of the Middle Bronze Age. Gonen further distinguishes another indigenous burial practice characterized by intramural interment. The study concludes with a presentation of eight foreign burial types that originated in different places and arrived in Canaan during different phases of the Late Bronze Age: bench burial caves; loculi burial caves; bilobate burial caves; open pits; structural chambers; and larnax, coffin, and jar burials. Tell Dothan's Tomb 1 clearly falls within the general category of cave burials for multiple interments and shares the specific characteristics of the loculi burial caves.

Unlike those burials that used natural caves (such as Tell Jedur and Khirbet Rabud), or those that reused Early or Middle Bronze Age burial sites (Tel Regev, Beth-shean, Gibeon, Jericho, Tell el-Far^cah [N], and certain ones at Gezer and Megiddo), Tell Dothan's Tomb 1 was a newly constructed burial site of the Late Bronze Age. However, Tomb 3 was a nearby burial cave that was originally used as a cistern. As Gonen has correctly observed, a typology of Late Bronze Age tombs is impossible to establish at the present time and probably for the immediate future as well.

Like most multiple burial caves of the Late Bronze Age, Tomb 1 was located outside of the settlement's fortifications on the western slopes of the mound. Other burial chambers located on the slopes of the mound are known from Megiddo, Lachish, Tell Jedur, Tell Beit Mirsim, and Beth-shemesh. While many settlements have only one associated burial cave, this tomb was part of a cemetery that consisted of three burial caves. Unfortunately, Tombs 2 and 3 were not well-preserved by comparison, though roughly contemporary (on the later side) with Tomb 1. Nevertheless, there is no clear tomb organization in the western cemetery, consistent with Gonen's observation that the positioning of Late Bronze Age burial caves in relation to associated settlements is irrelevant.

Again, consistent with the majority of Late Bronze Age cave burials, Tomb 1 was used for multiple interments, with the well-known Middle Bronze II practice of removing old bones to the sides of the chamber to make room for new burials. This practice is well documented at Jericho, Megiddo, Beth-Shean, Gibeon, and Safed. The number of interments in multiple burial tombs varies from a handful, though this circumstance is relatively infrequent, to the numbers represented in Tell Dothan's largest burial chamber. The types and numbers of funerary objects detailed above are quite characteristic of the larger Late Bronze Age burial caves. Pottery vessels of various types, mostly local, represent the largest class of funerary deposits. Approximately five percent of the Tomb 1 assemblage is imported. This datum, too, is con-

sistent with the typical multiple burial cave of this period.

While Tomb 1 shares the general characteristics of cave burials for multiple interments, Gonen classifies this tomb among the categories of foreign burials, specifically caves with loculi burials (Gonen 1992: 132–33). As is clear in the accompanying plan, Tomb 1 had six rock-hewn and two constructed crypts or loculi. Similar roughly contemporary tomb constructions are known from Tell el-^cAjjul (Petrie 1931: 127, pl. 57, fig. 6; pl. 54); Lachish (Tufnell 1953: pl. 128; 1958: 228, 240, 280–87); and Megiddo (Guy 1938: 127, 129; pls. 41, 42, 140, 141). Though some would suggest a slightly earlier chronology, the typical tomb with loculi was introduced at the beginning of the Late Bronze Age. This burial design obviously was intended for individual burials but in the context of the group, often the family.

While noting that loculi burial caves in Canaan display hybrid features of Greek and Cypriot origin, Gonen finds the parallels closer to Cypriot models, where the design was common, beginning with the Early Cypriot period (Gonen 1992: 24–25). She studies Tumulus #7 at Paleoskutela in the center of the Karpas Peninsula as representative of the Cypriot loculi burial cave (Sjökvist 1940: fig. 45:10; Gjerstad 1934: 427–38). The parallels between this tomb construction and that of Tell Dothan's Tomb 1 are striking. The burial chamber of the Cypriot example is roughly circular, with four loculi cut into the walls. Access to the burial chamber was achieved by means of a well-cut shaft with three steps that opened into a stomion. A blocking stone was located at the entrance to the tomb chamber. Seven skeletons were found in the four loculi, two burials in each of three loculi, and an individual burial in the fourth. Seven additional burials were discovered on the floor of the tomb chamber. Although the number of burials in the Tell Dothan tomb is significantly larger, the parallels in tomb construction are instructive.

BRIEF INTRODUCTION TO
TOMBS 2 AND 3

Tombs 2 and 3 also were discovered in Area K, the former during the 1962 season and the latter in 1964. The construction of both tombs involved the reuse of cisterns that had been quarried into the soft limestone. Neither tomb was as well preserved as Tomb 1, and neither evidenced the stratification of the latter. In both instances, the complete architectural definition of the tomb complex was lost to later quarrying, which also resulted in extensive damage to tomb deposits. Although Tomb 1 is the primary focus of this article, a few details will be presented for Tombs 2 and 3, since these burial contexts complete the picture of the western cemetery.

Tomb 2 was a small shaft-type tomb constructed in Area K-23 (just southwest of Tomb 1), an area originally used for cisterns. Cistern D was used as the shaft for Tomb 2. It was elliptical, 1.40 m (north–south) × 1.60 m (east–west). The depth of this cistern shaft was 1.30 m. In its eastern side an opening was cut to serve as the entrance into the chamber of Tomb 2. Cisterns B (1.50 m × 1.05 m with a depth of 1.25 m) and C (1.47 m × 1.56 m with a depth of 2.20 m) were contiguous with the cistern shaft (Cistern D) on its southern side. Cistern E (1.70 m × 1.90 m with a depth of 2.00 m) was located just north of the cistern shaft, though not contiguous with it. This cistern, however, did adjoin the chamber wall of Tomb 2. The chamber of Tomb 2 was basically rectangular, with rounded corners measuring approximately 5.50 m × 4.0 m. Five crypts were located around the chamber's northern, eastern, and southern sides.

Tomb 2 skeletal remains are extremely fragmentary. Some 500 objects, including sherds, were registered from this tomb and cistern complex, suggesting chronological horizons similar to these of Tomb 1.

Tomb 3 was discovered some 35 m west–southwest of Tomb 1. Originally, this area also was used for cisterns. Three intact cisterns, labeled A, B, and C, were completely excavated during the 1964 season and another (D) was partially cleared. When Cistern B no longer functioned in that capacity, the chamber was utilized as a tomb. This bell-shaped cistern-tomb (Tomb 3), with rounded bottom, measured 1.80 m (north–south) × 1.70 m (east–west). The maximum depth of the tomb chamber was 1.60 m.

The soft limestone into which the cistern–tomb had been cut was quarried at a later time, resulting in extensive damage to the chamber and its contents. Most of the pottery was broken and widely scattered over the area of the tomb. The skeletal remains were in similar disarray. Despite the level of disturbance, there was no evidence of stratification as in Tomb 1. Only one level of burials was distinguished.

Tomb 3 yielded 89 vessels in the following categories: lamps (12), juglets (27), chalices (11), jugs (28), bowls (9), jar (1), and pyxis (1). The handful of bronze objects included a knife handle with rivets and two rings. Also noteworthy was a small assortment of beads. The skeletal remains were extremely fragmentary, including two skull fragments and teeth from an adult and an infant. The lack of data precludes observations on burial orientation or positioning.

The pottery indicates that the chronological horizons of this tomb correspond to the later levels of Tomb 1. Several examples of the diagnostic Iron I lamps and black dipper juglets with bulbous body were present, as well as vessels with wheel burnishing on the inside and outside. There are no indications of continued usage in the Iron II period.

CONCLUSION

Archaeological investigation at numerous sites throughout the Levant has yielded abundant data concerning burials and burial rituals (for summaries, see Gonen 1987; 1992; Bloch-Smith 1992; Abercrombie 1979; Meyers 1970; Rahmani 1981). The nonepigraphic data of archaeology are hardly sufficient, however, for an understanding of death, death rituals, and the theological and sociological inferences of mortuary practice. The archaeological data must be viewed in light of the literary evidence; and here too, the horizons of our knowledge have been expanded through discovery of pertinent epigraphic evidence, notably the Ugaritic texts, among other sources (Lewis 1989; Tromp 1969; Healey 1977). The final publication of Tell Dothan's western cemetery will provide a wealth of information for numerous areas of research in biblical, archaeological, and ancient Near Eastern studies, especially the study of death and burial rituals in the world of Canaanite–Hebrew culture.

NOTES

[1] Joseph Free (1911–1974) was professor of biblical archaeology at Wheaton College during the nine seasons of excavation between 1953 and 1964. In 1965, he retired to northern Minnesota to pursue his publication projects.

Soon thereafter, however, he accepted the position of professor of archaeology at Bemidji State College in Bemidji, Minnesota, where he served until his death.

[2] The excavated materials from Dothan are presently housed in several locations: a small collection in the Jordan Archaeological Museum in Amman; several collections totaling over 2000 pieces in Jerusalem at the Rockefeller Museum, Saint George's College, and in the Siriganian Building; a large collection of artifacts and some of the field records at Wheaton College, Wheaton, Illinois; and most of the field records and a representative collection of artifacts at Gordon-Conwell Theological Seminary in South Hamilton, MA. The latter collection originally was housed at Southwest Missouri State University in Springfield, MO., and was transferred to the seminary in July 1981.

[3] All plans and photographs in this publication were used with permission from The Dothan Archaeological Project under the direction of Robert Cooley. The pottery drawings were done by Abbas Alizadeh.

[4] A project of this magnitude has generated a lengthy list of acknowledgments, of which only a few will be noted here. We thank Joseph Cunningham, Bonnie Hanson, and Carl Taeschner for their generous financial support, and Anita Free Wilhelmi, David Free, and Abed Ismail for their dedicated support of the Dothan Archaeological Project. A special word of thanks to Alfred Hoerth for years of work with the Wheaton College collection of Tell Dothan artifacts and for his facilitation of our research efforts with this corpus.

BIBLIOGRAPHY

Abercrombie, J. R.
  1979 *Palestinian Burial Practices from 1200 to 600 B.C.E.* Unpublished Ph.D. dissertation, University of Pennsylvania, Philadelphia.

Baramki, D. C.
  1959 A Late Bronze Age Tomb at Sarafend: Ancient Sarepta. *Berytus* 12: 129–42.

Bloch-Smith, E.
  1992 *Judahite Burial Practices and Beliefs about the Dead.* JSOT/ASOR Monographs Series 7. Sheffield: JSOT.

Cooley, R. E.
  1968 *The Canaanite Burial Pattern in the Light of the Material Remains.* Unpublished Ph.D. dissertation, New York University, New York.
  1983 Gathered to His People: A Study of a Dothan Family Tomb. Pp. 47–58 in *The Living and Active Word of God: Studies in Honor of Samuel J. Schultz*, eds. M. Inch and R. Youngblood. Winona Lake, IN: Eisenbrauns.

de Vaux, R.
  1951 La troisième campagne de fouilles à Tell el-Fâr[c]ah, près Naplouse. *Revue Biblique* 58: 566–90.
  1952 La quatrième campagne de fouilles à Tell el-Fâr[c]ah, près Naplouse. *Revue Biblique* 59: 551–83.

Dothan, T.
  1982 *The Philistines and their Material Culture.* New Haven: Yale.

Free, J. P.
  1953 The First Season of Excavation at Dothan. *Bulletin of the American Schools of Oriental Research* 131: 16–20.
  1954 The Second Season at Dothan. *Bulletin of the American Schools of Oriental Research* 135: 14–20.
  1955 The Third Season at Dothan. *Bulletin of the American Schools of Oriental Research* 139: 3–9.
  1956a The Fourth Season at Dothan. *Bulletin of the American Schools of Oriental Research* 143: 11–17.
  1956b The Excavation of Dothan. *Biblical Archaeologist* 19: 43–48.
  1956c Dothan, 1954. *Annual of the Department of Antiquities of Jordan* 3: 79–80.
  1957 Radiocarbon Date of Iron Age Level at Dothan. *Bulletin of the American Schools of Oriental Research* 147: 36–37.
  1958 The Fifth Season at Dothan. *Bulletin of the American Schools of Oriental Research* 152: 10–18.
  1959 The Sixth Season at Dothan. *Bulletin of the American Schools of Oriental Research* 156: 22–29.
  1960 The Seventh Season at Dothan. *Bulletin of the American Schools of Oriental Research* 160: 6–15.
  1962 The Seventh Season at Dothan. *Annual of the Department of Antiquities of Jordan* 6–7: 117–20.
  1972 *Archaeology and Bible History.* Wheaton, IL: Scripture.
  1975 Dothan. Pp. 157–60 in *The Zondervan Pictorial Bible Encyclopedia*, ed. M. C. Tenney. Grand Rapids: Zondervan.

Gittlen, B. M.
1977   *Studies in the Late Cypriote Pottery Found in Palestine*. Ann Arbor, MI: University Microfilms.

Gjerstad, E.
1934   *The Swedish Cyprus Expedition. I. Finds and Results of the Excavations in Cyprus 1927–1931*. Stockholm: Swedish Cyprus Expedition.

Gonen, R.
1987   Structural Tombs in Canaan in the 2nd Millennium B.C. Pp. 128–35 in *The Architecture of Ancient Israel*, eds. H. Katzenstein, A. Kempinski, and R. Reich. Jerusalem: Israel Exploration Society (Hebrew).

1992   *Burial Patterns and Cultural Diversity in Late Bronze Age Canaan*. ASOR Dissertation Series 7. Winona Lake, IN: Eisenbrauns.

Guy, P. L. O.
1938   *Megiddo Tombs*. Oriental Institute Publications 33. Chicago: University of Chicago.

Hankey, V.
1974   A Late Bronze Age Temple at Amman 1. The Aegean Pottery; 2. Vases and Objects Made of Stone. *Levant* 6: 131–78.

Healey, J. F.
1977   *Death, Underworld and Afterlife in the Ugaritic Texts*. Unpublished Ph.D. dissertation, University of London, London.

James, F. W.
1966   *The Iron Age of Beth Shean: A Study of Levels IV–VI*. University Museum Monograph 28. Philadelphia: University of Pennsylvania.

Lewis, T. J.
1989   *Cults of the Dead in Ancient Israel and Ugarit*. Harvard Semitic Museum Monographs 39. Atlanta: Scholars.

Loud, G.
1948   Megiddo II. Chicago: University of Chicago.

McGovern, P. E.
1986   *The Late Bronze and Early Iron Ages of Central Transjordan: The Baqᶜah Valley Project, 1977–1981*. University Museum Monograph 65. Philadelphia: University of Pennsylvania.

Meyers, E. M.
1970   Secondary Burials in Palestine. *Biblical Archaeologist* 33: 2–29.

Oren, E.
1973   *The Northern Cemetery at Beth Shan*. Leiden: Brill.

Petrie, W. M. F.
1931   *Ancient Gaza 1*. London: British School of Archaeology in Egypt.

Pritchard, J. B.
1963   *The Bronze Age Cemetery at Gibeon*. University Museum Monograph 25. Philadelphia: Museum of the University of Pennsylvania.

1980   *The Cemetery at Tell es-Saᶜidiyeh, Jordan*. University Museum Monograph 41. Philadelphia: University of Pennsylvania.

Rahmani, L. Y.
1981   Ancient Jerusalem's Funerary Customs and Tombs: Part Two. *Biblical Archaeologist* 44: 229–35.

Schaeffer, C. F.
1939   *The Cuneiform Texts of Ras Shamra-Ugarit*. London: Oxford.

Sjökvist, E.
1940   *Problems of the Late Cypriot Bronze Age*. Stockholm: Swedish Cyprus Expedition.

Tromp, N. J.
1969   *Primitive Conceptions of Death and the Nether World in the Old Testament*. Rome: Pontifical Biblical Institute.

Tufnell, O.
1953   *Lachish III: The Iron Age*. London: Oxford.
1958   *Lachish IV: The Bronze Age*. London: Oxford.

Ussishkin, D.
1975   Dothan. Pp. 337–39 in *Encyclopedia of Archaeological Excavations in the Holy Land*, Vol. 1, ed. M. Avi-Yonah. Jerusalem: Israel Exploration Society.

Yadin, Y.
1958   *Hazor I: An Account of the First Season of Excavations, 1955*. Jerusalem: Magnes.

1960   *Hazor II: An Account of the Second Season of Excavations, 1956*. Jerusalem: Magnes.

1961   *Hazor III–IV: An Account of the Third and Fourth Seasons of Excavations, 1957–1958*. Jerusalem: Magnes.

SUPPLEMENTAL READINGS

Albright, W. F.
1938   *The Excavation of Tell Beit Mirsim, 2: The Bronze Age*. Annual of the American Schools of Oriental Research 17. Cambridge, MA: American Schools of Oriental Research.

Alesksin, V. A.
1983   Burial Customs as an Archaeological Source: Reply to Comments. *Current Anthropology* 24: 137–49, 373–79.

Amiran, R.
1970   *Ancient Pottery of the Holy Land*. New Brunswick, NJ: Rutgers.

Anderson, W. P.
1990   The Beginnings of Phoenician Pottery: Vessel Shape, Style, and Ceramic Technology in the Early Phases of the Phoenician Iron Age. *Bulletin of the American Schools of Oriental Research* 279: 35–54.

Bailey, L. R.
1979   *Biblical Perspectives on Death*. Philadelphia: Fortress.

Binford, L. R.
1971   Mortuary Practices: Their Study and Their Potential. Pp. 6–29 in *Approaches to the Social Dimensions of Mortuary Practice*, ed. J. A. Brown. Memoirs of the Society for American Archaeology, 25. Washington: Society for American Archaeology.

Brichto, H. C.
1973   Kin, Cult, Land and Afterlife—A Biblical Complex. *Hebrew Union College Annual* 44: 1–54.

Dajani, R. W.
1970   A Late Bronze-Iron Age Tomb Excavated at Sahab, 1968. *Annual of the Department of Antiquities of Jordan* 15: 29–34.

Dever, W. G.
1992   The Chronology of Syria-Palestine in the Second Millennium B.C.E.: A Review of Current Issues. *Bulletin of the American Schools of Oriental Research* 288: 1–25.

Dever, W. G., *et al.*
1974   *Gezer II: Report of the 1967–70 Seasons in Fields I and II*. Annual of the Hebrew Union College/Nelson Glueck School of Biblical Archaeology. Jerusalem: Hebrew Union College.
1986   *Gezer IV: The 1969–71 Seasons in Field VI, the "Acropolis."* Annual of the Hebrew Union College/Nelson Glueck School of Biblical Archaeology. Jerusalem: Hebrew Union College.

Dornemann, R. H.
1982   The Beginning of the Iron Age in Transjordan. Pp. 135–40 in *Studies in the History and Archaeology of Jordan: 1*, ed. A. Hadidi. Amman: Department of Antiquities of Jordan.
1983   *The Archaeology of the Transjordan in the Bronze and Iron Ages*. Milwaukee, WI: Milwaukee Public Museum.

Dothan, T.
1972   Anthropoid Clay Coffins from a Late Bronze Age Cemetery near Deir el-Balah. *Israel Exploration Journal* 22: 65–72.
1979   *Excavations at the Cemetery of Deir el Balah*. Qedem 10. Jerusalem: Hebrew University.

Franken, H. J.
1969   *Excavations at Tell Deir ꜥAlla: A Stratigraphical and Analytical Study of the Early Iron Age Pottery*. Leiden: Brill.

Free, J. P.
1953a   Excavating Ancient Dothan. *Sunday School Times* 95: 491–92.
1953b   Further Digging at Dothan: Some of the Finds and What they Indicate. *Sunday School Times* 95: 624–25.
1953c   A 4000 Year Old Skeleton at Dothan: Does It Point to Child Sacrifices by the Canaanites? *Sunday School Times* 95: 930, 941–43.
1954   What Have Archaeologists Found? *Sunday School Times* 96: 807–8.
1955   Light on the Bible From the Near East. *Sunday School Times* 97: 750–51, 762–63.
1957b   Archaeological Excavation in 1956 and 1957. *Sunday School Times* 99: 928–29.
1958   Excavating at Dothan in 1958. *Sunday School Times* 100: 871–73.
1960   Digging Up the Past in Dothan: Archaeological Discoveries and Reports of Late 1959 and Early 1960. *Sunday School Times* 102: 689, 692, 702–3.

Furumark, A.
1944   The Mycenaean IIIC Pottery and its Relation to Cypriote Fabrics. *Opuscula Archaeologica* 3: 194–265.

Gittlen, B. M.
1981   The Cultural and Chronological Implications of the Cypro-Palestinian Trade During the Late Bronze Age. *Bulletin of the American Schools of Oriental Research* 241: 49–59.

Gonen, R.
1981   Tell el-ꜥAjjul in the Late Bronze Age-City or Cemetery. *Eretz Israel* 15: 69–78 (Hebrew).
1984   Urban Canaan in the Late Bronze Period. *Bulletin of the American Schools of Oriental Research* 253: 61–73.

Helms, S. W.
1977   Early Bronze Age Fortifications at Tell Dothan. *Levant* 9: 101–14.

James, F. W.
1977   *The Iron Age of Beth Shean: A Study of Levels IV–VI*. University Museum Monograph 28. Philadelphia: University of Pennsylvania.

James, F. W., and McGovern, P. E.
1993   *The Late Bronze Egyptian Garrison at Beth Shan: A Study of Levels VII and VIII*. Vols. 1 and 2. Philadelphia: University of Pennsylvania.

Leonard, A.
1981   Considerations of Morphological Variation in the Mycenaean Pottery From the Southeastern Mediterranean. *Bulletin of the American Schools of Oriental Research* 241: 87–101.

1989   The Late Bronze Age. *Biblical Archaeologist* 52: 4–39.

Loffreda, S.
1968   Typological Sequence of Iron Age Rock-Cut Tombs in Palestine. *Liber Annuus* 18: 244–87.

May, H. G.
1935   *Material Remains of the Megiddo Cult.* Oriental Institute Publications 26. Chicago: University of Chicago.

Morris, I.
1987   *Burial and Ancient Society: the Rise of the Greek City-State.* Cambridge: Cambridge University.
1992   *Death-Ritual and Social Structure in Classical Antiquity.* Cambridge: Cambridge University.

Oren, E.
1969   Cypriote Imports in the Palestinian Late Bronze I Context. *Opuscula Athiensia* 9: 127–50.

Petrie, W. M. F.
1932   *Ancient Gaza 2.* London: British School of Archaeology in Egypt.
1933   *Ancient Gaza 3.* London: British School of Archaeology in Egypt.
1934   *Ancient Gaza 4.* London: British School of Archaeology in Egypt.

Pitard, W.
1994   The "Libation Installations" of the Tombs at Ugarit. *Biblical Archaeologist* 57: 20–37.

Pritchard, J. B.
1962   *Gibeon—Where the Sun Stood Still.* Princeton: Princeton University.
1965   The First Excavations at Tell es-Saᶜidiyeh, Jordan. *Biblical Archaeologist* 28: 10–17.
1975   *Sarepta: A Preliminary Report on the Iron Age.* University Museum Monograph 35. Philadelphia: University of Pennsylvania.

Smith, M. S., and Bloch-Smith, E.
1988   Death and Afterlife in Ugarit and Israel. *Journal of the American Oriental Society* 108: 277–84.

Stager, L. E.
1985   The Archaeology of the Family in Ancient Israel. *Bulletin of the American Schools of Oriental Research* 260: 1–35.

Stern, E.
1984   *Excavations at Tel Mevorakh (1973–1976). Part Two: The Bronze Age.* Qedem 18. Jerusalem: Hebrew University.

Stiebing, W. H., Jr.
1970   *Burial Practices in Palestine During the Bronze Age.* Unpublished Ph.D. dissertation, University of Pennsylvania, Philadelphia.

Stubbings, F. H.
1951   *Mycenaean Pottery from the Levant.* Cambridge: Cambridge University.

Ucko, D.
1969   Ethnography and Archaeological Interpretation of Funerary Remains. *World Archaeology* 1: 262–80.

TOMB PROVENANCE FOR THE POTTERY
OF FIGURES 19–35

		Vessel Type	Registration No.	Tomb Provenance (L=Level)			Vessel Type	Registration No.	Tomb Provenance (L=Level)
Fig.	19:1	Pyxis	1338	L1–8F		20:4	Biconical jar	1170	L1–7E
	19:2	Pyxis	1102	L1–6E		20:5	Biconical jar	1235	L1–8D
	19:3	Pyxis	1129	L1–7C		20:6	Biconical jar	1198	L1–8B
	19:4	Pyxis	1004	L1–5D		20:7	Biconical jar	1340	L1–8F
	19:5	Pyxis	1025	L1–5E					
	19:6	Pyxis	1186	L1–7E	Fig.	21:1	Chalice	998	L1–5D
	19:7	Pyxis	220	L1–2F		21:2	Chalice	199	L1–2E
	19:8	Pyxis	1334	L1–8F		21:3	Krater mug	927	L1–4D
	19:9	Pyxis	950	L1–4E		21:4	Lamp	1150	L1–7D
	19:10	Pyxis	1034	L1–5E		21:5	Lamp	933	L1–4E
	19:11	Pyxis	948	L1–4E		21:6	Multihandled krater	1273	L1–8E
	19:12	Pyxis	1097	L1–6E					
					Fig.	22:1	Multihandled krater	114	L1–3C
Fig.	20:1	Biconical jar	56	L1–4B		22:2	Multihandled krater	960	L1–4G
	20:2	Biconical jar	1300	L1–2F		22:3	Multihandled krater	966	L1–5B
	20:3	Biconical jar	108	L1–3C					

		Vessel Type	Registration No.	Tomb Provenance (L=Level)			Vessel Type	Registration No.	Tomb Provenance (L=Level)
Fig.	23:1	Multihandled krater	1224	L1–8D		29:5	Biconical jar	2023	L3–5E
	23:2	Multihandled krater	924	L1–4C		29:6	Biconical jar	2128	L3–6F
Fig.	24:1	Pyxis	1431	L2–5B	Fig.	30:1	Chalice	2155	L3–7D
	24:2	Pyxis	1703	L2–7D		30:2	Chalice	2000	L3–5C
	24:3	Pyxis	1888	L2–8G		30:3	Chalice	2018	L3–5E
	24:4	Pyxis	1647	L2–6F		30:4	Chalice	1984	L3–5C
	24:5	Pyxis	1356	L2–4C		30:5	Chalice	2097	L3–6E
	24:6	Pyxis	1672	L2–7C		30:6	Chalice	550	L3–2E
	24:7	Pyxis	1701	L2–7D		30:7	Stirrup jar	2218	L3–8C
	24:8	Pyxis	368	L2–3B		30:8	Flask	713	L3–4F
	24:9	Pyxis	1432	L2–5B		30:9	Stirrup jar	2044	L3–6C
	24:10	Pyxis	1581	L2–6C					
	24:11	Pyxis	505	L2–4G	Fig.	31:1	Krater mug	2143	L3–7C
	24:12	Pyxis	335	L2–2F		31:2	Krater mug	537	L3–5B
						31:3	Krater mug	2071	L3–6D
Fig.	25:1	Biconical jar	1769	L2–7F		31:4	Lamp	677	L3–3E
	25:2	Biconical jar	1764	L2–7F		31:5	Lamp	1899	L3–4B
	25:3	Biconical jar	1818	L2–8D		31:6	Lamp	2244	L3–8D
	25:4	Biconical jar	1660	L2–6G					
	25:5	Biconical jar	1774	L2–7F	Fig.	32:1	Pyxis	2296	L4–4D
	25:6	Biconical jar	1388	L2–4E		32:2	Pyxis	2392	L4–6C
						32:3	Pyxis	2393	L4–6C
Fig.	26:1	Chalice	1712	L2–7D		32:4	Pyxis	2474	L4–7D
	26:2	Chalice	1461	L2–5D		32:5	Pyxis	2372	L4–5E
	26:3	Chalice	1454	L2–5C		32:6	Pyxis	2328	L4–4G
	26:4	Chalice	1828	L2–8D		32:7	Pyxis	742	L4–2B
	26:5	Chalice	1480	L2–5D		32:8	Biconical jar	2431	L4–6E
	26:6	Chalice	1744	L2–7E		32:9	Biconical jar	898	L4–1E
	26:7	Lamp	1477	L2–5D					
	26:8	Lamp	1699	L2–7D	Fig.	33:1	Biconical jar	2351	L4–5D
	26:9	Lamp	424	L2–3E		33:2	Biconical jar	912	L4–4E
						33:3	Chalice	2316	L4–4F
Fig.	27:1	Multihandled krater	339	L2–2F		33:4	Chalice	782	L4–3C
	27:2	Multihandled krater	1646	L2–6F		33:5	Chalice	837	L4–3D
	27:3	Multihandled krater	1722	L2–7C		33:6	Krater-mug	2415	L4–6E
						33:7	Krater-mug	2338	L4–5C
Fig.	28:1	Pyxis	2084	L3–6D					
	28:2	Pyxis	2046	L3–6C	Fig.	34:1	Lamp	2302	L4–4D
	28:3	Pyxis	2184	L3–7E		34:2	Lamp	2444	L4–6F
	28:4	Pyxis	2147	L3–7D		34:3	Lamp	2442	L4–6E
	28:5	Pyxis	679	L3–3E		34:4	Stirrup jar	2522	L4–8D
	28:6	Pyxis	635	L3–4B		34:5	Multihandled krater	2427	L4–6E
	28:7	Pyxis	2052	L3–6C					
	28:8	Pyxis	2274	L3–8F	Fig.	35:1	Pyxis	2665	L5–7D
	28:9	Pyxis	2088	L3–6E		35:2	Pyxis	2663	L5–7D
	28:10	Pyxis	2134	L3–7C		35:3	Pyxis	2564	L5–5C
	28:11	Pyxis	2224	L3–8C		35:4	Pyxis	2692	L5–7E
	28:12	Pyxis	2136	L3–7C		35:5	Jar	2676	L5–7D
						35:6	Pyxis	2673	L5–7D
Fig.	29:1	Biconical jar	2151	L3–7D		35:7	Chalice	2580	L5–5E
	29:2	Biconical jar	2072	L3–6D		35:8	Lamp	2548	L5–4E
	29:3	Biconical jar	2120	L3–6F		35:9	Lamp	2587	L5–5F
	29:4	Biconical jar	2015	L3–5E					

Fig. 19. Pyxides of Level 1.

0   5   10 cm

Scale = 1:3

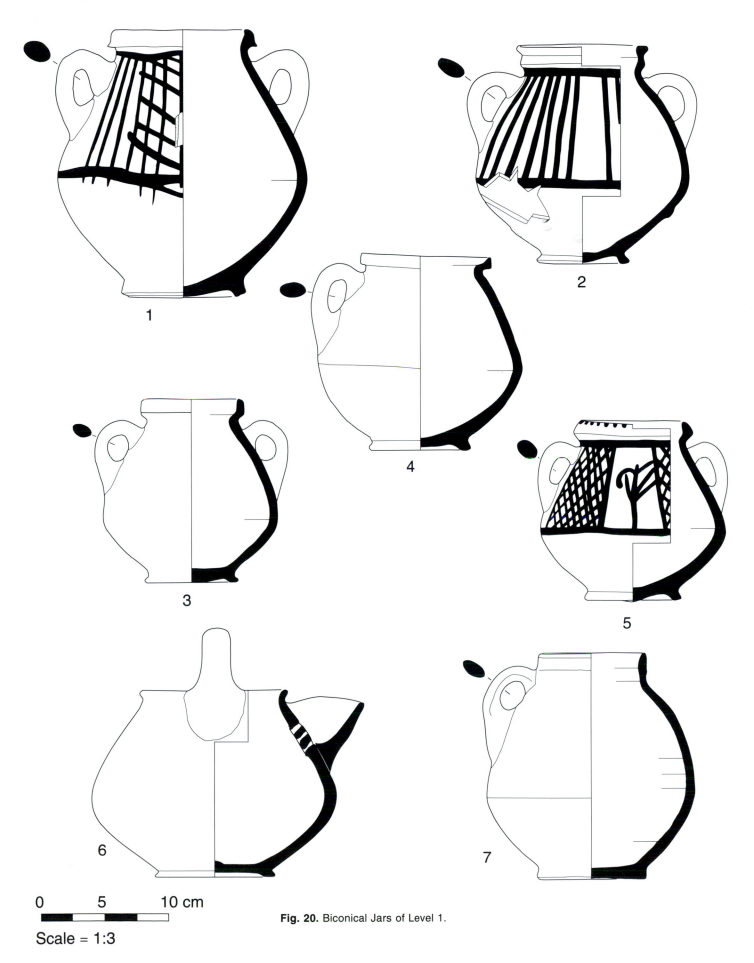

Fig. 20. Biconical Jars of Level 1.

0   5   10 cm

Scale = 1:3

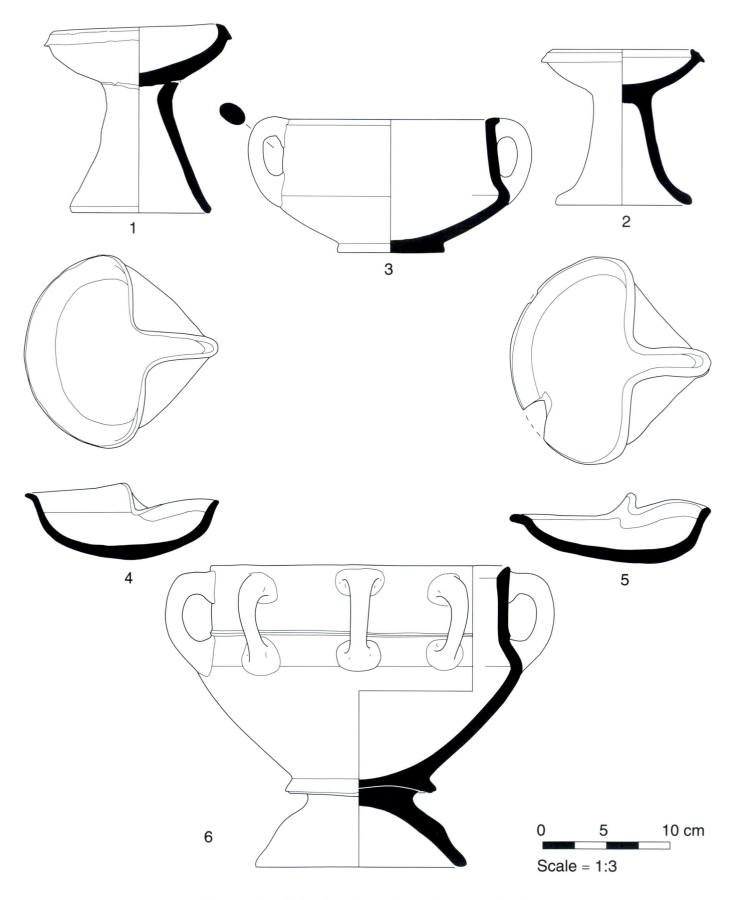

Fig. 21. Pottery of Level 1 (Chalices, Lamps, Krater-Mug, and Multihandled Krater.

0   5   10 cm

Scale = 1:3

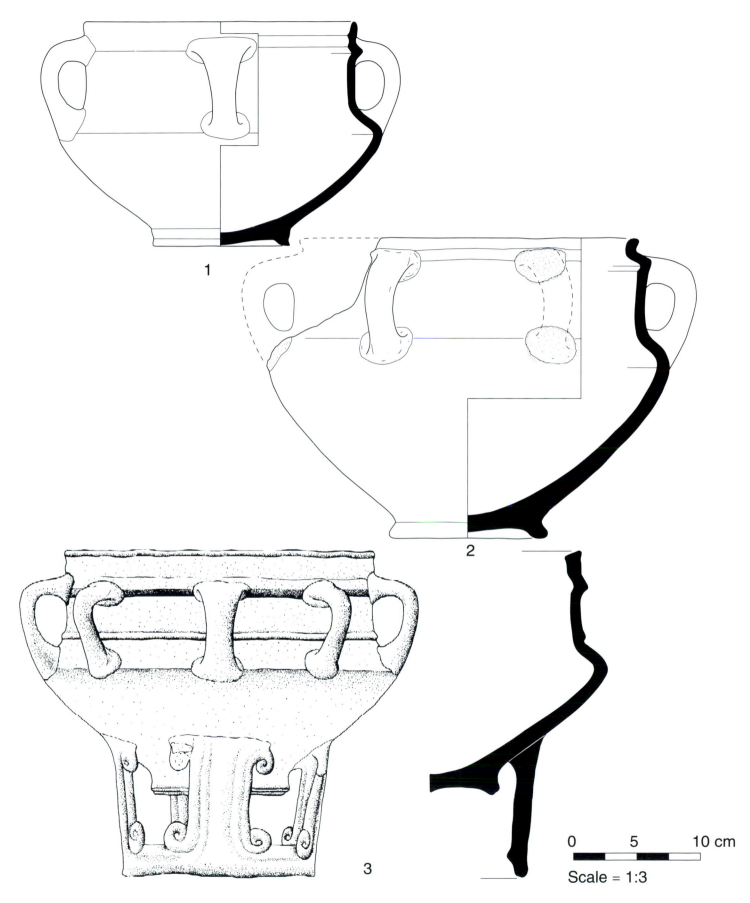

Fig. 22. Multihandled Kraters of Level 1.

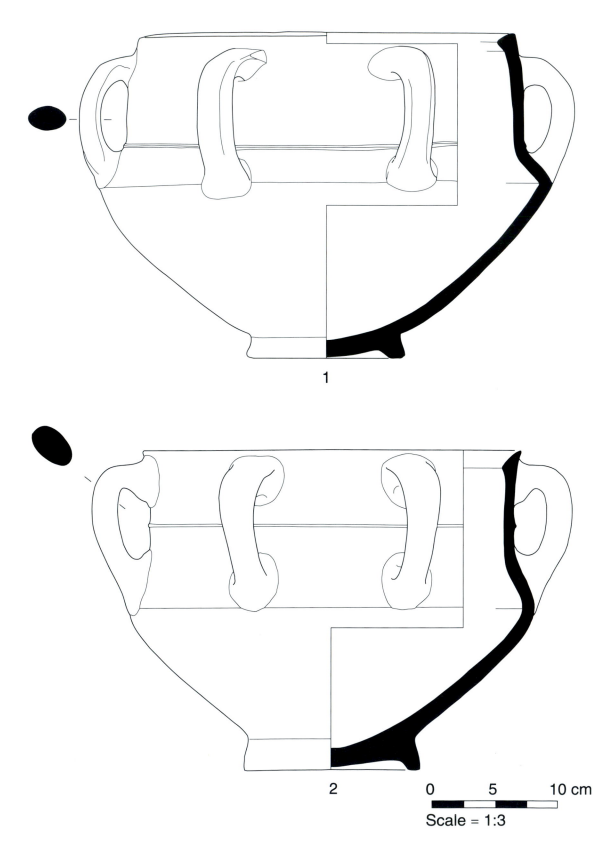

Fig. 23. Multihandled Kraters of Level 1.

Fig. 24. Pyxides of Level 1.

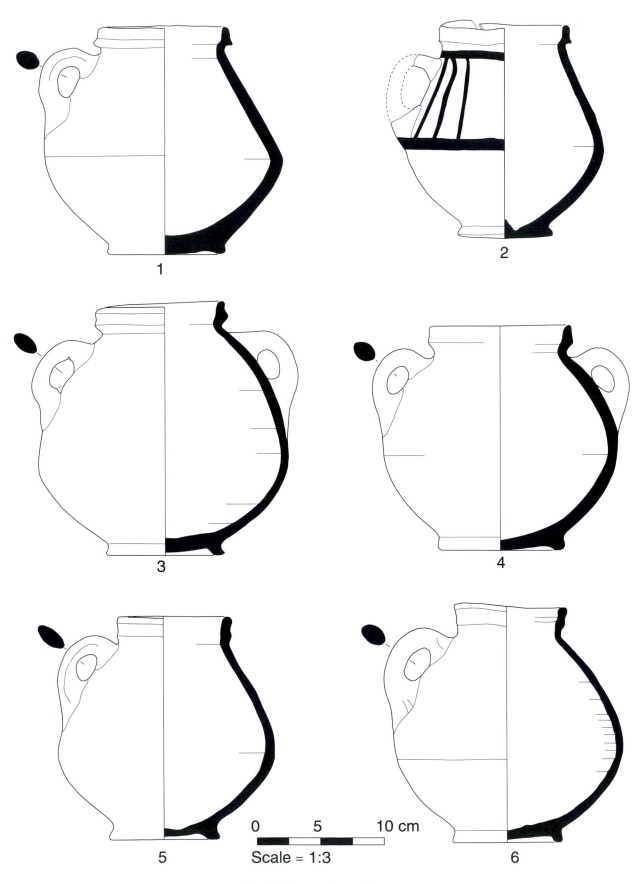

Fig. 25. Biconical Jars of Level 1.

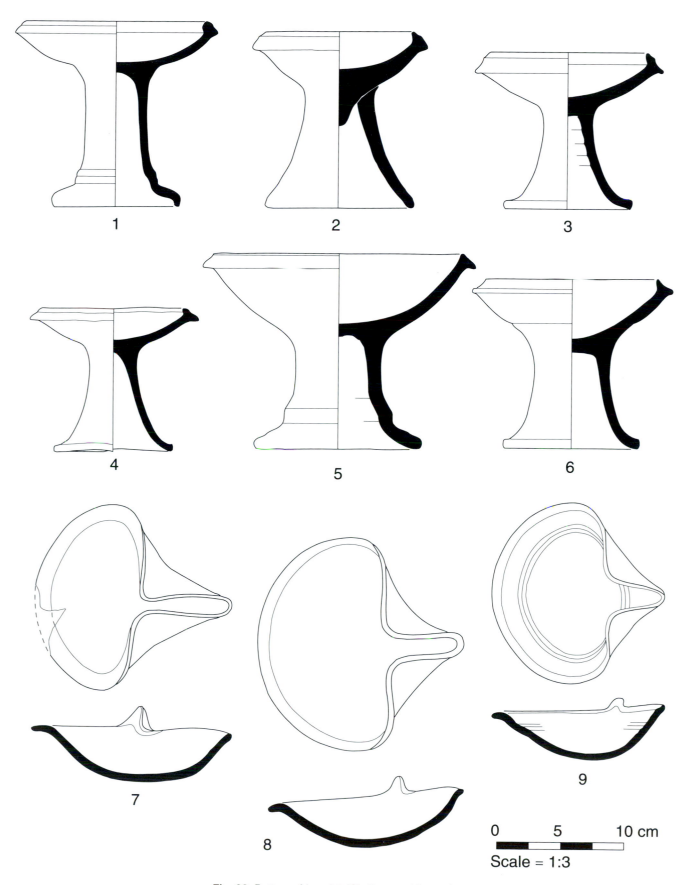

Fig. 26. Pottery of Level 2 (Chalices and Lamps).

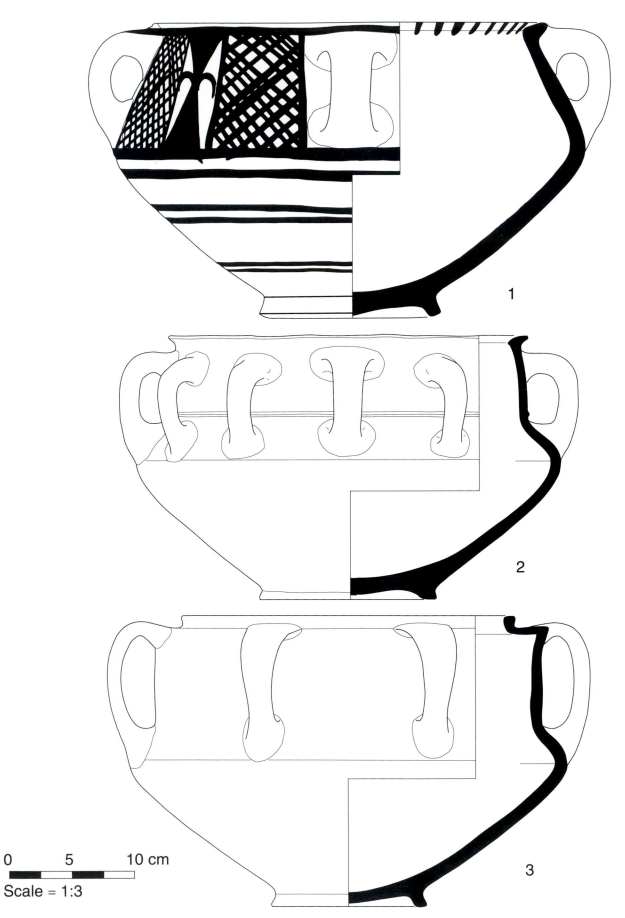

Fig. 27. Multihandled Kraters of Level 2.

Fig. 28. Pyxides of Level 3.

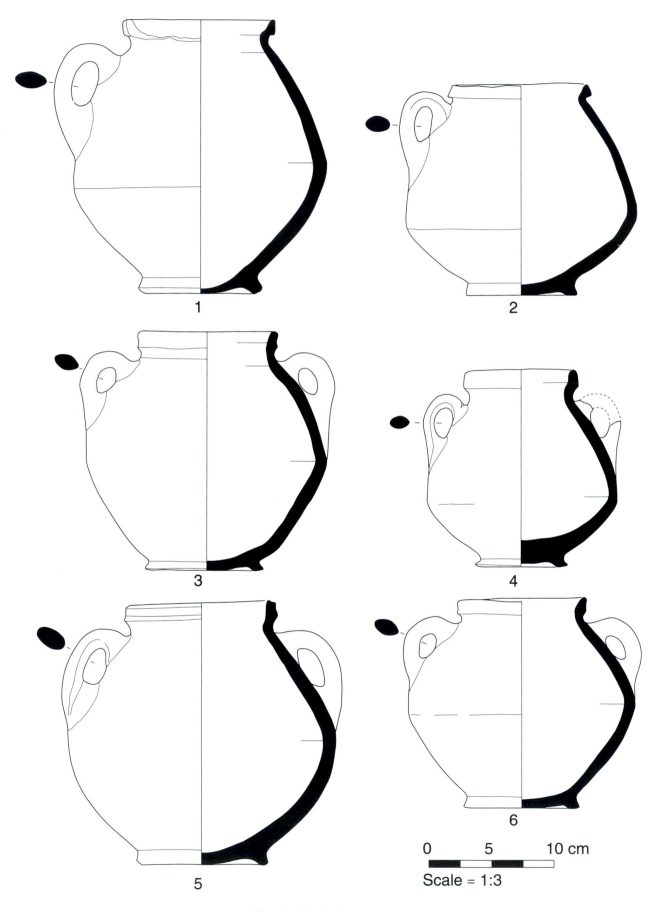

Fig. 29. Biconical Jars of Level 3.

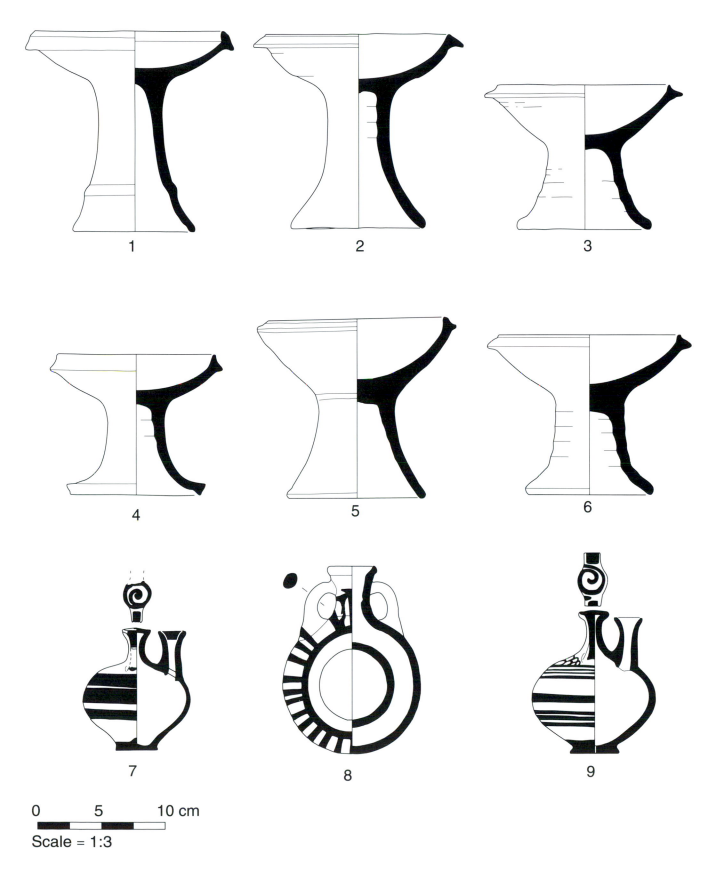

0   5   10 cm

Scale = 1:3

Fig. 30. Pottery of Level 3 (Chalices, Stirrup Jars, Flasks).

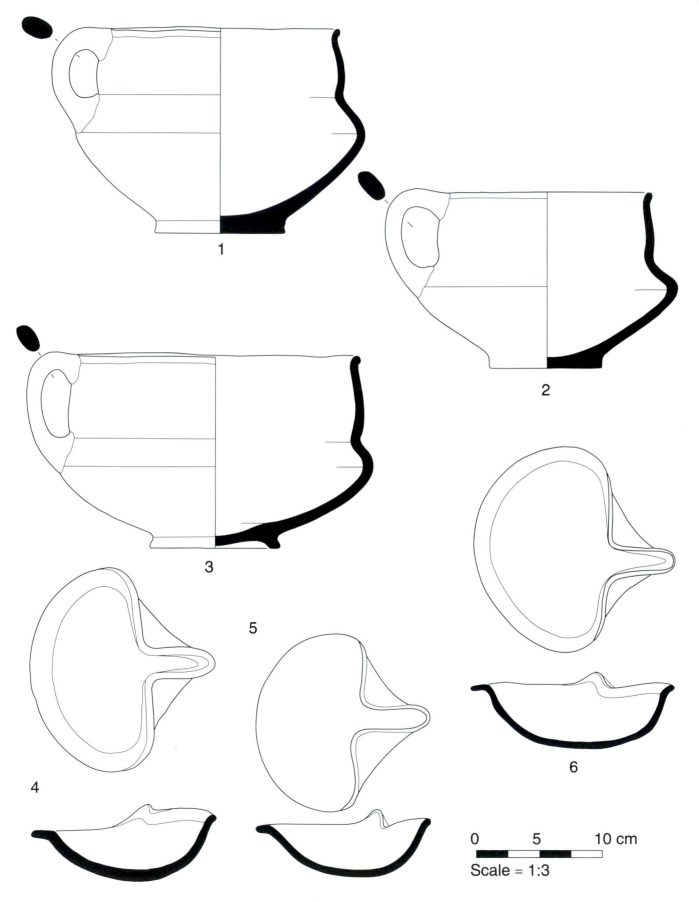

Fig. 31. Pottery of Level 3 (Krater-Mugs and Lamps).

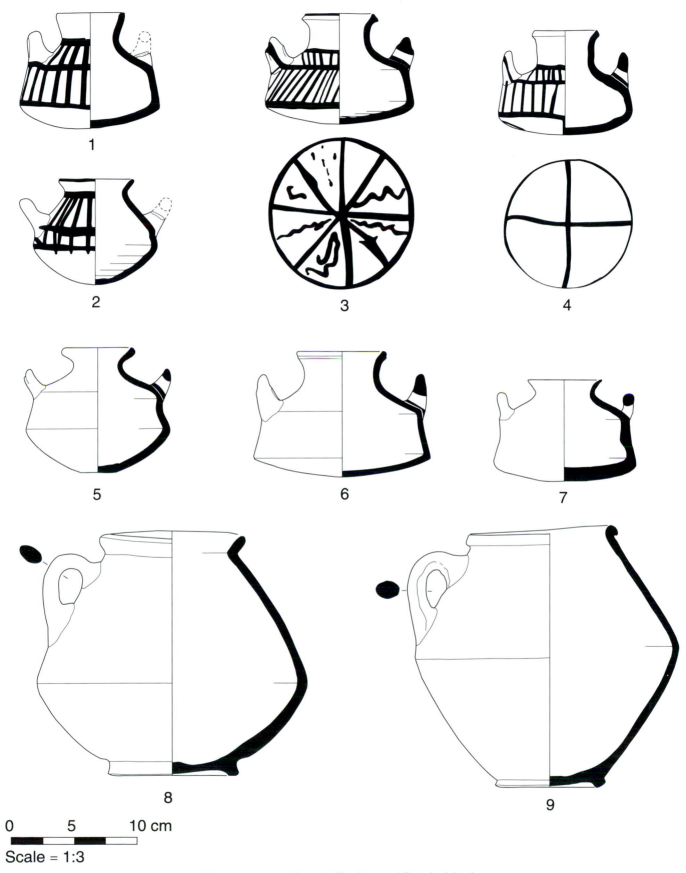

Fig. 32. Pottery of Level 4 (Pyxides and Biconical Jars).

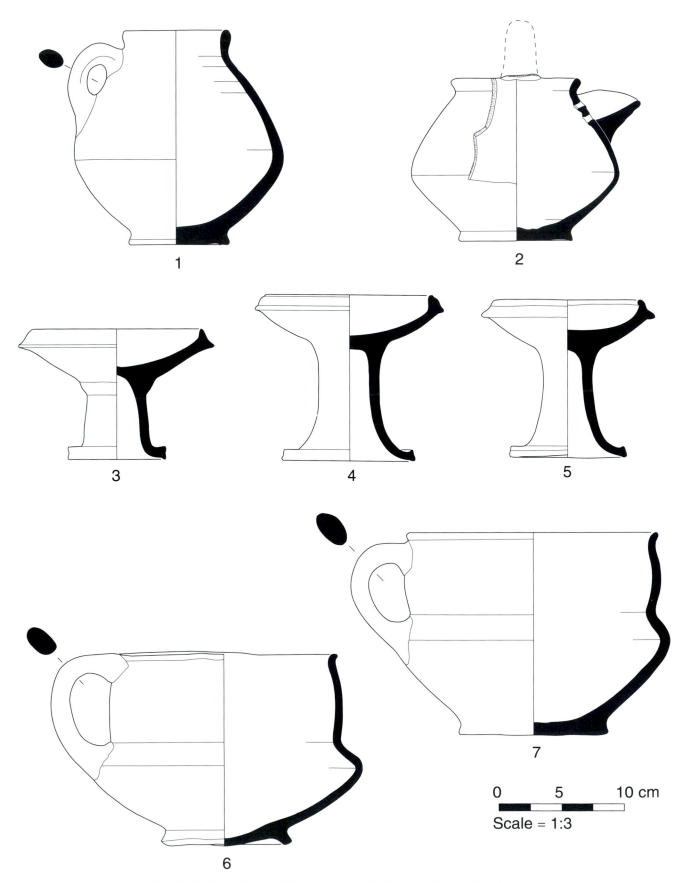

Fig. 33. Pottery of Level 4 (Biconical Jars, Chalices, and Krater-Mugs).

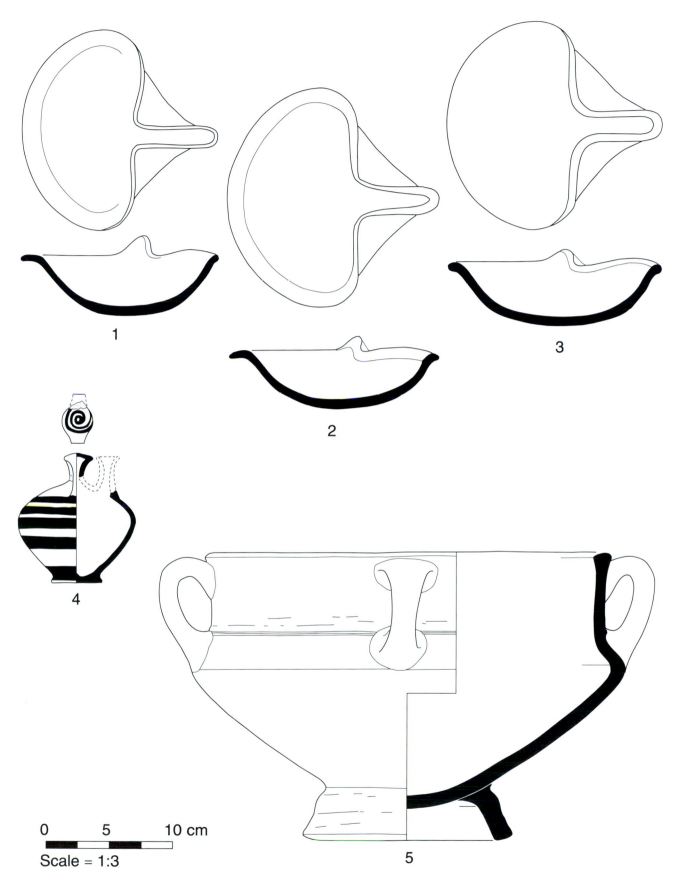

Fig. 34. Pottery of Level 4 (Lamps, Stirrup Jar, and Multihandled Krater).

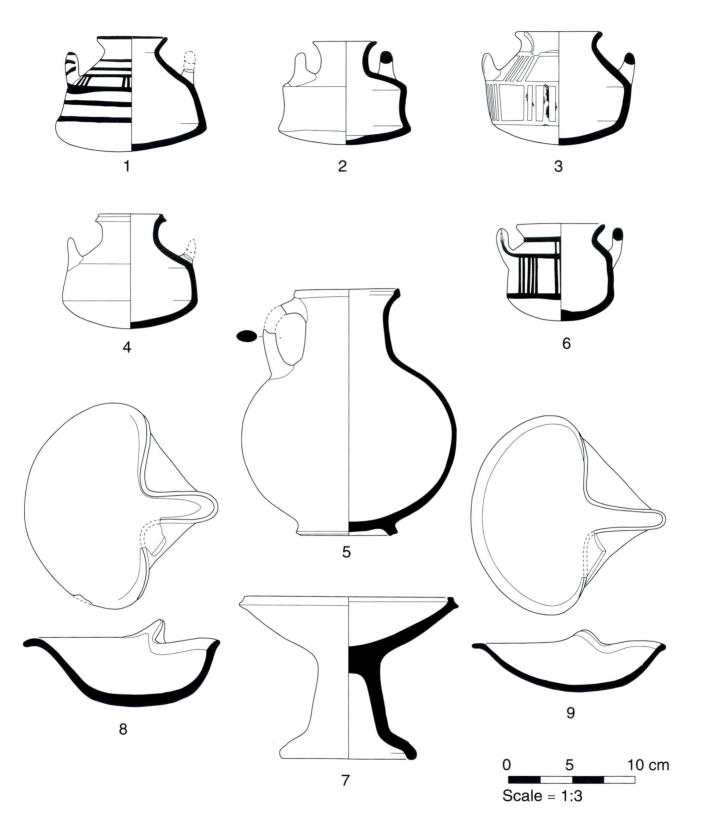

Fig. 35. Pottery of Level 5 (Pyxides, Lamps, Chalice, and Jar).